The Madder Stain

Contemporary Psychoanalytic Studies

Contemporary Psychoanalytic Studies (CPS) is an international scholarly book series devoted to all aspects of psychoanalytic inquiry in theoretical, philosophical, applied, and clinical psychoanalysis. Its aims are broadly academic, interdisciplinary, and pluralistic, emphasizing secularism and tolerance across the psychoanalytic domain. CPS aims to promote open and inclusive dialogue among the humanities and the social-behavioral sciences including such disciplines as philosophy, anthropology, history, literature, religion, cultural studies, sociology, feminism, gender studies, political thought, moral psychology, art, drama, and film, biography, law, economics, biology, and cognitive-neuroscience.

VOLUME 21

The titles published in this series are listed at *brill.com/cps*

The Madder Stain

A Psychoanalytic Reading of Thomas Hardy

By

Annie Ramel

BRILL
RODOPI

LEIDEN | BOSTON

Cover illustration: "Madder Root", painting 100 × 65 cm., Francis Glénat (glenat.guidarts.com)

Library of Congress Cataloging-in-Publication Data

Ramel, Annie.
The madder stain : a psychoanalytic reading of Thomas Hardy / by Annie Ramel.
pages cm. -- (Contemporary psychoanalytic studies)
Includes bibliographical references and index.
ISBN 978-90-04-29340-3 (pbk. : alk. paper) -- ISBN 978-90-04-29662-6 (e-book)
1. Hardy, Thomas, 1840-1928--Criticism and interpretation. 2. Psychoanalysis and literature--England--History--19th century. 3. Psychoanalysis and literature--England--History--20th century. 4. Voice in literature. 5. Psychology in literature. I. Title.

PR4757.P8R36 2015
823'.8--dc23

2015009908

This publication has been typeset in the multilingual "Brill" typeface. With over 5,100 characters covering Latin, IPA, Greek, and Cyrillic, this typeface is especially suitable for use in the humanities. For more information, please www.brill.com/brill-typeface.

ISSN 1571-4977
ISSN 978-90-04-29340-3 (paperback)
ISSN 978-90-04-29662-6 (e-book)

This book is printed on acid-free paper.

Printed by Printforce, the Netherlands

To Jacques Ramel, Josiane Paccaud-Huguet, Michel Cusin

Contents

The Madder Stain: A Psychoanalytic Reading of Thomas Hardy

Introduction: The Madder Stain

Why should the "sticky blights" that Tess rubs off her naked arms as she wends her stealthy way through the garden at Talbothays, "though snow-white on the appletree-trunks," leave "madder stains"[1] on her skin? That is a moot point indeed, for the madder stain works as a blind spot in the narrative discourse of *Tess of the d'Urbervilles*, an enigmatic point that defies interpretation. If Tess is "pure," as the authorial subtitle indicates ("a Pure Woman, Faithfully presented by Thomas Hardy"), why should Nature and Man conspire to inscribe a red stain on her flesh? Even before the age of "deconstruction," several critics had pointed out the "confusion of many standards"[2] which, they said, impaired the value of the novel. The subtitle appeared particularly offensive to many Victorians, for whom it shockingly contradicted their own conventional interpretation of Tess as a "fallen woman." Then, in the 1980's, criticism started drawing attention to the modernity of Hardy, reassessing *Tess of the d'Urbervilles* in the light of deconstruction:

> Hardy's novel, then, well-ahead of its time, *seems* to be dismantling the bourgeois-humanist (patriarchal and humanist) notions of the unified and unitary human subject, and to be doing so by way of a discourse so self-reflexive and defamiliarising about representation, so unstable and dialogical, that it deconstructs itself even as it creates.[3]
>
> WIDDOWSON, p. 20

1 "Madder" is a plant from whose roots red dye is made. In the earlier editions, up to the 1895 edition, Hardy had written "blood-red stains," but then he revised his text (Tanner, p. 188).

2 Paris, pp. 57–79. See also Lodge, p. 178: "Hardy's undertaking to defend Tess as a pure woman by emphasizing her kinship with Nature perpetually drew him towards the Romantic view of Nature as a reservoir of benevolent impulses, a view which one side of his mind rejected as falsely sentimental. Many Victorian writers, struggling to reconcile the view of Nature inherited from the Romantics with the discoveries of Darwinian biology, exhibit the same conflict, but it is particularly noticeable in Hardy" (a point also made by Boumelha, 1993, p. 56). See also Jacobus, pp. 318–338.

3 Here is a selection of post-deconstruction articles, which focused on the undecidability of Tess's "purity." Kathleen Blake shows that "in his verbal habits, Hardy only partially separates himself from Angel's mental ones, while the irony of the overlap draws attention and actually

 | DOI 10.1163/9789004296626_002

The madder stain that appears on Tess's arm in the garden at Talbothays, and more generally speaking the "chain of red things"[4] in the novel, may be construed differently, depending on perspective: whether it is the perspective of the prudish Victorian reader (like Mrs Oliphant, the typical "Grundyist"), the "colonizing male gaze" (Silverman, p. 132), the empathetic gaze of the "primary narrator,"[5] Tess's contradictory views of herself, the perspective of the modern reader, etc. Rather than "couch" the female body in terms of moral censure (Morgan, 1991, p. x), rather than view the "madder stain" as an indelible "scarlet letter" branding Tess as fallen,[6] modern readers see it as the mark of a lush, voluptuous sexuality. Rosemarie Morgan indeed was foremost in stressing

---

extends the novel's interest as a commentary on the heroine as pure woman" (Blake, p. 704). Penny Boumelha also points to "the overlapping of contradictory and conflictual points of view" (Boumelha, 1993, p. 55) and shows how the dislocations of the text "threaten the dominance of the dispassionate and omniscient narrator, and so push to its limits the androgynous narrative mode that seeks to represent and explain the woman from within and without" (p. 58). Laura Claridge wonders about Tess's purity: "Tess's purity is maintained throughout the dominant narrative line precisely on these terms: in spite of men's abuse, she is pure. Yet again, this position causes formal discontinuities: if this purity is so potent an ingredient in her makeup, why did she open up her lips and take in the strawberry—and continue to eat? Why, finally, does Eve not refuse Satan?" (Claridge, p. 71). But, Claridge concludes, some readers enjoy the novel precisely insofar as it deviates from textual coherence (p. 77). Patricia Ingham argues that Hardy attempts to replace "the fallen woman as sign" with the positive image of Tess as an "explicitly sexual being" (Ingham, p. 81), but the last-minute addition, "A Pure Woman," by measuring her against the old norms, fails to rehabilitate her (p. 83). Hardy constructs her as "generic" woman, who is "up for moral assessment," "and it is in respect of sexual morality that it is felt appropriate, even essential, to assess her: is she pure or not pure? To that extent the text colludes with the familiar pattern" (p. 85). Charlotte Thomson writes about "a disease in language" (the "literal understanding of primitive metaphors"): "This 'disease in language' has the power virtually to obliterate reality by systematically replacing a living event with a construction of the past, just as Angel replaces a living Tess with his biblical and mythological women [...] From the past a scenario of guilt and sacrifice in blood imprints itself upon the cultural mind" (Thomson, p.114). Kaja Silverman shows how the gaze of the novel "*constructs* its object through a process of colonisation, delimitation, configuration, and inscription" (Silverman, p. 132). For instance the painter of religious slogans constructs Tess as "a figure sharply edged in the red letters of damnation" (pp. 136–137).

4 Hillis Miller, p. 123.

5 Cf Morgan (1991, p. xvii): "I use the term primary narrator to mean the voice and perspective that, when distinguished from all others, proves to be recognisably coherent, consistent, and stable."

6 For that sort of reading (which views the garden as "dirty"), see Marilyn Stall Fontane's, "The Devil in 'Tess'," *The Thomas Hardy Society Review*, 1982, pp. 250–254.

"the palpability of female sensation" in Hardy's novels (Morgan, 1991, p. IX). In her perspective, the "Garden scene" is "an erotic scene" evoking "sexual readiness" (Morgan, 1991, p. 86). Tess assimilates the physical world to her own erotic consciousness, so that the sticky blights that wet and stain her person resemble "the mucosa and emissions of biological sex" (Morgan, 1991, p. 87).

Far from rejecting that view, I wish to draw attention to the "madder stain" as a radical enigma, which no ideological discourse(s) can fully circumscribe. I will focus on the *oxymoronic* nature of those white "blights" that turn red as they touch Tess's arm—those "blights" which inscribe Tess's "passing corporeal blight" on her skin, even though Tess is "pure." Kaja Silverman has noted that "instability" reaches a climax on Tess's wedding night, "when the heirlooms jewels transform her from a peasant girl into a woman of fashion, and when she is twice identified with the portraits of her d'Urberville ancestors" (Silverman, p. 137). When she begins to unfold her tale to Angel, a strange metamorphosis threatens to turn the jewels she has donned "as if by magic" into the winking eyes of an ugly toad: "She bent forward, at which each diamond on her neck gave a sinister wink like a toad's" (*Tess* p. 222). Could not a perceptive ear overhear "witch" in "at which"?[7] The brilliantly adorned woman, the bright star adored by Angel, may all too easily be changed into a blighted one, to be discarded as useless refuse.[8] Bright and blight are interchangeable, so are white and red. Why should *agalma*, the precious object, be so easily overturned to reveal *palea*,[9] on the side of horror?

My concern then is not the enigma resulting from ideological hesitancy (for an enigma may eventually be solved), it is the sheer, absolute, insoluble mystery of the "madder stain" as a point of contact with the unspeakable Real, the Lacanian Real that could be defined as what cannot be integrated into the symbolic order and remains undifferentiated, outside language.[10] Roland

---

7 A reading of "which" encouraged by its textual proximity to "toads."

8 In a similar way, Knight in *A Pair of Blue Eyes* casts away Elfride when he finds that there is "a blight" upon her (*APBE* p. 309).

9 Lacan opposes *agalma* (a Greek word meaning an "ornament") to *palea*, a Latin word which means "waste." In his seminar on *Anxiety*, he distinguishes between the true object-cause of desire, which tends to be on the side of *palea*, and the object "aimed at" in love, *agalma*, which is a false object. Cf Jacques-Alain Miller's Seminar, 2nd June 2004 (Miller, 2009):

"Le statut éthique de l'objet-visée, c'est l'agalma, alors que, par excellence, l'objet-cause est plutôt de l'ordre de *palea*. Au grec *agalma*, la chose précieuse, Lacan oppose le latin *palea*, le déchet."

10 Lacan (1966, p. 388): "le réel en tant qu'il est le domaine de ce qui subsiste hors de la symbolisation."

Barthes's concept of the *punctum* can help us understand my meaning here. In *Camera Lucida*, after introducing the *studium* (the first element in the photograph he is analysing), Barthes moves on to the second element:

> The second element will break (or punctuate) the *studium*. This time it is not I who seek it out (as I invest the field of the *studium* with my sovereign consciousness), it is this element which rises from the scene, shoots out of it like an arrow, and pierces me. A Latin word exists to designate this wound, this prick, this mark made by a pointed instrument: the word suits me all the better in that it also refers to the notion of punctuation, and because the photographs I am speaking of are in effect punctuated, sometimes even speckled with these sensitive points; precisely, these marks, these wounds are so many points. This second element which will disturb the *studium* I shall therefore call *punctum*; for *punctum* is also: sting, speck, cut, little hole – and also a cast of the dice. A photograph's *punctum* is that accident which pricks me (but also bruises me, is poignant to me).
>
> BARTHES (2000, pp. 26–27)

If we transpose these distinctions from the field of photography to textuality, the "madder stain" is not part of the *studium* of the narrator's discourse: it is not just a sign that makes sense in an ideological reading of the text, in a view of Hardy's texts as offering a political testimony to be enjoyed culturally by a given readership (the stain as a metaphor for woman's "fault," for instance). The stain, or speck, or spot, cannot be invested by the reader's (or writer's) "sovereign consciousness," it somehow eludes his understanding, it is something that may (or may not) pierce the reader, affect him. It is poignant, both enjoyable and painful. It is a *punctum*, very precisely. In that sense, because it lies enigmatically beyond the scope of "sovereign consciousness," the "madder stain" pertains to the Real. So do the fiery red letters painted on a stile by a religious fanatic in *Tess of the d'Urbervilles*, another form assumed by the madder stain, sent back to Tess as a mirror-image of her supposed "fault": they form a "tex" riddled with holes, broken by mad, erratic punctuation (as the man places a comma after each word "as if to give pause while that word was driven well home to the reader's heart" *Tess* p. 85).[11] The holes which pierce the reader's heart/the readers' hearts cannot fail to remind us of Barthes's *punctum* effect.

---

11 We could almost use Lacan's metaphor of "a punctuation without a text" (Lacan, 1966, p. 388).

But, one might argue, it is no great revelation to claim that the "madder stain" (or any poignant scene in Hardy's fiction) belongs to the realm of the inexpressible/unspeakable. It was Virginia Woolf who first situated Hardy on "the margin of the unexpressed" (Woolf, 1932/1953, p. 248).[12] Tony Tanner's analysis of the red stain *motif* comes very close indeed to a Lacanian reading, with its assertion that Hardy makes us *experience* the "awesome mystery" of "that red ribbon marking out the little girl in the white dress, which already foreshadows the red blood stain on the white ceiling" (Tanner, pp. 205–206). Tanner's reading has the merit of conjoining the issues of sexuality, death, and origin, which are three figures of the Lacanian Real: "Hardy is dealing here with the simplest and deepest of matters. Life starts in sex and ends in death, and Hardy constantly shows how closely allied the two forms of blood-letting are in one basic, unalterable rhythm of existence" (Tanner, pp. 191–192). Blood, and the spilling of blood, in one set of circumstances, "can mean sexual passion and the creation of life, and in another can mean murderous passion and death—two forms of 'red energy'[13] intimately related—this is the *substance* of Tess's story" (Tanner, p. 205, my italics). The four-poster bed erected by the d'Urbervilles over the family vault at Kingsbere, reduplicated with the "enormous four-post bed" decked with "crimson damask hangings" found later by Tess (*Tess* p. 375, Tanner, p. 195), is the very symbol of that impossible, nonsensical mixing of origin, sexuality and death.

Why then resort to a Lacanian term, "the Real," to refer to what has already been said. The answer is that the concept of the Real, which in the later Lacan is inseparable from the *objet petit a* and *jouissance,*[14] can help us read the text more attentively, paying special attention to the death drive at work in it.[15] For the concept of *jouissance*, not easily translatable (the English "enjoyment" is not wholly satisfactory), is radically ambivalent: "it involves a combination of pleasure and pain, or, more accurately, pleasure *in* pain" (Homer, p. 89). Moreover, pre-Lacanian formulations of the "Real" tend to exteriorize it, to view it as the real of science (i.e. what cannot be comprehended in scientific discourse), a menace that lies beyond the limits of human understanding, like

12 The expression was first used by Virginia Woolf in her *Common Reader*, second series, and later taken up by Roger Ebbatson as a title to his study on Hardy (Sheffield Academic Press, 1993).

13 Tanner's "red energy" is very close to Hillis Miller's assertion that "all these red things are marks made by that creative and destructive energy underlying events to which Hardy gave the name 'Immanent Will'" (Hillis Miller, p. 124).

14 Homer, pp. 81–82.

15 Again, this is no novelty: see Hillis Miller's Freudian pages on *Tess of the d'Urbervilles* in *Fiction and Repetition* (pp. 137–138).

the "gloomy spectres" waiting like wolves just outside "the circumscribing light" that enveloped Tess (*Tess* p. 195, Tanner, pp. 206–208). The Real understood as *jouissance* does not lie beyond, it is *extimate* to man, at the same time exterior and interior, like the two faces of a Moebius strip. It knows of no limit, no distinction, either between self and Other, between near and far. It takes a poet to find the right words to express this: "There was not distinction between the near and the far, and an auditor felt close to everything within the horizon" (*Tess* p. 127). *Jouissance* inhabits the "fleshly tabernacle" (*Tess* p. 301) with which Nature had endowed Tess. It is both the hungry wolves lying outside, biding their time, and Tess's innermost truth, what she fears and what she unconsciously yearns for. Neither outside nor inside, it is *on the littoral*. Which helps us to understand why the "madder stain" is both a mark of enjoyment and the mark of death and suffering. And most importantly, the Real as liminal/littoral appears as the proper domain of literature,[16] in that the *jouissance* it involves inhabits the "fleshly tabernacle" of a text, its very *letter*. Being aware of that poetic dimension is not insignificant when attempting to read a text. In the light of this I will try to define a specifically Hardyan "sublime."

At this stage, a closer look at "the chain of red things" in some of Hardy's novels appears necessary. In *Tess of the d'Urbervilles* the chain starts with the red ribbon tied in Tess's hair, which distinguishes her from the other girls (*Tess* p. 37). It ends with "a large red-brick building" (*Tess* p. 384), the prison where Tess awaits her execution. The most striking occurrence is perhaps the "spot" like a paint-mark made by the sun on Tess's skirt:[17] "the sun [...] formed a golden staff which stretched across to her skirt, where it made a spot like a paint-mark set upon her" (*Tess* p. 215). In *The Return of the Native*, the chain includes Diggory Venn the reddleman, first seen as "a sinister redness [...] dull and lurid, like a flame in sunlight" (*RN* p. 149), but then cleansed of the red stain associated with his trade once the tragedy is over ("red, and all approach to red, was carefully excluded from every article of clothes upon him" *RN* p. 388). The central figure who bears the red stain as a distinctive mark is of course Eustacia, the "fallen" woman of the novel: she, like Tess, is identified by "a red ribbon round her neck," which she wears beside her dark dress (*RN* p. 360). Like Tess, whose chin is pricked by a thorn of the rose offered her by Alec

16 Cf Joseph Conrad, about the "meaning" of a tale for Marlow: "[...] to him the meaning of an episode was not inside like a kernel, but outside, enveloping the tale which brought it out only as a glow brings out a haze, in the likeness of one of these misty halos that sometimes are made visible by the spectral illumination of moonshine" (Conrad, p. 138).

17 Arguably, the spot here is not red, but Tony Tanner has shown "the convergence of redness and the sun" (Tanner, p. 194).

(*Tess* p. 47), Eustacia has blood oozing on her skin in a scene when she and Clym try to draw water from her grandfather's well: she draws blood from her hand as she holds fast to the rope tied to the bucket.[18] And on the very same day she has been pricked with a long needle by a woman who believes her to be a witch; she shows Clym the "scarlet little puncture" on her round white arm, "a bright red spot [...] like a ruby on Parian marble" (*RN* p. 186). The bonfire on the heath at Mistover, meant by Eustacia as a signal to Wildeve, is also one of the "red things" in the novel that represent her (one might object that it is Diggory Venn who is characterized by redness, I will argue later that the red hue metaphorizes the tragic disruption brought into the community by Eustacia, whose disappearance quite logically restores the colours of life). Fire is indeed the distinctive feature of Eustacia: "You could fancy the colour of Eustacia's soul to be flame-like. The sparks from it that rose into her dark pupils gave the same impression" (*RN* pp. 63–64). The red spot can be a blood-stain marking Tess as a "murderess" (as when Tess is "splashed from face to skirt with the crimson drops" of the horse's blood after the accident *Tess* p. 37), a scarlet puncture on Eustacia's arm, a paint-mark on her Tess's skirt, a bonfire on the heath, etc. The bonfire may be read as the fire of passion and desire, just as the blood shed by Tess has been associated with the loss of her virginity.[19] In all cases, whether it is blood or fire, or even "liquid fire" (*Tess* p. 92), the stain seems to materialize an enjoyment which the reader's gaze (as well as the writer's) ascribes to Tess and Eustacia—an enjoyment which is somewhat in excess of what their community considers acceptable, and for which they are cruelly punished.

Then a question arises: what if that enjoyment, presumably derived from sexual intercourse with a man, were other than sexual? What if the red stain as a figure of sexual enjoyment were a (partial) misapprehension of the *jouissance* that is really involved? How can one read *The Return of the Native* and *Tess of the d'Urbervilles* after Lacan's twentieth Seminar, *Encore*, which posits that women (and those situated on the feminine side in Lacan's graph of sexuation, i.e. artists) have access to an "Other" *jouissance*, a surplus enjoyment which is "more than" phallic *jouissance*, "beyond" the phallus, beyond the Symbolic and the signifier? And what if the red stain were to be deciphered not only on the side of the heroine, but also on the side of the writer (or of the reader), as the form assumed by his own enigmatic (and feminine) *jouissance*? What strange *kinship* between the male writer and the feminine heroine, like

18 "She opened her hands. One of them was bleeding; the rope had dragged off the skin. Eustacia wrapped it in her handkerchief" (*RN* p. 186).

19 Tanner, p. 186.

that fantasized by Ella Marchmill between herself and Robert Trewe in "An Imaginative Woman," could then be deduced from such an analysis? I will try to bring a few answers to these questions in a chapter oriented by Lacanian psychoanalysis.

One reason why I believe the red spot should be reassessed in the light of psychoanalysis is the *vocal* quality of the stain. Barthes's metaphor of the *punctum*, derived from photography, is a visual concept. Transposed to the realm of fiction, the *punctum* may acquire a resonance, it may become audible as well as visible. Audible, but in an oxymoronic way: the red stain is "silence audible," in the same way as darkness is said to be "visible" in *Paradise Lost*. Just as a colour in English can be said to be "loud" or "clamorous," the madder stain seems to shout like a silent cry. That is what Hardy's text says: "these staring vermilion words shone forth. They seemed to shout themselves out, and to make the atmosphere ring" (*Tess* p. 85). Colour rings out like a voice, whether red or blue ("On the sheltered side was a turnip-slicing machine, whose bright blue hue of new paint seemed almost vocal in the otherwise subdued scene" *Tess* p. 305). It seems as though the stain spoke *in Tess's place*: where language fails, the red stain appears, a soundless clamour that one *hears with one's eyes*. We will try to understand why silence and the red stain are so strangely interrelated.

Most of the time, it is Tess's voice which fails to make itself heard.[20] The voice of "soft and silent Tess" (*Tess* p. 151) has a peculiar quality: it seems almost choked, throttled, stuck in her throat—a point that will be developed. Like Eustacia Vye in *The Return of the Native* (Gribble pp. 524–542), like Henchard in *The Mayor of Casterbridge*, like Elfride Swancourt in *A Pair of Blue Eyes*, Tess proves unable to tell her story when it would be vital for her to do so. When she finally breaks her silence and makes her confession to Angel, she is struck dumb as she realises that Angel rejects her. No cry resonates, but a silent cry forms on her lips, soundlessly ("her mouth had almost the aspect of a round little hole" *Tess* p. 227)—exactly like the mouth of Munch's homunculus in *The Scream*. In both cases the madder stain *is* a silent cry. The stain disappears in Hardy's novel the very minute Tess is hanged, that is to say when Tess's throttled voice is hushed for ever by the hangman's rope—when that disturbing silent cry of hers ceases to make itself heard as "silence audible." Which raises a few questions: about Hardy's fascination with hanging scenes (that is to say with the *silencing* of voice), and also about the enjoyment we readers derive from a literary text, which by definition is a silent text.

---

20 About voice in *Tess of the d'Urbervilles*, see Higonnet, pp. 14–31.

One concept will be particularly helpful: the Lacanian concept of *object-voice*, or *voice qua object* (in Žižek's formulation).

Not that we should restrict ourselves to things red in Hardy's fiction. The spot can be black, as when Alec intrudes into Tess's field of vision at Flintcomb Ash: "[...] far beyond the ploughing-teams, a black speck was seen; it had come from the corner of a fence, where there was a gap" (*Tess* p. 305).[21] Or when a policeman emerges as a black dot against the rising sun on the Salisbury Plain: "something seemed to move on the verge of the dip eastward—a mere dot. It was the head of a man [...]" (*Tess* p. 381). It is often at such precise *points* that a threat erupts that will bring disaster, it is there that life is engulfed, as if sucked into an abyss. No wonder such points, whether they be stains, spots, specks, flecks, blots, dots, splotches or mere points, are particularly poignant, they rise from the *studium*, they shoot out of it like so many arrows, and pierce us.[22] In a short-story by Hardy, "The History of the Hardcomes," a young man and a young woman are rowing away from the shore, from which two other characters (the man's wife and the woman's husband) are watching them. They form "a mere speck" on the horizon, they are about to disappear for ever, as if swallowed up by an ocean of nothingness:

> The heedless pair afloat now formed a mere speck in the films of the coming night, which thickened apace, till it completely swallowed up their distant shapes. They had disappeared while still following the straight course away from the world of landlivers, as if they were intending to drop over the sea-edge into space, and never return to earth again.
>
> THOMAS HARDY, *CSS* p. 528

In another short-story, "A Mere Interlude," a newly married couple are sitting on a cliff, gazing at the sea. The man decides to go for a swim by himself. Having crossed "the white fringe of foam," he walks into "the undulating mass of blue," while his wife watches him. He remains a long time in the water, so that she withdraws her eyes from the "spot" (*CSS* p. 766). A moment later, he has disappeared. She peers at the horizon, in search of a trace of his presence, but to no avail: "Not a *speck* or *spot* resembling a man's head or face showed anywhere" (*CSS* p. 767). The man has drowned, his body sucked under by the current in a "small area of water" whose peculiar aspect (comparable to that of a "foul patch" in a meadow) suggests the presence of a turmoil. It is there, in that

21 André Topia, introduction to *Tess d'Urberville*, Paris: Livre de Poche, 1939, 1995, p. 25.

22 Seen in that perspective, the moment when Alec breaks into our field of vision at Flintcomb Ash is proleptic of the fatal blow that will pierce his heart.

"dreaded spot," that the married life of Baptista and Charles has been swallowed up (*CSS* pp. 767–768).

The *punctum* effect may be produced by various means, without being necessarily triggered by words like "spot" or "speck." *A Pair of Blue Eyes* is punctuated by moments that repeat the same experience: losing an ear-ring, giving a kiss, standing on the verge of a precipice, etc. Repetition appears essential to the *punctum* effect, for it is the Real, defined as what "always returns to the same place,"[23] which breaks through the *studium* at those "sensitive points" focused on by Barthes. Most actions in *A Pair of Blue Eyes* occur at the *precise spot*[24] where they have already taken place. For instance, Elfride and Stephen are sitting together on "a flat tomb, showing itself to be newer and whiter than those around it" (*APBE* p. 72): it is the tomb of young Jethway, who was once in love with Elfride, and has died of consumption. "Strange conjunctions of phenomena" (*APBE* p. 69) result in Elfride sitting with her second[25] sweetheart on the very spot where the first lies buried. When some time later Elfride and Henry Knight are taking a walk at nightfall in the self-same churchyard, their steps take them automatically to the same tomb:

> [...] the moonlight returned again, irradiating that portion of churchyard within their view. It brightened the near part first, and against the background which the cloud-shadow had not yet uncovered stood, brightest of all, a white tomb—the tomb of young Jethway.
>
> *APBE* p. 308

The key-signifier as regards young Jethway's tomb is not "spot" but "here." Troubled by Elfride's admission that she has already had a sweetheart, Stephen asks: "Where is he now?" Her answer comes as a sting to his heart:

> 'HERE'.
> 'Here! What do you mean by that?'
> 'I mean that he is here'.

23 Lacan (1973, p. 49): "le réel est [...] ce qui revient toujours à la même place."

24 Coincidence being essential to the plot, the expression is recurrent: "the precise spot from which she had parted from Stephen" (*APBE* p. 70), "his family are living in precisely the same spot in England as yours" (*APBE* p. 84), etc.

25 The young man's mother insists that her son died of a broken heart because Elfride encouraged him and then rejected him, an accusation which Elfride denies indignantly. The whole point is that there is no telling who was Elfride's first lover—that there is no traceable origin.

> 'Where here?'
> 'Under us. He is under this tomb. He is dead, and we are sitting on his grave'.
>
> *APBE* p. 77

"Here," a recurring signifier in *A Pair of Blue Eyes*, is of paramount importance. The deictic refers to the place of Stephen's origin ("To think YOU, the London visitor, the town man, should have been born here [...]" *APBE* p. 75), the place where Elfride and her father live ("This part about here is West Endelstow" *APBE* p. 13), the setting of the scenes of love-making, first between Elfride and Stephen, then between Elfride and Henry Knight. It is also the locus of death: young Jethway's tomb in the churchyard, which is of course the very place where Knight finds Mrs Jethway buried under a heap of rubble (his hand lights on a "stringy and entangled" mass that he can hardly see at first: "the deep shadow from the high wall prevented his seeing anything here" *APBE* p. 315). In the same paradigm is Lord Luxellian's family vault, the setting of a most awkward encounter between Knight, Elfride, and Stephen (Stephen had been "here" two or three times when his father did some work in the vault, Knight meditates ponderously on "these who lie here" *APBE* p. 256, etc.). The vault is the final destination of Elfride's coffin ("She died in London, you know, and has been brought here by this train" *APBE* p. 363). "Here" is the point where a small river finds an "inglorious end," running over a precipice ("the small stream here found its death" *APBE* p. 200). "Here" rhymes with "bier" in "The Flight of Love," a poem by Shelley quoted by Hardy:

> O Love, who bewailest
> The frailty of all things here
> Why choose you the frailest
> For your cradle, your home, and your bier.
>
> *APBE* p. 23

"Here" works as a *punctum* in the field of vision, it pinpoints the visible spot where the Real erupts, but at the same time, because of the homophony between "here" and "hear," the flat white tomb causes us to *hear* something like a silent cry, it seems to shine forth, to shout itself out and to make the atmosphere *ring*. It is silence audible. A phenomenon which should not surprise us in a novel where "hear," "ear," as well as "ring" (either verb or noun, as in "earring") are key-signifiers. "Here" and "hear" are brought into close proximity in Stephen's words to Elfride when she, in desperation, knocks at his bedroom-door: "Let us come down to the drawing-room [...] he will *hear* us *here*" (*APBE* p. 94, my italics). I will therefore argue that, in *A Pair of Blue Eyes* as well as in *Tess of the d'Urbervilles*, the *punctum* makes you hear (as well as see) the silent cry of those whose voice cannot be heard. The concept of "object-voice" will be useful here too.

The signifier "here," we have seen, is insistently connected in *A Pair of Blue Eyes* with three Lacanian figures of the unknowable Real: origin, sexuality, and death. So is another signifier, which is one of Hardy's favourites, the word "spot." "Spot" in English is rich in multiple connotations because, unlike the French *tache* or the German *Fleck*, it is polysemous: it can refer both to a stain and to a place. In Hardy texts, meaning often flickers between the two senses of the word. The series where "spot" refers to a place is heard *against* the paradigm of "red things,"[26] which adds its tune to the main theme, like a counterpoint. For instance when Tess, on the outskirt of the garden at Talbothays, feels unable to leave the "spot" where Angel is playing the harp ("Tess, like a fascinated bird, could not leave the spot" *Tess* p. 127), is she drawn to a particular *place*, or to the *stains* that appear on her naked arms, to the glowing weed-flowers dotting the juicy grass with their dazzling polychrome? In *The Return of the Native*, is the "spot" chosen by the reddleman to park his van (*RN* pp. 236, 368) merely a place on Egdon Heath, or another form assumed by the "stain" through which we can hardly see him blushing ("Venn flushed through his stain" *RN* p. 150), the "moving spot," of a "lurid red" colour (*RN* p. 6) whose appearance on Egdon heath in Chapter II marks his entry into the diegesis? The "spot" from which a long flame arises as Susan Nunsuch melts above a turf-fire the wax figure modelled in Eustacia's likeness, while the pins thrust into the image fall one by one and are heated red by the embers, is both the precise *point* on the pile of turf where the wax drops, and the "red thing" which presentifies Eustacia—the creature of fire and blood who wears a scarlet ribbon round her neck (*RN* pp. 360–361). The word "spot" is always loaded with affect, whether it denotes the place of origin, the locus of death, or whether it materializes some form of enjoyment, like the stain marking Tess, Eustacia, or Lucetta's Paisley shawl with a red centre in *The Mayor of Casterbridge*. It works as a sort of nodal point in the text, a "quilting point" (to use another metaphor by Lacan): like the upholstery-buttons used in mattress-making, the signifier "spot" serves as a *point de capiton*, a quilting-point that knots together the two

---

26 The spots may be black, or white: in *A Pair of Blue Eyes*, where Elfride appears to Stephen as "a white speck in motion" and Knight as "another moving speck, as different from the first as well could be, insomuch that it was perceptible only by its blackness" (*APBE* p. 219). The chess metaphor has been convincingly studied by Mary Rimmer (Rimmer, 1993).

paradigms, the chain of red things and the series where "spot" has a spatial meaning. The *punctum* effect is the direct result of such quilting operations.[27]

Examples showing that the spatial spot is often the place of origin and/or the locus of death are innumerable. The word appears in the very first line of *The Life and Work of Thomas Hardy*: "June 2nd, 1840. It was in a lonely and silent spot between woodland and heathland that Thomas Hardy was born" (*Life* p. 7). And to remain forever in the place of origin is a desire keenly felt by the young Hardy: "[…] he did not want at all to be a man, or to possess things, but to remain as he was, in the same spot" (*Life* p. 20). The poem "Domicilium" describes the garden where grow "such hardy flowers as flourish best untrained," and Hardy wonders about the primeval times when his father's mother first settled there: "I once inquired of her / How looked the spot when first she settled here" (*Life* p. 20). In *Tess of the d'Urbervilles*, Marlott is, for Angel, "the spot of his dear Tess's birth" (*Tess* p. 360), Kingsbere is "the historic spot" (*Tess* p. 350), the cradle of the d'Urberville family ("the spot of all spots in the world which could be considered the d'Urbervilles' home" *Tess* p. 348). And strikingly, the *womb* is also a *tomb*, for it is *there* that Tess's dead ancestors lie buried, rows and rows of them in their vaults.[28] Wellbridge, chosen by Angel for their honeymoon because it is an old d'Urberville seat, is both the place of origin for Tess ("Welcome to your ancestors' mansion" are Angel's greeting words, *Tess* p. 214), and the place where her life ends ("'My wife—dead, dead!' he said" *Tess* p. 243), the stone coffin where Angel lays her down while sleep-walking, only a few steps from the lonely "spot" (*Tess* pp. 243, 244) where he nearly drowned her by carrying her on a narrow plank across the tumultuous river. No sexual consummation[29] takes place there, but the "spot" betraying Tess "fault" appears on her skirt as the low sun makes "a spot like a paint-mark set upon her" (*Tess* p. 215). Here, as often, the word "spot" is used in a scene that conjoins origin, death, and sexuality—as Tony Tanner noted, "life starts in sex and ends in death" (Tanner, pp. 191–192).

Hardy's churchyards are most of the time referred to as "spots": not only the d'Urbervilles' vault at Kingsbere, but also the churchyard at East Endelstow in *A Pair of Blue Eyes* (*APBE* p. 241), the one at West Endelstow where the old church collapses ("the spot of the tragedy" *APBE* p. 316), Weatherbury graveyard in *Far From the Madding Crowd* (*FFMC* p. 239), in particular the reprobate

27 It is perhaps interesting to note that a "counterpane," which is a quilted bedspread, is the same word as "counterpoint," a word derived from the old French *contrepointe*.

28 Cf Tanner, p. 205.

29 Death is the only consummation "devoutly to be wished": "If they could only fall together, and both be dashed to pieces, how fit, how desirable" (*Tess* p. 243).

quarter where Fanny lies buried ("a spot which until lately had been abandoned to heaps of stone and bushes of alder" *FFMC* p. 239, a "spot" which Bathsheba "dreaded to see," p. 246). On that precise spot the marble tombstone is "spotted" with the stains made by brown mud, and the flowers brought by Troy lie uprooted, "on the spots whither they had been splashed by the stream" (*FFMC* p. 243)—another instance of Hardy playing with the two meanings of "spot." Bathsheba will finally wipe the "mud spots" from the tomb (*FFMC* p. 246). In "An Imaginative Woman," another grave-yard scene shows us "a crouching object beside a newly-made grave": lighting on a "spot" where the soils is trodden, William Marchmill discovers his wife Ella mourning the loss of the dead poet Robert Trewe (*CSS* p. 399). In another short-story, "The Grave by the Handpost," the "spot" is the burial place under the handpost of Luke Holway's father, the old man having committed suicide and been refused a grave in consecrated ground (*CSS* pp. 664, 670, 673). "This spot" in "A Few Crusted Characters" is both the village churchgyard and the birth-place of Mr Lackland, where he suddenly decides to return and re-establish himself (*CSS* p. 566).

If the womb and the tomb, the beginning and the end, coincide exactly in the signifier "spot," how can movement be achieved in the diegetic world of Hardy's novels? Here lies the paradox of Hardy's fiction: though we labour under the illusion that the characters are constantly moving from place to place, that Tess, or Jude, or Henchard follow their own desire on the path of life, no movement can ever take them anywhere. Hardy's tragic characters cannot be *displaced,*[30] all they can achieve is "a circuitous peregrination" (Tanner, p. 205). When Tess, the daughter of a professed poulterer, goes away from home, she finds herself in a poultry-yard.[31] When she marries, she goes no further than her ancestors' manor. The carriage which is to take her and Angel to church, which reminds Angel of the legendary d'Urberville coach, is a cumbrous and creaking structure, driven by a venerable postilion afflicted with rheumatism, a conveyance hardly fit for a young couple engaging on the roads of life. When Tess is caught by the police on the Salisbury plain, she at last finds that one of her mother's people "was a shepherd here about," and she exclaims "So now I am at home" (*Tess* p. 379). The first word of the novel is "on" ("On an evening in the latter part of May" *Tess* p. 13), so is the last word ("joined hands, and went on" *Tess* p. 384). We seem to have come full circle. The last chapter begins with "The city of Wintoncester [...]" (*Tess* p. 383), and ends with words that sound like an echo of the first line: "went on." Though the novel is haunted

30 A distinction should be made between tragic and non-tragic characters: for instance between Boldwood and Gabriel Oak in *Far from the Madding Crowd.*

31 Cf Escuret, pp. 576–635.

by the adverb "on," repeatedly associated with verbs of movement ("went on," "drove on," "sped on," "rode on," "walked on," "walks on," "moved on," etc.), another motif plays a similar tune ("bone," "stone," "skeleton," "skillentons," "tons and tons,"[32] etc.), heard like an ironical counterpoint against the series of movement. All is immobilized, as though turned into stone, or bone.[33]

The theme of immobilization is introduced in *Tess of the d'Urbervilles* with the accident scene in Chapter IV, when the heroine's course to Casterbridge is arrested by an "object" blocking the way: "Something terrible had happened. The harness was entangled with an *object* which blocked the way" (*Tess* p. 36, my italic). The way will remain blocked for Tess, who will have no choice but "to bide here" with her "load": "We can't go on with our load—Prince is killed" (*Tess* p. 37). From that moment, Tess does not fully belong to living humanity,[34] she lingers in that in-between area which Lacan, referring to Antigone, has called "Between-Two-Deaths" (*L'entre-deux-morts*): she is "on the wrong side," not just the wrong side of the road ("You was on the wrong side" *Tess* p. 37), or the wrong side of the entrance to the d'Urberville vaults ("Why am I on the wrong side of this door!" *Tess* p. 351), but on the wrong side of the limit called *Atè*: Like Antigone, "although she is not yet dead, she is eliminated from the world of the living" (Lacan, 1986a/2008, p. 345). Like the Greek heroine, she "suspends everything that has to do with transformation, with the cycle of generation and decay or with history itself," she "finds herself in the position of synchrony in opposition to diachrony" (Lacan, 1986a/2008, p. 351). What is suspended is temporal flux, whether natural or historical.[35] The point I wish to make here is that it is an object that blocks the way, a *surplus object* that jams the system, and that this object is precisely the "spot" I am writing about. Unlike the *jeu de taquin* ("15-puzzle"), in which the parts can move freely within the frame because there is a hole somewhere (a missing square), all is blocked

32 One might object that the phonemes of "on," "stone," "bone," "skeleton," "tons," are not exactly the same. But the same *graphemes* are repeated.

33 To give a few examples: "Under the church of that there parish lie my ancestors—hundreds of 'em—in coats of mail and jewels, in gr't lead coffins weighing tons and tons. There's not a man in the county o' South-Wessex that's got grander and nobler skillentons in his family than I" (*Tess* p. 16), "Tess's feet were quite bare, and the stones hurt her, and chilled her to the bone [...] He thus beheld in the pale morning light the resolve to separate from her; not as a hot and indignant instinct, but denuded of the passionateness which had made it scorch and burn; standing in its bones; nothing but a skeleton, but none the less there" (*Tess* p. 245).

34 Cf "You don't live anywhere. You are extinct [...]" (*Tess* p. 15) are Parson Tringham's words to John Durbeyfield.

35 See Reinhard Lupton (2009).

in the tragic world because no such gap exists, because a surplus object occupies the place that should be left vacant. No wonder Tess gets "splashed from face to skirt with the crimson drops" from the horse on "the spot of the accident" (*Tess* p. 37): the disaster that strikes her is a "spot."

It is fairly easy to show that things go wrong in Hardy's tragic world because of an object which comes in excess of reality—in other words, an object *added* to the *studium*, a *punctum*. A *punctum* in the diegesis which is not evanescent (as it is in works of art, that one may choose to look at or not), but is here to stay. In *Far from the Madding Crowd*, Boldwood is unbalanced by an uncanny object, a Valentine card that Bathsheba has bought and does not know what to do with (*FFMC* p. 78). An object that disrupts the peace of his home when it finds its way to the mantel-shelf: "Upon the mantel-shelf was a time-piece, surmounted by a spread eagle, and upon the eagle's wings was the letter Bathsheba had sent" (*FFMC* pp. 79–80). The object, on which a red seal is affixed, fascinates Boldwood "till the large red seal [becomes] as a blot of blood on the retina of his eye" (*FFMC* p. 80). We will see that a similar construction serves to introduce Eustacia as she first appears on the heath in *The Return of the Native* (*RN* p. 11). Eustacia is an anomaly in the landscape, a protrusion that will have to be removed to leave room for the villagers' bonfire. When the "red suns and tufts of fire [...] flecking the whole country around" (*RN* p. 13) begin to disappear one by one, their fuel having been spent, only one remains, "the moon of the whole shining throng," the private bonfire lit by Eustacia on her own barrow as a signal to Wildeve, a fire "that nobody else may enjoy" (*RN* pp. 26–27). That bonfire, a "quiet eye" representing Eustacia, is clearly a surplus object that disrupts communal order on the heath. Characteristically, after her death, reality becomes smooth again, with no more protruding objects piercing the sky above the barrows (except Clym).[36]

One particular example will help us understand the significance of the Hardyan "spot." When Angel leaves Sandbourne after seeing Tess, he "unconsciously" looks back, and his gaze is arrested by an object which forms a stain on a particular point of his field of vision, the vanishing point of perspective: "The tape-like surface of the road diminished in his rear as far as he could see, and as he gazed a moving spot intruded on the white vacuity of its perspective" (*Tess* p. 371). It is Tess, trying to run after him after murdering Alec.[37] Here too

36 "From a distance there simply appeared to be a motionless figure standing on the top of the tumulus, just as Eustacia had stood on that lonely summit some two years and a half before" (*RN* p. 411). But there is a major difference: the erect form piercing the sky is not alone, and it *speaks*.

37 In Polanski's film, Tess here appears in a beautiful crimson dress.

the spot comes as a surplus, it fills a place that is normally empty. Slavoj Žižek writes that, in a mirror image (or in any image), there is always "more than meets the eye" (Žižek, 2001, p. 127), because there is a *surplus* in the image that eludes the eye. That point, which eludes the grasp of the eye, is the subject's own gaze, "the *unheimlich* surplus forever missing in the mirror image, i.e., 'unspecularizable'" (Žižek, 2001, p. 126). Lacan has given it a name, the "object-gaze" (also translated by Žižek as "the gaze *qua* object"). When Tess appears as a spot on "the white vacuity" of the perspective, she adds to the picture what is usually missing to it, the something more "than meets the eye," normally "unspecularizable." Angel, who had been "staring at nothingness" while eating his breakfast (*Tess* p. 371), "unconsciously" looks back as he walks to the station, impelled to the act by "something" he cannot explain (*Tess* p. 371). With the uncanny inclusion in the field of vision of what is not normally visible (the hidden side behind one's back), we step into an eerie world where perception goes awry. Something is definitely out of joint in Hardy's tragic universe.

I will of course explain as best as I can the Lacanian concept of "object-gaze," not many people being familiar with its subtle complexities. The basics of the concept being that object-gaze is a form of *objet a*, "the object cause of desire" which Lacan introduced in his *Seminar* on anxiety (1962–63). To the Freudian partial objects, Lacan then added two objects, "object-gaze" and "object-voice," which he claimed were interrelated forms of *objet a*. It is important to understand that *objet a* is an object forever missing: in Joël Dor's words, it "inscribes the presence of a hollow which any object may come into."[38] For Sarah Kaye *objet a* may be defined as "a pure deficit in the symbolic order that does not have any imaginary protrusion to fill it out [...] As such, it acts as a vacuum, sucking other objects into its place."[39] It is an object, but an *extracted* one. For our experience of reality to acquire consistency, *objet a* has to be excluded from it:

> Lacan pointed out that the consistency of our 'experience of reality' depends on the exclusion of what he calls the *objet petit a* from it: in order for us to have normal 'access to reality', something must be excluded, 'primordially repressed'. In psychosis, this exclusion is undone: the object (in this case, the gaze or voice) is *included* in reality, the outcome of which, of course, is the disintegration of our 'sense of reality', the loss of reality.
>
> ŽIŽEK (1996, p. 91)

38 Dor, p. 185.

39 Kaye, p. 56.

My point is precisely that in Hardy's fiction the extraction of *objet a* (whether it is voice or gaze) is problematic, because the course followed by the tragic characters takes them "on the wrong side" of the limit barring access to "l'entre-deux-morts," or at any rate places them in a liminal position which is dangerously close to the destructive, unknowable Real. Hardy's modernity probably lies in this: a proximity to "the horror" laid almost bare by the disappearance of Victorian semblances, "the Real as opposed to everyday social reality—the real [...] as the price to be paid for peeling off the deceptive layers of reality."[40] This does not mean in any way that the characters or the author suffer from psychosis (except perhaps Boldwood). It simply means that the "madder stain," as it comes to occupy the blind spot that normally elides the field of the gaze, is a poetic device that punctuates Hardy's writing, giving it pulse and substance. It is Hardy's signature, in a way, something like a red seal affixed on the page. "Read me," it seems to say. My approach will by no means be psychological, it is Hardy's *texts* that I will seek to read. And reading with Lacan is a fascinating and rewarding enterprise to embark on. One advantage is that Lacan's twofold concept of "object-gaze" and "object-voice" allows readings that can knot together the visual dimension of Hardy's fiction and the "audible silence" which, I will argue, is both a diegetic specificity in Hardy's novels and the very essence of the literary. For what is the literary, after all, if not a silent voice? Does not the "textual voice"[41] bear a great resemblance to the plaintive note of November winds on Egdon Heath, "a worn whisper, dry and papery" (*RN* p. 51), which brushes distinctly across the ear if the reader lends it his voice, but otherwise lies dormant on paper leaves, silent letters that no one can hear?

---

40 Žižek (2002, pp. 5–6). To Žižek, the emergence of the Real is the hallmark of the XXth century, which "aimed at delivering the thing itself" (p. 5).

41 A concept elaborated by Claude Maisonnat, who defines the "textual voice" as "a fictional version of the Lacanian object-voice" (Maisonnat, 2012, p. 167).

CHAPTER 1

The Letter Killeth

1.1 The Littoral in *A Pair of Blue Eyes*

To introduce the question of the *literal* in Hardy's fiction, it may be instructive to give some thought to the *littoral*[1] in *A Pair of Blue Eyes*. Indeed the littoral in that novel is much more than the setting of the fiction—the parish of Endelstow on the coast of north Cornwall, so strangely reminiscent of St Juliot, where Hardy met and courted his first wife Emma Gifford. It is an essential theme in the novel, which dwells insistently on the question of limits, for instance in the famous scene that shows Knight literally suspended between life and death as he clings to the "Cliff without a Name" overhanging the "unplummetted ocean" (*APBE* p. 212) beneath his feet—a black sea edged with white foam which appears to him as "his funeral pall and its edging" (*APBE* p. 212). In his desperate attempt to resist gravity, he suddenly catches sight of "an embedded fossil, standing forth in low relief from the rock":

> It was a creature with eyes. The eyes, dead and turned to stone, were even now regarding him. It was one of the early crustaceans called Trilobites. Separated by millions of years in their lives, Knight and this underling seemed to have met in their place of death. It was the single instance within reach of his vision of anything that had ever been alive and had had a body to save, as he himself had now.
>
> *APBE* p. 209

The passage has been commented upon to show the impact of Darwinism and Lyell's geology on Victorian thought.[2] The reader might be arrested by the Medusa-like gaze of the "creature with eyes" staring Knight in the face. But my point here is to draw attention to a different problematic, in a Lacanian perspective: I will focus on the question of *limits* in the diegesis of the novel,

1 Whether the pun is justified or not will be for the reader to decide. Of course the pun was once made by Lacan: "Rature d'aucune trace qui soit d'avant, c'est ce qui fait terre du littoral. *Litura* pure, c'est le littéral" (Lacan, 2001a, p. 16).

2 Beer, p. 236. For Marjorie Garson, the scene evokes "The Mystery of Human Consciousness: A Post-Darwinian Mystery, A Geological Sublime" (Garson, 2006, p. 108). See also Gossin, 2007, and Radford, 2010.

 | DOI 10.1163/9789004296626_003

more precisely on the failure of the Symbolic to provide a *rim* around the void of the Real. For in this particular novel, as well as in many others by Hardy, what goes wrong is the "paternal metaphor" (Lacan's "Name-of-the-Father"), which is inoperative. That function being the organizing principle that normally cuts out reality into discrete units and articulates them together,[3] its dysfunctioning can only bring about chaos, and tragedy. Limits in *A Pair of Blue Eyes* are uncertain, porous, easily transgressed. They only seem to be there for daring trespassers to overstep them and put their lives at risk. When Elfride goes to Endelstow church tower with Knight, she remembers "a giddy feat" she had performed the year before: "It was to walk round upon the parapet of the tower—which was quite without battlement or pinnacle, and presented a smooth flat surface about two feet wide, forming a pathway along the four sides" (*APBE* p. 160). Later, when Knight finds himself in a perilous position on the Cliff without a Name, Elfride remembers the previous episode and sees the present as a repetition of the past: "This is the moment I anticipated when on the tower. I thought it would come" (*APBE* p. 205). Falling, or rather *nearly* falling into precipices, is a recurrent pattern in the novel, too insistent to be meaningless. Limits are inefficient, they fail to act as barriers against the tempting void opening beneath the characters' feet.

Limits may appear precarious in the diegetic world, but in the *text* they are a strong poetic element. It is important to note that from the outset, even though I will only develop the idea later: Hardy's texts owe most of their beauty to a particular concern with the liminal;[4] it is there, on the "margin of the unexpressed" (Woolf, 1932/1953, p. 248), on "the 'outer limit'—the place where order shades into chaos, light into darkness,"[5] that the text acquires its "literariness," its *sublime*[6] dimension—a point once made by Conrad in a powerful passage (Conrad, p. 138). The literary letter is traced along the *littoral*, following its contours "like curves and arabesques flourishing round a centre of complete emptiness" (Woolf, 1927/1995, p. 193). One example can illustrate this point. Elfride, standing upon "the edge of the terrace, close to the stone balustrade," facing the sun, is observed by Knight who cannot help looking at her face flooded with

3 See Marc Strauss about the paternal function: "Il faut à ce monde [...] un principe organisateur. Ce principe est la fonction paternelle. C'est elle qui est la clé de la signification, à partir de laquelle le monde incohérent prend sens" (Strauss, p. 67). "This world [...] requires an organizing principle. That principle is the paternal function. The paternal function is the key to signification, thanks to which the incoherent world begins to make sense" (my translation).

4 See *The Hardy Review*, xv–i, on the subject of liminality in Hardy's work.

5 See Burgin, 1990, pp. 115–116.

6 "Sublime" is derived from the Latin *sublimis*, from *sub* + *limen* threshold.

the warm light. The "bright rose colour" of the girl's cheek being heightened to "a vermilion red," it is only at the point where it curves round into shadow that its "natural tone" may be glimpsed, and it is what *surrounds* her—the ends of her hair and the fringes of her dress, what might be called her "extremities"—that catches the light and becomes resplendent like a sublime aura:

> The ends of her hanging hair softly dragged themselves backwards and forwards upon her shoulder as each faint breeze thrust against or relinquished it. Fringes and ribbons of her dress, moved by the same breeze, licked like tongues upon the parts around them, and fluttering forward from shady folds caught likewise their share of the lustrous orange glow.
> *APBE* p. 158

Fringes in the novel, like the "thready silk fringe" (*APBE* p. 315) around Mrs Jethway's shawl, on which Knight's hand lights when he discovers her dead body under the *debris* of the fallen church tower, are both the uncertain limit edging the horror and a metatextual representation of the literary text—the text as *fabric*, a fabric with frayed edges. For a literary text makes us enjoy beauty, which works as "a barrier prohibiting access to a fundamental horror."[7] *A Pair of Blue Eyes* is a novel in which Hardy makes ample use of the *silhouette*, as J.B. Bullen has noted (Bullen, p. 55). No doubt because the outline is of prime importance in Hardy's aesthetics.

For want of a strong barrier edging the abyss, everything falls in *A Pair of Blue Eyes*: hats, telescopes, ear-rings, towers, words (*APBE* 297), people, especially women of course. One particular scene is enlightening because it shows the connection between the fall *motif* and the collapse of the Symbolic order: the scene in which Knight "lets down" Elfride because he has realized that the kiss he gave her was not the first she had received. His desertion of the girl is paralleled by the fall of the Endelstow church tower—demolition had been going on for days, but the tower falls one day too soon, unsupervised by the team of masons who had been pulling it down, and a woman is killed in the accident. Elfride, who has so far seen Knight as her worthy "knight," as a tower of strength against adversity, understands that he is about to fail her. In the dialogue with him, she quotes *The Book of Common Prayer* ("Thou hast been my hope, and a strong tower for me against the enemy" *APBE* p. 304). At that very moment, the church tower collapses:

7 "[…] ce que nous avons démontré, dans la tragédie, de la fonction de la beauté: barrière extrême à interdire l'accès à une horreur fondamentale" (Lacan, 1966, pp. 774–775). My translation.

> 'The strong tower moves', said Knight, with surprise.
> A corner of the square mass swayed forward, sank, and vanished. A loud rumble followed, and a cloud of dust arose where all had previously been so clear.
>
> *APBE* p. 304

It is the *name* (in other words the Symbolic order) that the fall of the "tower of strength" affects: for in the Bible the "tower of strength" is "the name of the Lord," and in *Richard III* it is "the King's name."[8] The name in *A Pair of Blue Eyes* appears "wounded," like Tess's "poor wounded name"[9] —the "Cliff without a Name" being symptomatic of that disorder.

The most striking example to illustrate my point is the story of Elfride's grandmother, "Lady Elfride," who ran away with a singer and married him without her father realizing what was happening: "She fell in love with this young man of hers, and their banns were asked in some church in London; and the old lord her father actually heard'em asked the three times, and didn't notice her *name*, being gabbled on wi' a host of others" (*APBE* p. 246, my italics). The name, gabbled out and undistinguishable from others, generates a sense of indistinctness—just as the collapse of the tower raises a cloud of dust which blurs what had been so clear previously. The paternal function fails to make reality legible in *A Pair of Blue Eyes*. The deficiency of the Symbolic affects language and the capacity of nomination: quite logically, when Knight's hand lights on the "thready silk fringe," he cannot at first *name* the substance he is touching,[10] as he finds it "differing in the greatest possible degree from what he had expected to see" (*APBE* p. 315). When the symbolic falters, the Real is no longer contained within limits, it is then "the horror, the horror" that confronts us directly. No words can define the "stringy and entangled" thing trailing upon the rubble of the fallen tower (*APBE* p. 315), the unnameable substance of the Real.[11] The collapse of the tower must be seen as a metaphor for the decline of

8 The origin of the phrase is biblical: "The name of the Lord is a strong tower" (Proverbs, 18, 10). The "tower" turns into a "tower of strength" in *The Book of Common Prayer* and in *Richard III* ("the King's name is a tower of strength," v, 3, 12).

9 "Poor Wounded Name! My Bosom as a Bed Shall Lodge Thee" (*Two Gentlemen of Verona*, I.ii.115–116). The quotation from Shakespeare is placed in epigraph to *Tess of the d'Urbervilles*. See Ramel, 1991.

10 He makes several fruitless attempts at nomination ("a tressy species of moss or lichen [...] a tuft of grass [...] a mason's whitewash brush" *APBE* p. 315), until he realizes that it is the fringe of a dead person's shawl.

11 Žižek made an attempt at giving a figure to the Real: "this 'grey and formless mist, pulsing slowly as if with inchoate life', [...] the pulsing of the presymbolic substance in its abhorrent

the Symbolic in the Victorian age—an age in which belief in patriarchal figures of authority (Father, King, God) was gradually being eroded by the discourse of science and the crisis of faith it engendered.[12]

Elfride's father, Parson Swancourt, reacts in a typically Victorian way to the fall of the ancient tower. Far from regretting the loss of "an interesting piece of antiquity," as Knight and Elfride do, he rejoices over the event: "'Ah, but my dear sir, we shall have a new one', expostulated Mr Swancourt; 'a splendid tower—designed by a first-rate London man—in the newest style of Gothic art' (*APBE* p. 305). Ironically, he has been presented to us as a man with a particular interest in the past, especially "genealogies [...] and patrician reminiscences" (*APBE* p. 81), and who is so convinced of Stephen Smith's "blue blood" (*APBE* p. 20) that he allows his daughter to roam about the countryside alone with him. He is in fact the worst possible father for Elfride, the motor that drives the plot to its tragic resolution. All his decisions concerning his daughter prove disastrous: his total lack of concern as to her whereabouts at first, his rejection of Stephen, his intrusion in Knight's flat when Elfride has run away to her fiancé to try to make him relent, his harsh treatment of her after her return from that escapade (*APBE* p. 369), which leaves her no choice but to accept a loveless marriage with Lord Luxellian—a marriage that ends in death for her.

1.2 Gaps and Gashes

Fathers are often absent or deficient in Hardy's novels, leaving daughters and sons to follow a tragic course. By contrast, an effective paternal figure makes a comic resolution possible, as Marjorie Garson has noted about Bathsheba: "with a father-figure in his right place, a woman is free to dwindle into a properly bourgeois wife" (Garson, 1991, p. 55). In *The Return of the Native*, writes Marjorie Garson, "there are no effective fathers, and things accordingly unravel: all the plot developments in this novel begin with a missing, or deficient, father or father-figure" (Garson, 1991, pp. 55–56). In Hardy's fiction, "mothers tend to be redundant, fathers deficient" (Garson, 1991, p. 55). Eustacia Vye runs into trouble because she is brought up by a grandfather who has no authority over

---

vitality" (Žižek, 1992, p. 14). The quotation inside the quotation is from a science-fiction novel by Robert Heinlein, *The Unpleasant Profession of Jonathan Hoag*.

12 I do not wish to develop that point, which was the subject of my habilitation paper, "L'Autre à l'époque victorienne: Shorthouse, Hardy, Dickens" (unpublished). That paper was based on the (unpublished) seminar of Jacques-Alain Miller and Éric Laurent: "L'Autre qui n'existe pas et ses comités d'éthique" (1996–1997).

her (Garson, 1991, p. 56). In *Tess of the d'Urbervilles*, paternity is a gap that can never be filled, a missing link in the chain of generations which has deprived Tess of her true *name*, Tess d'Urberville.[13] Tess's father having gone to the public house to "get up his strength" (*Tess* p. 27) for his journey to Casterbridge the next day, Tess and her little brother Abraham (a parodic father figure) have to replace him: it is clearly paternal disability that causes disaster. Jack Durbeyfield fails to be the "bread-winner" of his family: it is the horse, Prince (from the Latin *princeps*, the first), which assumes this function ("the bread-winner had been taken away from them" *Tess* p. 38)—a function devolved to Tess after the horse has been killed. Tess is never referred to as her father's daughter: she is "a fresh and virginal daughter of Nature" (*Tess* p. 124), "a daughter of the soil" (*Tess* p. 131). It is Jack Durbeyfied who, just returned from his weekly booze at Rolliver's Inn, declares that no parson is to enter his house (*Tess* p. 98), thereby compelling Tess to baptize the child herself "in the Name of the Father" (*Tess* p. 99). That mock baptism performed in private has no validity, so the parson logically refuses to give the infant a Christian burial. Access to the Symbolic world is denied it because of a deficiency in the paternal function.[14]

It has been acknowledged that in *The Mayor of Casterbridge*—a novel often compared to *King Lear*—paternity is the problem. For when Henchard sells his wife on a fair, he also severs himself from his daughter: "Paternity is the central subject of the book, far more important than conjugal love" (Showalter, p. 57). Henchard will be unable to restore "the tenderest human tie" (*MC* p. 125), the one binding him to Elizabeth-Jane, whom he believes to be his daughter. In that novel, what happens is a rupture in historical continuity: the symbolic chain binding the hero to his ancestors and to his offspring is broken, as Henchard re-enters society alone, "the new Adam, reborn, self-created, unencumbered" (Showalter, p. 57). Jan Gordon made a similar analysis in his reading of *Tess of the d'Urbervilles* (Gordon, pp. 366–388). That tragic breach is both a rupture in symbolic succession—therefore involving the question of paternity—and a severance that alienates the hero from his community. In *The Mayor of Casterbridge*, Susan pulling off her wedding-ring and flinging

13 Tess's name ("Durbeyfield") is a degraded form of "d'Urberville" ("our names are worn away to Durbeyfield" *Tess* p. 44). The title of the novel ("Tess of the d'Urbervilles") shows that Hardy's attempt at repairing the heroine's "wounded" name is doomed to failure: the repetition of the preposition "of" (first in English and then in its French form, "d'") suggests ineffectuality, the radical impossibility of such a restoration. Tess is unnameable.

14 In the context of the Victorian crisis of faith, and in the light of Hardy's own unbelief, that deficiency must also be understood as the failure of God the father to reply to Tess, as the "silence of infinite spaces" that fills one with awe (Blaise Pascal). The Other does not exist. The place of the Father is a void.

it in her husband's face is the moment when the "alliance" between Henchard and his community is broken—it is interesting to note that the French word for "wedding-ring" is *alliance*. The next morning, Henchard awakes and discovers the ring, "a little shining object" among the litter strewn over the floor.

From now on, the "ring" will be a recurrent image in the novel, but not as a metaphor for human symbolic relations: it is a hole, a gaping void, like for instance the Ring at Casterbridge, "the frequent spot for appointments of a furtive kind," often used for "tentative meetings" after "divisions and feuds," but never visited by happy lovers (*MC* p. 71), the sinister place where Susan and Henchard, and then Henchard and Lucetta, meet in fruitless attempts to heal breaches. There stood the town gallows at Casterbridge when executions were carried out in public, and sanguinary games were performed in Roman times. A "ring" is also formed by the cups disposed on the circular oak table at the Three Mariners Inn where Henchard goes to put an end to his term of abstinence from drink: "Forty at least might have been seen at this time in the large room, forming a ring round the margin of the great sixteen-legged oak-table, like the monolithic circle at Stonehenge in its pristine days" (*MC* p. 231)—the connotation of sacrifice is obvious, prefiguring *Tess of the d'Urbervilles*. The ring is also the "stout copper ring" (*MC* p. 205) welded onto the nose of the bull that has run loose and terrifies Lucetta and Elizabeth Jane, a parodic ring that does not work as a sign of *wed*lock but is *weld*ed on to the flesh of the sacrificial victim.[15] The ring metaphor is one of several that punctuate the novel and give form to the tragic breach: crevices, rents, chinks, cracks, gaping mouths, nostrils, pools, holes of all kinds—like Ten-Hatches-Hole, for instance, where Henchard intends to take his life. The "crevices in the canvas"[16] through which the sun filters when he awakes in the tent the morning after selling his wife (*MC* p. 17) are part of that motif. They must be read as a sign that the symbolic fabric of Henchard's life has been ripped beyond the possibility of repair.

The tragic gash is also a major theme in *Tess of the d'Urbervilles*: the motif begins with the pointed shaft of the mail-cart entering the breast of the unfortunate Prince "like a sword" (*Tess* p. 37), allowing the horse's blood to gush forth—try as she may, Tess cannot close the wound by putting her hand on the hole. She only gets splashed from head to foot. The horse's wound has metonymically become hers. The next occurrence is her "violation" by Alec: "she too, like the stoical Prince [is] brutally pierced on a darkened road far from home" (Tanner, p. 186). By attempting to "claim kin," in the fond hope of

15 An interesting parallel has been made between Henchard and a "bull breaking fence" (Holloway, p. 345).

16 See Ramel, 1998.

restoring historical continuity, Tess has only succeeded in opening another gap, between "The Maiden" (phase the first) and "Maiden No more" (phase the second): "an immeasurable social chasm was to divide our heroine's personality thereafter from that previous self of hers [...]" (*Tess* p. 77). The narrator here tries to mend the torn fabric of history by his commentary on the event as a possible "retribution" for similar acts of violence committed by Tess's ancestors on defenceless peasant girls, but that is of no avail: "But though to visit the sins of the fathers upon the children may be a morality good enough for divinities it is scorned by average human nature; and it therefore does not mend the matter" (*Tess* p. 77). The tragic gash can only be repeated, again and again, all along the novel. Metonymically, the wound is passed on to Alec, whose heart will be pierced by a carving-knife in Mrs Brooks's lodging-house. The symbolic gap—the missing link in the chain of generations—has turned into a gash in living flesh. An unsymbolized "wound" in Tess's name that will never be healed.

But then, in a Lacanian perspective, one important question arises: that void opening in the lives of Hardy's protagonists, is it the *structural* hole which is at the core of human existence? In the very last lines of the novel, once the tragic scapegoat has been excluded and the passions are supposedly "purged," the reader is struck by the recurrence of negative prefixes or suffixes ("unknowing," "speechless," "motionless" *Tess* p. 384). Isn't some truth expressed here about the "ontological void" (Žižek, 1999a, p. 138) that defines subjectivity? My answer will be twofold. First, the tragic gash must be distinguished from what can be called *structural* holes. The hole in the middle of a wedding-ring is part of a structure, like the hole in the middle of the King's crown: the "hollow crown" in *Richard II*[17] is emblematic both of the rift within the speaking subject (the "ontological void") and of all the texts that culture weaves around this fundamental void. Such is the function of human culture: to erect ramparts that encircle the abyss of the Real[18]—but the abyss is still there. And there would be no culture, no art without it. Lacan, using as a starting-point Heidegger's theorizing on the function of the vase (perhaps the most primitive form of art), shows that art is always a creation *ex-nihilo*:

> It creates the void and thereby introduces the possibility of filling it. Emptiness and fullness are introduced into a world that by itself knows not of them. It is on the basis of this fabricated signifier, this vase, that

17 "[F]or within the hollow crown/That rounds the mortal temples of a King/Keeps death his court" (Shakespeare, *Richard II*, III.ii.160–162).

18 In *The Ethics of Psychoanalysis*, Lacan speaks of *Das Ding* rather than of the Real (Lacan, 1986a/2008, p. 148, on the function of the vase as surrounding *Das Ding*).

> emptiness and fullness as such enter the world [...] If the vase may be filled, it is because in its essence, it is empty. And it is exactly in the same sense that speech and discourse may be full or empty."
>
> LACAN, 1986A/2008, p. 149

In the scene at the Three Mariners', where the "ring" formed by the circular table and the forty cups disposed on it threatens to engulf the tragic hero, no such fate awaits the choir members: *they* are safely seated on the margin of the pit, because they belong to a community, and because as singers they are participants in the production of human culture. For them the hole in the middle is part of a symbolic structure which articulates fullness and emptiness. For Henchard the void is not caught in a structure, it is sheer abysmal hollowness.[19] So are the "crevices in the canvas" at the beginning of the novel: radically different from the holes woven into a cloth by the interlacing threads, they are the figure given to a tragic wound that cannot be healed. Similar questions could be raised about the signifier "ring" in *A Pair of Blue Eyes*: are the ear-rings structural like those made by a jeweller, or are they a figure of the nothingness towards which the story tends? In Hardy's tragic novels, the gash is an *unsymbolizable* hole.

1.3 The Missing Blank

But matters are a little more complex than that. For what strikes the reader of Hardy's novels, rather than a gaping hole threatening to engulf the tragic heroes, is the obtrusive presence of a surplus object, as I have announced in my introduction. The paradigmatic example of this being the unidentified object blocking the way on the night of the accident that kills the horse of the d'Urbervilles ("the harness was entangled with an object blocking the way *Tess* p. 36). The way is barred for Tess, who cannot "go on" with her load (*Tess* p. 37)—and as we have seen all *displacement* will be impossible for her. The two seemingly

19 For Henchard, the "ring" cannot be measured, contained, or circumscribed. It is unfathomable. Into that void he is about to plunge, as he puts an end to his long term of abstinence. The measurelessness of tragic *jouissance* is conveyed by the words of the choir-leader: "Whatever servant David were thinking about when he made a Psalm that nobody can sing without disgracing himself, I can't *fathom*" (*MC* p. 233, my italics). By contrast, the description of the forty church-goers seated round the table in front of forty cups of exactly half-a pint of liquor each insists on measure and reckoning. And the first task undertaken by Abel Whittle once Henchard is dead is "to get a man to measure him" (*MC* p. 333).

antithetical readings (one focusing on the tragic gash, the other on the surplus object) are in fact perfectly coherent: there are tragic holes *because* what is missing is a structural hole that could serve as the initial gap in the signifying chain. It is *the lack of a lack* which makes life impossible in tragedy—and which in real life causes anxiety.[20] Lacan was much influenced in the 1970s by two mathematicians, Peano and Frege, who showed that the sequence of natural numbers rests entirely on zero counting as one: 2 proceeds from zero and one, 3 from zero, one, and two, etc. The property that makes possible the progression from n to n + 1 comes from the initial move from 0 to 1, which can be repeated along the chain of numbers. In other words, zero is a prerequisite for moving on along the chain of numbers (Maleval, 2000). No *displacement* is feasible without the gap where the sequence originates.[21] From that Lacan deduced the logical equivalence of the function of the Father to that of zero in Peano's axiomatic. The Father is not the first, but should occupy the position of zero in the sequence—which is another way of saying that the Symbolic Father is the dead Father. The function of The Name-of-the-Father achieves symbolic castration, that is to say it prohibits *jouissance*: the *jouissance* of the Other (in both senses of the preposition "of"), either maternal or paternal.

But, as Žižek argues, the Oedipal father, the agent of symbolic law, "is necessarily redoubled in itself, it can exert its authority only by relying on the superego figure of the Father-of-Enjoyment" (Žižek, 1992, p. 24). Because of that dependence of one "version" of the father on the other, there is always the possibility of "perversion,"[22] that is to say the risk for the "Father-of-Enjoyment" to prevail upon the symbolic Father. In that case symbolic castration fails to operate, and the paternal Other is not the dead Father but the obscene Father-of-Enjoyment. Then the paternal Other is not an empty place but a radically perverse figure, the embodiment of satiety. Something of that kind happens in Hardy's tragic novels: the place of the Other is not vacant, it is filled by the cruel Other of tragedy, "the President of the Immortals" who sports with Tess

---

20 About Freud's story of the child playing with a wooden reel, Lacan writes: "Ce qui provoque l'angoisse [...] ce n'est pas, contrairement à ce qu'on dit, le rythme ni la présence-absence de la mère[...] Il ne s'agit pas de perte de l'objet, mais de la présence de ceci, que les objets ça ne manque pas [...] Qu'est-ce que cela veut-il dire?—sinon que ce qui est craint, c'est la réussite. C'est toujours le *ça ne manque pas*." For Freud, what induces anxiety is separation from the mother; for Lacan it is the lack of such separation (Lacan, 2004, p. 67).

21 A parallel can be made with the *jeu de taquin* ("15-puzzle"), in which the parts can move freely within the frame because there is a hole somewhere (a missing square).

22 Which Lacan writes as *père-version* (Žižek, 1992, p. 25).

and is sated at the end of the novel.[23] The deficiency of the paternal function in Hardy's fiction has to be understood in such logical terms. The lack of an empty space—comparable to the lack of zero in a sequence of numbers—results in tragic immobilization. "This solidity, this mass seizure of the primitive signifying chain" (Lacan, 1973/1986b, p. 238), called "holophrasis" by Lacan,[24] is the very essence of the tragic. In Hardy's fiction, it is because some of the protagonists situate themselves on the locus of *origin*—disregarding the basic fact that the origin *is* a blank—that their lives become petrified. Henchard, reborn as "the new Adam," is doomed to endless wandering, "like the Canadian woodsman," around a centre formed by Casterbridge (*MC* p. 319).

A characteristic episode is the dialogue between Henchard and Farfrae, where the young man demonstrates to Henchard how an invention of his can "renovate" corn. Having tasted the processed corn, Henchard exclaims: "It's complete!—quite restored, or—well—nearly." To which Farfrae replies: "Quite enough restored to make good *seconds* out of it" (*MC* p. 48, my italics). Henchard, "corn-factor and hay-merchant" (*MC* p. 59), is not just a dealer in corn (and in hay), he is nothing short of the *seed* from which life originates.[25] However "unprincipled," parodic, and ineffectual a father-figure he may be, he is somehow the creator of life, the man whose thunderous voice, like the divine voice on Mount Sinai,[26] is heard reverberating at the town-pump (*MC* p. 113)—the "original fount" of Casterbridge, the source of "pure" water (*MC* p. 120). To him the renovation process makes regression to the origin possible: it turns the "unprincipled" bread (made from corrupt seed) into bread that might truly be called "principled," i.e. e. "the first," prepared from the original seed (for the Latin *princeps* means "the first"). Farfrae, who is not a tragic character, has a

23 The main function of tragedy is to give consistence to the Other—an important issue in an age that called into question the existence of God.

24 "[…] when there is no interval between S1 and S2, when the first dyad of signifiers becomes solidified, holophrased, we have the model for a whole series of cases" (Lacan, 1973/1986b, p. 237). See also Stevens, Alexandre, "L'holophrase, entre psychose et psychosomatique," *Ornicar?*, n° 42 (Autumn 87–88): "La solidification signifiante s'oppose à l'effet métaphorique. L'holophrase est même, dirons-nous, le nom que Lacan donne ici à l'absence de la dimension de la métaphore" (p. 66). ("Signifying solidification is opposed to the metaphoric effect. Holophrasis is even, shall we say, the name given here by Lacan to the absence of the metaphoric dimension," my translation).

25 The Latin origin of "factor" suggests that he is someone who *makes* corn, that is to say the prime cause of all seeds, the origin of life.

26 "a great voice, as of a trumpet" (*Revelation*, I, 10), "and when the voice of the trumpet sounded long, and waxed louder and louder, Moses spake, and God answered him by a voice" (*Exodus*, IX, 19).

different perspective and only believes in the possibility of making "good seconds" out of the adulterated corn. To that accomplished young man, who "does it all by ciphering and mensuration" (*MC* p. 107), arithmetics is an easy game, and counting up to two and even beyond is no problem at all.[27] Not so with Henchard, who is "bad at figures—a rule o' thumb sort of man" (*MC* pp. 49–50), and who can go no further than one. Another significant episode is the one that relates the visit of "a royal personage" to the town of Casterbridge—in a striking parallel with Prince Albert's visit to Dorchester in 1849. Henchard feels a strange compulsion to step into the "clear yards in front of the royal carriage, sanded" (*MC* pp. 265–66), thus occupying the vacant space *before* the "Prince," the first. He is roughly pushed back into his proper place by Farfrae, the Mayor, who represents the Law. Henchard has trespassed on forbidden ground—the place of zero in the chain of numbers. Such is the form assumed by *hubris* with that man, who attempts to fill a structural void, the place of God.

A development by Jean-Claude Maleval about the most typical representations of paternity, i.e. kings and popes, throws some light on the point I am making:

> Each of them owes his power not to the first of the monarchs bearing his name (e.g. Louis I or Gregory I), but to God, who founds the lineal succession, and counts for zero. In the n + 1 formula which governs the line, the initial n must be reduced to zero, thus confirming the Freudian intuition that the Symbolic Father is no other than the dead Father.
>
> MALEVAL, p. 115, my translation

The question of origin is at the core of Hardy's tragic fictions, as is manifest in the story of Tess d'Urberville, whose name contains the German prefix *Ur*, the signifier of origin. Jean-Jacques Lecercle points out that the dialect spoken by Tess, whose "characteristic intonation" is defined by Hardy as "the voicing approximately rendered by the syllable Ur, probably as rich an utterance as any to be found in human speech" (*Tess* p. 21), "far from being a corruption of pure English [...] appears as the rich *Ur-sprache* in which meaning is preserved ('as rich an utterance'), exactly as the country girl is the true descendant of the

---

27 When Farfrae is elected Mayor of Casterbridge, he wears "round his young neck the official gold chain with great square links like that round the royal unicorn" (*MC* p. 265): an ironical reversal makes him occupy the position of the "prince," the first—for the "unicorn" is not just the emblem of Scotland, aptly adorning the Scotsman neck (a symbol added to the English royal arms by James I in 1603), but also a word that conjoins "corn" with the signifier of unity, "uni-."

archaic nobility" (Lecercle, 1993, p. 151). Tess, we are told, is a "pure" woman, an "untinctured" (*Tess* p. 21) original d'Urberville.[28] There lies her problem: not in the gap of origin (which is structurally missing for any human being), but in the attempt to bridge it, to deny its essential vacuity.

A look at the text of A *Pair of Blue Eyes* will help us to understand the logic at work in Hardy's novels. What strikes the reader is the impossibility of *counting* in the diegesis. The series of defective arithmetics begins in a comic register, with the coach driver telling Stephen Smith about a Charles the Third having succeeded Charles the Second, to be soon followed by a Charles the Fourth—which causes Stephen to remark that he does not recollect anything about them in English history (*APBE* pp. 12–13). It is of course not insignificant that the mistake should be made in numbering *kings* and, of all kings, those supposed to have succeeded Charles the First. Figures, says Stephen's mother, are not Elfride's strong point ("if she'd learnt to make figures instead of letters when she was at school, 'twould have been better for her pocket" *APBE* p. 91). With the help of her maid, whose remarkable name is "Unity," the girl tries to count the number of times one of her ear-rings had a "hairbreadth escape"; they get lost in the reckoning, until Elfride, who is about to mount her horse and go for a ride, counts "one, two, three, and up!," expecting Stephen to lift her into her saddle—but Stephen staggers and the horse edges round, so that Elfride lights on the ground rather forcibly. One, two, three, and crash goes love—so the incident seems to say. The banns for the wedding of Elfride's grandmother were asked three times, to no avail. Windy Beak, the cliff where Elfride is kissed by Stephen and then by Knight, "was the second cliff in height along that coast, and [...] it enjoyed the reputation of being the first" (*APBE* p. 299)—just as Knight believes he is Elfride's first suitor while he is only second, or perhaps third. Strikingly, when the tragedy is over, counting the succeeding generations becomes possible again, as shown by the inscription on Elfride's coffin-plate: "Elfride, Wife of Spenser Hugo Luxellian, *Fifteenth* Baron Luxellian" (*APBE* p. 366, my italics).

Nobody seems to be able to count up to three, but everybody seems to know how to "put two and two together" (*APBE* 128). For the whole novel revolves around the "pair," which is its central motif: a pair of blue eyes, a pair of ear-rings—reduplicated when Knight attempts to buy a new pair to replace the missing ear-ring, then reconsiders his choice and has to buy a second one, etc. When Elfride loses her ear-ring, the loss is unbearable, for reasons that are not only conventional (fashion in those days made it imperative to wear a pair

28 "U" and "r," present in Tess's name, form a pair which is insistent in many of Hardy's texts (for instance in the passage quoted above about Tess's dialect, and also in *The Return of the Native*). That question will be explored later.

of ear-rings) but also *structural*. For people and objects go two by two in the novel, weddings in particular: Mr Swancourt marries a rich heiress on the very day when Elfride goes away to marry Stephen secretly (but the attempt aborts); Elfride's marriage with Lord Luxellian is celebrated on the same day as that between Unity and Martin Cannister ("it was a very quiet pair of weddings" *APBE* p. 370)—ironically, the woman believed by Knight to be "peerless" (*APBE* p. 333) marries "Spenser Hugo Luxellian, a Peer" (*APBE* p. 5). A first pair of lovers, Elfride and Stephen, is superseded by a second pair, Elfride and Knight, a situation all the more complex as Stephen and Knight form a pair too, in a pupil-master relationship. The repetition compulsion drives all the characters to repeat their acts (with different partners) in the very same place, or in settings evocative of previous events: Elfride and Stephen sit together on the tomb of a boy who once loved Elfride; Knight kisses Elfride on the same cliff where she received Stephen's first kiss (an event which Elfride sees as "a duplicate of the original arrangement with Stephen" *APBE* p. 299); Knight insists on Elfride giving him a "dwarf myrtle tree" (*APBE* p. 290) which was offered to her by Stephen as a keepsake. Knight's hairbreadth escape on the cliff reminds Elfride of her "elevated promenade" at the top of the church tower, which itself had been a repetition of a "giddy feat" performed the year before (*APBE* p. 160). The novel ends with Stephen and Knight following parallel courses: the two men stay in the same hotel in London, take the same train to Cornwall, find themselves in the same carriage, each intending to propose to Elfride. The courses finally converge at Endelstow,[29] where the two men understand that the final term of their journey is the gaping void of Elfride's grave.

All those reduplications are fairly obvious. What is more difficult to figure out is why every act is a repetition.[30] My explanation is that what underlies the text of *A Pair of Blue Eyes* is an unconscious desire to occupy what Žižek would call the "unhistorical kernel" of the Real (Žižek, 2001, p. 81), in other words Pascal Quignard's "sexual night" (Quignard, 2007), the blank of origin. Knight wants to be *the first*,[31] he will not "give way as to his desire"[32] which is to

29 Endelstow itself is divided between East Endelstow and West Endelstow.

30 Žižek's chapter entitled "Why is every Act a Repetition" in Žižek, 2001, pp. 69–110, throws a useful light on Hardy's novel.

31 "Inbred in him was an invincible objection to be any but the first comer in a woman's heart. He had discovered within himself the condition that if ever he did make up his mind to marry, it must be on the certainty that no cropping out of inconvenient old letters, no bow and blush to a mysterious stranger casually met, should be a possible source of discomposure" (*APBE* p. 186).

32 Žižek's translation of Lacan's formula "céder sur son désir" (Žižek, 2001, pp. 75–76). Lacan uses that phrase in "L'éthique de la psychanalyse" (Lacan, 1986a, p. 368). In "The Ethics of

position himself at the locus of origin—the place of zero in a chain of numbers. To be the first is an irresistible urge in the diegesis of the novel, a regressive force which is the exact opposite of the metonymy of desire, because it tends towards an aboriginal *jouissance*, fantasized as anterior even to the dawn of history.[33] It is not insignificant that Knight should find himself paired with a Trilobite embedded in the rock on the "Cliff without a Name," although he and the "creature with eyes" are "separated by millions of years in their lives" (*APBE* p. 209). The fascination with geology in this passage is perhaps not only due to Hardy's interest in Darwinism. Knight cannot bear the thought of being "second or third in the field" (*APBE* p. 313)—a position which cannot be explained only by the Victorian idealization of feminine chastity. Stephen too wants to be first: he does not like standing on young Jethway's tombstone: "Let us go away. I don't like standing by *him*, even if you never loved him. He was *before* me" (*APBE* p. 77). "Before" is a key-word in a novel whose main subject is *anteriority*: anteriority as the zero of origin, which is denied—but the repressed always returns. Of course no one can ever be *the first*, for counting is only possible through the acceptance of an initial nought. To be the first is always to be second, in a sense. "What a poor mortal I am to play second fiddle in everything!" (*APBE* p. 303), exclaims Knight. Angel Clare, too, despite his name, is a "poor mortal" who plays "a second-hand harp" (*Tess* p. 127). In the gap between first and second, between fantasy and reality, lies much of Hardy's irony.

Arithmetics is given a prominent place in the scene on the cliff where Knight kisses Elfride. Elfride has twice refused Knight's gift of a pair of ear-rings. The third attempt by Knight is successful:

> And the packet was withdrawn from his pocket and presented the third time. Elfride took it with delight. The obstacle was rent in twain, and the significant gift was hers.
>
> *APBE* p. 269

Psychoanalysis," the translation by Dennis Porter is "to give ground relative to one's desire" (Lacan, 1986a/2008, p. 392).

33 That refusal to give way as to one's desire amounts here to a refusal of symbolic castration as normally effected by the Name-of-the-Father, and it quite logically ends in the choice of the unsymbolized, "unhistorical" abyss of the Real. In *The Mayor of Casterbridge*, a typical example of the unhistorical kernel of the Real is the first Elizabeth-Jane, who is unrecorded in the family history. The second Elizabeth-Jane is forced into that position, which she is finally led to leave, a fortunate displacement.

So far so good. It seems as though a symbolic process were under way. Yet we cannot fail to hear echoes here of the banns asked "three times"[34] in a church in London (*APBE* p. 246) for the wedding of Elfride's grandmother—a regular proceeding that did not really work out as expected. Another detail jars with the apparent mood of jubilation, the expression "rent in twain": is it not proleptic of the happy pair being "rent in twain" very soon, at the end of that very chapter? Isn't a "pair" precisely what cannot, what must not be "rent in twain," in the logic of this novel? Then, Knight asks Elfride to allow him to put the ear-rings in their place: "Elfie, I should like to touch that seductive ear of yours. Those are my gifts; so let me dress you in them" (*APBE* p. 269). Elfride hesitates, so Knight suggests meeting half way: "Let me just put one in its place, then?" (*APBE* p. 269). The request being granted, Knight proceeds to hook the ear-ring on to Elfride's ear. The sensation felt by the lovers is exquisite:

> At the touch the sensation of both seemed to be concentrated at the point of contact. All the time he was performing the delicate manoeuvre Knight trembled like a young surgeon in his first operation.
>
> *APBE* p. 270

One ear-ring put in its place by Knight, one point of contact where Elfride and Knight are joined, as though it were possible for two human beings to become a "pair," fulfilling the Biblical prophecy that "they two shall be one flesh" (*Ephesians* 5: 31): it seems that "Unity" has at last been achieved.

But a look at the vocabulary used in the text makes us rather suspicious: why should Knight be compared to "a young surgeon in his first operation"? Why has he offered to "dress" Elfride in his gifts, as if he had to dress a wound—another meaning of "to dress" that can be overheard in the passage? That the "operation" should be the "first" performed by the surgeon is no surprise for us. But what is the wound, the breach that he has to heal? Is it the one that is about to be opened between himself and Elfride, when the pair is "rent in twain," or the wound common to the whole of mankind, the original trauma caused by symbolic castration? And is Knight the surgeon going to close that wound, or is he about to make the most painful cut into the living flesh, into the heart of Elfride? Denying the original cut of symbolic castration means inflicting the

---

34 For Tess's forthcoming wedding, Izz Huet remarks to Tess that "there must be three times of asking" (*Tess* p. 204). Nobody so far has heard Tess's or Angel's name called, and only two Sundays are left before the wedding-date. Angel will explain to Tess that he has opted for a licence ("a licence will be quieter for us" *Tess* p. 204), for which the "three times of asking" are not necessary.

cruelest wound on oneself or on others, because it is a tragic gash that cannot be symbolized. "Unity" is the choice made by the pair in this scene, as shown by Elfride's refusal to have Knight hook on the second ring: "'Now the other', said Knight in a whisper. 'No, no'. 'Why not?' 'I don't know exactly'" (*APBE* p. 270). A strange form of arithmetics prevails, where 1 + 1 = 1, and where in fact there is *no going further than one*. It is indeed the condition of being "mortal" that Knight objects to, the condition of being "second fiddle" in life.

Jean-Claude Maleval's reading of Lacan is extremely enlightening here:

> [...] One, when it comes into existence, is not univocal, but dual. The One which proceed from zero, that which is called 'unary', is not founded on sameness, but on sheer difference. It introduces a principle of distinction from which symbolic cutting out can order the real. This countable One is different from the unifying One, the 'unian' one, which tends towards the communal: it has a totalizing function, it erases differences."[35]

It now appears clearly that the "One" towards which the novel drives is the "unian" one, not the "unary" one which springs from zero. The "pair" in the novel is not formed by adding one to one (1 + 1 = 2). It is an indivisible unit, which cannot be broken, except through an unsymbolized rending "in twain." We understand now why it is unbearable for Elfride to lose one ear-ring: one ear-ring is the same as two. Losing one object is not losing an item in a series, it is losing all. And then one finds oneself left with *nothing*—absolute nothingness.[36] An object lost in *A Pair of Blue Eyes* is irreplaceable: when Knight's hat is blown away by the wind, he *has* to put his life at risk to retrieve it. Elfride's lost ear-ring is nowhere to be found—unlike Thomasin's glove in *The Return of the Native*, for which Diggory Venn searches the green under the maypole until the moonlight enables him to spot it. Or unlike Bathsheba's hat, caught by the wind, which Gabriel brings back to her. In these two episodes it is the logic of desire that prevails—not so with Knight and Elfride. All attempts at replacing

---

35 "[...] l'Un dans son surgissement n'est pas univoque mais 'bifide'. Celui qui opère du zéro, l'unaire, ne se fonde pas sur la mêmeté, mais sur la pure et simple différence. Il constitue un principe de distinction à partir duquel un découpage symbolique peut ordonner le réel. Cet Un comptable s'isole de l'Un unifiant, l'unien, dont l'idéal est de faire communauté: il totalise et gomme les différences" (Maleval, p. 116, my translation). Maleval's analysis is based on Lacan's XIXth *Seminar*, "*...ou pire*" (Lacan, 2011), especially Chapter IX (March 15 1972), "Dans le champ de l'Unien," pp. 125–135. "Unien" and "unaire" have not been translated, to my knowledge, so I try "unian" and "unary" (though "unaire" has sometimes been translated as "unitary").

36 For Knight, an ear-ring is "a mere nothing" (*APBE* p. 270).

a lost object in *A Pair of Blue Eyes* fail miserably: Stephen returns without the ear-ring, Knight is compelled to buy two pairs. Objects are either missing or proliferating. The redundant pair now in the possession of Knight is a *surplus* object—like the Valentine card that Bathsheba does not know what to do with, and which eventually finds its way to Boldwood's parlour, an incongruous object that will cause ravages in his life. The presence of a surplus object in the diegesis indicates that what has gone awry is the logic of *objet petit a*, which has been defined as "a pure deficit in the symbolic order that does not have any imaginary protrusion to fill it out [...] a vacuum, sucking other objects into its place" (Kaye, p. 56). That is perfectly consistent with my development on the missing zero for, as Jean-Claude Maleval remarks, "it is from Lacan's theorizing about incompleteness as the founding element of the signifying chain that he will deduce *objet petit a*" (Maleval, p. 118, my translation).

No such vacuum exists in the tragic world, or in psychosis.[37] There, *objet petit a* is included in reality, it is not *extracted*. A significant passage in *A Pair of Blue Eyes* shows us Elfride trying to *extract* the lost ear-ring from "a crevice in the rocky sedile" (*APBE* p. 301)—at the precise moment when Knight gives her a *second* kiss! Elfride's "instinctive act" is to try to secure the object "privately" (*APBE* p. 301), because she remembers the words she had inadvertently "let fall" when Knight first kissed her, about the other ear-ring that she lost "by doing this" (*APBE* 297). Unfortunately, her "surreptitious trials" (*APBE* p. 301) fail. It will take a *surgical* operation, performed by Knight armed with a knife, to extract the object, an irremovable[38] object embedded in Elfride's memory, as though inlaid in her very flesh:

> It was so deep in the crack that Elfride could not pull it out with her hand, though she made several surreptitious trials. [...]

---

37 Cf Žižek: "Lacan pointed out that the consistency of our 'experience of reality' depends on the exclusion of what he calls the objet petit a from it: in order for us to have normal 'access to reality', something must be excluded, 'primordially repressed'. In psychosis, this exclusion is undone: the object [...] is included in reality, the outcome of which, of course, is the disintegration of our 'sense of reality', the loss of reality" (Žižek, 1996, p. 91). That is what happens to Boldwood, who according to Rosemarie Morgan shows patent signs of psychosis (Morgan, 2013, p. 35). But Hardy's other characters are not psychotic of course, neither was Hardy himself. An *analogy* can be drawn between the tragic world and the experience of psychosis.

38 Like the "stout copper ring, welded on, and irremovable as Gurth's collar of brass" (*MC* p. 205), fixed on the nose of the bull that attacks Lucetta and Elizabeth-Jane in *The Mayor of Casterbridge*.

> Knight peered into the joint from which her hand had been withdrawn, and saw what she had seen. He instantly took a penknife from his pocket, and by dint of probing and scraping brought the earring out upon open ground.
>
> *APBE* p. 301

That the operation should have to be performed *surgically*—by a man whose first kiss made him tremble like "a young surgeon "— clearly shows that Knight's act is not a *symbolic* extraction of the primordial "object-cause" of desire. It delves into human flesh. And far from hollowing out reality (as symbolic castration normally does), it makes the object perennial, lodged in the flesh, *incarnated.* The knife cuts into Elfride's flesh.[39] *Expulsion,* as in child-birth, is not possible for her: when in London, "she could not be moved," and she died of a miscarriage (*APBE* p. 370). The rigour of Hardy's logic in this novel is faultless.

1.4 The Literal

"Incarnation" is a key-word to understand what happens in this particular novel, and in many others by Hardy. If "the Letter killeth," as the epigraph to *Jude the Obscure* announces, it is because the word is made flesh: language does not function metaphorically in the diegetic world—though of course it does in the text. For Tess, or for other characters in Hardy's fiction, the sign becomes "incarnated," or to put things the other way round, bodies are "intextuated."[40] An alternative formulation is that given by Elisabeth Bronfen: "Insigned Bodies—Embodied Signs."[41] Normally the metaphoric function of language substitutes words for things, it represents objects that are *not* present:

39 The operation that cuts into Elfride's flesh suggests that the "crevice" in the rock could represent the feminine sexual organ. But we should be mistaken if we saw gender as the main issue here, for what is essential is that the object should be *irremovable* (like the "stout copper ring" welded on to the nose of the bull in *The Mayor of Casterbridge*). Because the blank of origin is missing in both novels, the "crevice" is not the structural gap that serves to initiate the chain of numbers (and the signifying chain), it is a real wound, incarnated in human flesh. It takes a surgeon to deal with it. The lack of a lack makes symbolization impossible.

40 The expression is borrowed from Michel de Certeau: "Inscriptions de la loi sur le corps," *L'Invention du quotidien. Arts de faire*, 1, Paris: UGE, 10/18, 1980.

41 Bronfen, 1993, p. 66. On Tess as sign, see Ramel, 1991. Helena Michie shows how Tess becomes "a text to be read, interpreted, and edited by her two lovers," *The Flesh Made Word*, Oxford: OUP, 1987, pp. 112–114.

when the poet says "a flower," that flower is by necessity "what is absent from every bouquet."[42] Language draws a line between the signifier and the signified, between the sign and its referent. No such bar, no such clear line of demarcation exists in the diegesis of many of Hardy's novels, where signs are taken literally. That point is made by Hillis Miller about *The Well-Beloved*: Pierston, he writes, makes a "linguistic" mistake when he sees things and persons not in their uniqueness, but as signs pointing back to earlier things or persons; "such a character makes the fundamental error of taking figures of speech literally" (Hillis Miller, p. 13).

The same "error" is made in *Tess of the d'Urbervilles* when the sexual act in the forest of the Chase is described as a form of writing on Tess's body: "Why it was that upon this beautiful feminine tissue, sensitive as gossamer, and practically blank as snow as yet, there should have been traced such a coarse pattern as it was doomed to receive?" (*Tess* p. 77). A few pages further, the same mistaking of body for sign (or sign for body) is repeated: the "staring vermilion words" painted on a stile by a religious fanatic send back to Tess her own transfixed gaze, in a strange mirror relation that turns the "fiery lettering" into an inscription on her body—the writing causes a flush to appear on her face, the wall is described like a face, with its "strange unwonted mien" and the "hideous de*face*ment" it undergoes (*Tess* pp. 85–86, my italics). Tess in this passage becomes a text, a "tex." The "nice bit of blank wall" recalls the "blank" feminine tissue written upon by Alec. In this beautiful passage metaphor is an essential poetic element, but it fails to operate as such in the diegesis: the letters enter Tess "with accusatory horror" as though they were knives thrust into her heart ("that word was driven well home to the reader's heart" *Tess* p. 85), they are "crushing, killing" (*Tess* 85). The letter here "killeth," however vivifying it may be in the text.[43] That "linguistic" error is essential to the tragic, as these lines from Racine's *Iphigénie* make clear:

42 Stéphane Mallarmé: "Je dis: une fleur! et, hors de l'oubli où ma voix relègue aucun contour, en tant que quelque chose d'autre que les calices sus, musicalement se lève, idée même et suave, l'absente de tous bouquets" ("Crise de Vers," *Divagations*, Paris: Bibliothèque Charpentier, 1897, p. 251). "I say: a flower! And, out of the oblivion where my voice casts every contour, insofar as it is something other than the known bloom, there arises, musically, the very idea in its mellowness; in other words, what is absent from every bouquet."

43 Ramel, 2013a. The lethal power of the letter in Hardy's fiction has often been studied. In her thesis on Hardy, Annie Escuret points out that it is a collision with the mail-cart, carrying *letters*, that kills the horse of the d'Urbervilles (Escuret, p. 582). See also Goater, pp. 129–137. Elisabeth Bronfen writes that Tess "kills her body into a trope" (Bronfen, p. 75).

Vous armez contre Troie une puissance vaine
Si dans un sacrifice auguste et solennel
Une fille du sang d'Hélène
De Diane en ces lieux n'ensanglante l'autel.[44]

RACINE, *Iphigénie* I 1

The confusion that takes place here is between the *real* blood of Iphigenia, to be spilled on the altar in sacrifice to the goddess Diana, and the *symbolic* blood, the blood of filiation which ties her to Helen, and has a metaphoric value. The metaphor of Helen's "blood" ceases to function as such when it has to be shed, when the word is taken literally.[45] Tragedy often results from such a linguistic "error," which conflates bodies and tropes—in Lacanian terms, when a deadly confusion takes place between the Real and the Symbolic, or between nature and culture. Then, in that perspective, it would appear that the disorder in Hardy's tragic novels is not caused by culture interfering with nature (which, if left untampered with, would make for universal welfare), but by a deficiency in culture itself—a flaw in the Symbolic order.[46]

A brief parenthesis might be useful here to remind the reader that "metaphor" in the Lacanian perspective[47] is a process of substitution that prohibits *jouissance*. Following Jakobson's identification of metaphor with the paradigmatic (or substitutive) axis of language, Lacan developed the concept of the "paternal metaphor" as what substitutes a signifier, the Name-of-the-Father, for another signifier, the "desire of the mother" (to be understood as both the child's desire for the mother, and the mother's desire for the child). The Name-of-the-Father, the "Nom-du-Père" in French, is both the name ("nom") and the "No-of-the Father" ("Non-du-Père"), because it says "no" to the "desire of the mother." It allows entry into the Symbolic world, while simultaneously laying down the incest taboo—the two actions being conditioned by each other and concomitant. In other words there can be no regression to *Das Ding* for anyone

44 "You arm against Troy a vain force if you do not spill over Diana's altar the blood of a daughter of the same blood as Helen" (my translation).

45 A similar linguistic disorder happens in *The Mill on the Floss* when Maggie Tulliver, the daughter of a "bankrupt" father, drowns in a flood caused by the rupture of banks ("at the very worst, the banks would be sure to break lower down the river when the tide came in with violence," Eliot, p. 511).

46 More precisely, the flaw affects the "Borromean" knotting of Real, Symbolic and Imaginary.

47 At any rate in the perspective that was Lacan's when he gave predominance to the Symbolic, in the early days of his teaching—as opposed to the later phase that gave pride of place to the Real.

who inhabits language,[48] because the paternal metaphor substitutes language for the Thing. Symbolic castration also means that an end is put to the boundless enjoyment of the primitive Father: the biblical episode of "the sacrifice of Abraham" (*Genesis* XXII:1–13), where a ram is finally sent by God to be sacrificed *instead of* Isaac, clearly shows how a process of signifying substitution can "bar" the big Other (the "Father-of-Enjoyment") and put a limit to its unsatiable appetite for human sacrifices. What is sacrificed in that episode (which logically should have been called "the sacrifice of Isaac") is the Father's *jouissance*, it is indeed the "sacrifice of Abraham." Anticipating psychoanalytic theory, the Bible shows us how *metaphor* works. Seen in that light, the confusion of bodies with signs appears rather ominous in Hardy's diegetic world: because metaphor is inoperative for Tess, the *jouissance* of the Other is unlimited. No victim will be substituted for her when she awaits sacrifice on an altar-stone at Stonehenge: the woman will have to pay with her own flesh and blood,[49] as has been shown by Elisabeth Bronfen. Hardy's "ensigned bodies," or "embodied signs," must be understood in that perspective. The logic of tragedy is one where the unbarred Other exists—a "red tyrant" (*Tess* p. 315) that Hardy's heroines are there to serve. And the nature of that error is "linguistic."

One striking example to illustrate the "linguistic" disorder that prevails in *Tess of the d'Urbervilles* is the famous d'Urberville coach which, to ordinary people, is a *legend*, i.e. e. some kind of *legible* text, that one may read about, or hear about. For Tess, the carriage due to take her and Angel to church is not a sign representing an absent object (the legendary d'Urberville coach), it is that very coach. Her perception is a direct experience of the *thing*, unmediated by language and culture. She has never heard *of* it ("I have never heard of it to my knowledge" *Tess* p. 212), she can only see it, or hear it ("'I don't remember hearing it before', she murmured. 'Is it when we are going to die, Angel, that

48 Yet, paradoxically, *Das Ding* is an effect of language (Braunstein, pp. 35, 78–80). On the paternal metaphor, see Lacan, 1966, p. 557 (Lacan, 1977, p. 200), and Lacan, 1994, p. 379. On the Name-of-the-Father, see Lacan, 1966, p. 278 (Lacan, 1977, p. 67).

49 Ramel, 1997, pp. 75–89. One of the points made in that article was that in the diegetic world money is substituted for speech, that "to pay" is "to say." An association between words like "money" or "cash" with "answer," "demand," "response," is frequently made in the opening chapter. Money ceases to function as a token representing some value, it has become "real money" (*MC* p. 14), as the text insists on its materiality (the banknotes are "weighed by the shillings on the table" *MC* p. 14), and as Susan warns that *contact* with the money will make her go ("if you touch that money, I and this girl go with the man" *MC* p. 14). Later when Henchard encloses five guineas in the envelope containing the few lines written to Susan, the word "note" is ambiguous (both a bank-note and a written note). Henchard is merely repeating the original equation of "paying" with "saying."

members of my family see it?'" *Tess* p. 212). The legend has turned real, the sign has become "incarnated." "Embodied" signs or "ensigned" bodies form motifs all along the novel: the red letters painted on a stile that are "driven home" to the reader's "heart" foreshadow the fatal blow dealt by Tess with a carving-knife in Mrs Brooks's lodging house ("the point of the blade had touched the heart of the victim" *Tess* p. 370)—what might have been understood as a figurative sense of "heart" is taken literally. Tess's "trump-card," which John Durbeyfield ventures might be "her d'Urberville blood" (*Tess* p. 55), turns out to be, not her aristocratic "blue" blood, but the real blood of Alec d'Urberville, forming a "gigantic ace of heart" on the ceiling. Retaliation means that Alec's heart, and his blood, have become readable tropes.

In *The Mayor of Casterbridge*, the most striking example is the phrase "unprincipled bread," used by the Casterbridge people to describe the distasteful bread made from Henchard's degraded flour. In fact the bread is "unprincipled" because the "cornfactor" who provided the wheat lacked principles when he sold his wife like a mare at Weydon-Priors fair—a fact of which the angry villagers are ignorant at this stage, but which nevertheless affects the quality of the bread. "Unprincipled bread" is a metaphor, more precisely a form of hypallage, where the quality of being "unprincipled" is erroneously applied to bread—for it is the "cornfactor" who is an unprincipled man. But the rhetorical figure ceases to work as a metaphor when the bread actually becomes distasteful, when the moral judgment it carries materializes in the concrete reality of things—just as Tess's "corporeal blight," which many Victorians viewed as a moral "fault," turns into "sticky blights" adhering to her skin. Similarly, Lucetta's "fault" acquires substantiality in the red stain ear-marking her: the "Paisley shawl with a red centre" (MC p. 118), the cherry-coloured dress that cannot be removed.

Basically, *The Mayor of Casterbridge* is the tragic story of a man whose words are taken *literally*: the offer of his wife to the highest bidder may appear as a joke (Susan warns him that the "joke" might be made too often and carried too far MC p. 11), but it is taken at face-value. Later, Henchard will regret that his wife "had taken him so *literally*" (MC p. 18, my italics). The theme of jokes that are no jokes but fearful "practical jokes" played for real is a recurrent theme in the novel: Henchard, who claims to be "a fearful practical joker" when he chooses (MC p. 235), comes very close to murdering Farfrae, an attempt which he views as "some practical joke" (MC p. 239). His reading to her husband of Lucetta's love letters to him is "only a sort of practical joke" (MC p. 251), the skimmity-ride is "a great jocular plot" (MC 268). Henchard's lie to Newson about Elizabeth-Jane's death is an unpremeditated fabrication which he had expected to be unmasked in five minutes—yet it is taken seriously, and causes

Newson to depart immediately without asking questions. Later, Newson will look upon the incident as a good joke ("Ha—ha—'twas a good joke, and well carried out" *MC* p. 316), a light-hearted view which is not shared by his daughter (*MC* p. 316). Henchard, we are told, is but "a gamester" (*MC* p. 327) who loves Elizabeth-Jane's affection more than his own honour. The world of tragedy allows of no flicker of meaning between signifier and signified, sign and referent, no metaphoric disparity between tenor and vehicle. When Susan Nunsuch, in *The Return of the Native*, makes a wax image of Eustacia Vye, thrusts pins into it and then melts it over the fire, she carries out the actual destruction of her enemy: as the flames eat into the substance of the figure, it is Eustacia herself who is devoured, not some figure somehow resembling her.

1.5 Texts and Textiles

In the perspective that I have opened, it may be of some interest to look into the question of clothes in Hardy's fiction, because after all, textiles are texts[50] — whether or not one accepts that the two words have a common etymology. And what can be made of the "sartorial metaphor" (Bullen, p. 110) in a fictional world where metaphor is problematic? A striking passage in *The Mayor of Casterbridge* is the scene in which Henchard is about to drown himself in Ten-Hatches-Hole. As he watches "a something" floating on the circular pool he intends to make his death-bed, he soon distinguishes an object that finally takes shape, "a human body lying stiff and stark upon the surface of the stream":

> In the circular current imparted by the central flow the form was brought forward, till it passed under his eyes; and then he perceived with a sense of horror that it was *himself*. Not a man somewhat resembling him, but one in all respects his counterpart, his actual double, was floating as if dead in Ten-Hatches-Hole.
>
> *MC* p. 297

Elizabeth-Jane will provide a rational explanation for that strange object ("The effigy [...] They must have thrown it into the river higher up among the willows at Blackwater, to get rid of it" *MC* p. 298), it is after all only a bundle of old clothes. Yet to Henchard it remains "an appalling miracle": he persists in viewing the thing as his actual double, not as a representation of himself.

50 "Textile is first of all a text" (Lacan, 1986a/2008, p. 281).

What can be read as metaphoric[51] or symbolic by ordinary people is undecipherable for him.

The same identification process may be observed with Lucetta. She is, writes J.B. Bullen, a mere show, nothing but "visual appearance," often associated with "artfulness" and false appearances (Bullen, p. 112).[52] When two dresses arrive at High Place Hall, Lucetta spreads them on the bed and wonders which "person" she is going to be: "'You are that person (pointing to one of the arrangements), or you are *that* totally different person' (pointing to the other), 'for the whole of the coming spring'" (*MC* p. 167). She eventually makes up her mind: "It was finally decided by Miss Templeman that she would be the cherry-coloured person at all hazards." The choice of the verb "to be" is quite remarkable. Unlike Elizabeth-Jane, writes J.B. Bullen, "Lucetta believes that clothes make the woman, and Lucetta's misplaced faith in the value of appearances is the immediate cause of her death" (Bullen, p. 113).

I would argue that the cause of death is the same for Lucetta as for Henchard: a structural incapacity for both of them to dissociate themselves from the "texts" or "textiles" that cling to their skin and have become "embodied signs." When Lucetta's effigy is carried along the streets of Casterbridge in the "skimmity-ride," Lucetta sees the effigy of herself through the window, and her words are significant: "''Tis me', she said, with a face pale as death" (*MC* p. 278). Complete identification is achieved when she exclaims: "She's me—she's me—even to the parasol—my green parasol" (*MC* p. 279). Lucetta *is* her own clothes in a relation of perfect adequacy that conjoins her to her dress, without any semiotic hesitancy (if the dress worked as a sartorial metaphor, a vacillation between similarity and dissimilarity, between "she is her dress" and "she isn't her dress," would be maintained). Similarly, Henchard clings doggedly to the vesture of his former prosperity, "the fretted and weather-beaten garments of bygone years" (*MC* p. 265), "clothes of frayed and threadbare shabbiness—the very clothes which he had used to wear in the primal days" when he had presided over the town-council (*MC* p. 262). Only when he is about to jump into Ten-Hatches-Hole does he sever himself from his coat and hat—in contrast to Elizabeth-Jane, who is constantly seen donning and doffing her hat and

51 Stylisticians will object to my use of the term "metaphoric," which does not take into account the finer distinction between metaphor and metonymy (Henchard's soiled and shabby clothes are a metaphor for his social degradation, but also a metonym for his person). I use "metaphor" in a wider sense, because the proper functioning of the paternal metaphor is a prerequisite for the "oscillation" between metaphor and metonymy (Guy Rosolato, *La relation d'Inconnu*, Paris: Gallimard, 1978, pp. 52–80).

52 Like Felice Charmond in *The Woodlanders*.

her coat according to circumstance, and adapting her vesture to her station in life. That Henchard should be unable to take off his clothes except through the very act of self-destruction is symptomatic of a structural disability: because the "paternal metaphor" (the Name-of-the-Father) is unavailing in his case, severance cannot be metaphorized, it can only be experienced in the flesh. Thus taking off his hat and coat means nothing short of death for him—as it does for Abel Whittle ("Yes—I'll go to Blackmoor Vale half-naked as I be, since he do command it; but I shall kill myself afterwards; I can't outlive the disgrace" *MC* p. 99).

The impossibility of severance is a point that has been made by Marjorie Garson about Clym Yeobright: "Mother and son are one flesh—he was a part of her" (223). That his link with this woman is so intense that separation from her means dismemberment, emasculation, sexual death, is one inevitable meaning of the narrative" (Garson, 1991, p. 74). The failure of the Name-of-the-Father is of course obvious in the relation between Clym and his mother. In Hardy's tragic novels, what threatens life is precisely the lack of a clear line of demarcation between bodies and texts/textiles. Seen in that light, the description of Eustacia's clothes appears rather ominous:

> [...] her out-door attire [...] always had a nebulousness about it, devoid of harsh edges anywhere, so that her face looked up from its environment as from a cloud, with no noticeable line of demarcation between flesh and clothes."
>
> *RN* p. 260

The restoration of order at the end of the novel will be signified by the erasure of the red "stain" which had been ingrained in the very flesh of Diggory Venn the reddleman, so much so that it was part of his identity.

Yet it is important to underline that, unlike the texts/textiles of the diegesis, the text that relates the story owes its "literariness" to the flicker of meaning that the poetic creates all along the signifying chain. There may be too much sense in the diegetic world, where human bodies turn into signs—as when a comma is placed after each word to ensure that the biblical message in red letters is properly hammered in, conveyed to Tess without any ambiguity as to its target or its signification ("placing a comma after each word, as if to give pause while that word was driven well home to the reader's heart" *Tess* p. 85). But ambiguity inhabits literature: in the present example, "the reader" is either Tess or the person reading the book, or both. The indomitable voice of an omnipotent Other is hushed by the poetics of the text, which makes meaning uncertain, not guaranteed—for one may choose to read the text or not, and the effect produced on the reader is variable. No meaning is ever "driven well home" to the reader of a literary text. Playing with language is impossible in the diegesis of Hardy's tragedies, where all jokes are "practical jokes" acted out in the real world.[53] But playing with *lalangue*[54] is what Hardy the poet is constantly doing, as he pleases our ears with those sonorous "orts, scraps and fragments"[55] that ring out in the silence of the literary text—alliterations, assonances, consonances, paronomastic chains (for instance the phonematic chains which run through *The Mayor of Casterbridge*, linking words like "ear," "weir," "near," and "hear," or moving from "revel" to "riveted," "reverberation," "reverie," "revelation," "revelry," "rivalry," in the skimmity-ride scene). When the Name-of-the-Father does not work, there may be other ways of "barring" the cruel Other of tragedy. And that "other way"[56] does not merely suppress *jouissance*: it turns it to good account, as a few fragments of it are kept for the reader to enjoy, left-overs from a massive and destructive enjoyment that the literary text enables us to share in a pleasurable form.

I wish to take one last example, this time from *The Woodlanders*, to show how the Name-of-the-Father can be restored by a dress working as a text/textile distinct from the human body—to put it in other words, how "a dress" can restore intersubjective relations and make "an address" possible (it may be

53 All the world's a stage in *The Mayor of Casterbridge*: Lucetta and Elizabeth-Jane watch the drama of life on the *carrefour* from their windows, but they are part of the play ("the incidents that occur always happen to bear on the lives of the adjoining residents" *MC* p. 166). Worse still, that stage is one in which the actors play for real, and where their lives are at stake. It is an arena where the participants and the spectators alike are put to death: Lucetta is killed by the dress she was wearing "when she sat in the front-seat at the time the play-actors came to the Town-Hall" (*MC* p. 278). In Henchard's own words, she is killed by a "performance" (*MC* p. 298). The "performances" in the notorious Casterbridge Ring were sanguinary games that ended in death for the gladiators, or for those who were executed when the town-gallows stood there (*MC* p. 91). All play is impossible in the world of tragedy.

54 "Lalangue" is a pre-Symbolic linguistic form, produced by our encounter with the maternal language, it is the language of affects, loaded with a palpitating substance of enjoyment/*jouissance*. It is from *lalangue* that the poet draws the material he writes with. "Lalangue" associates language and *jouissance*. See Lacan, 1975, p. 130.

55 "Look at ourselves, ladies and gentlemen! Then at the wall; and ask how's this wall, the great wall, which we call, perhaps miscall, civilization, to be built by (here the mirrors flicked and flashed) orts, scraps and fragments like ourselves?" (Woolf, 1941/1998, p. 169). Woolf's phrase is an approximate quote from *Troilus and Cressida*, v, ii.

56 To that "other way," Lacan will give the name of "suppléance" ("replacement") in his seminar on "Le sinthome" (Lacan, 2005), where he shows how writing enabled Joyce to make do with a deficient Name-of-the-Father.

interesting to note here that Grace had been unable to write to her husband Fitzpiers "in the absence of an address" *W* p. 222). I will not dwell on the question of paternity, which is strikingly deficient in the novel: Grace's father makes her forget her childhood sweetheart Giles and encourages her to marry Fitzpiers, who turns out to be an incorrigible philanderer; Marty South's father is an invalid unable to make a living for his family, and whom his daughter has to replace in his trade, the making of spars—a man's occupation which makes her hands rough. Necessity forces Marty, who is "pressed" (*W* p. 10) by a "hair-dresser" (*W* p. 28), to sell her beautiful tresses to a rich lady, Felice Charmond. Severance here is problematic, as Marty's "tresses" (which rightly belong to her body) are severed from her to adorn the body of another woman. A strange confusion between nature and culture turns a natural element into a cultural sign transferable to another person, to be misread as natural (it is the exact opposite of Henchard and Lucetta identifying with their clothes, but implies a similar structural disorder). Marty is logically very much affected by "this distressing business" (*W* p. 29), while the lady wearing those ill-acquired tresses, who once was a "play-actress" (*W* p. 172) and who is now the "mistress" of Hintock House (*W* pp. 68, 95, etc.), will become the "mistress"[57] of Fitzpiers—thus making it plain that those false tresses were indeed "mis-tresses." One might expect things to go from bad to worse, but a tragic ending is only just avoided in the novel, thanks to a "dress," in a fascinating scene which is the reverse of what happens in *The Mayor of Casterbridge* or in *Tess of the d'Urbervilles*.

Grace Melbury and Edred Fitzpiers are a married couple who are separated owing to Fitzpiers's infidelity. But they are gradually becoming reconciled, and they are to meet one night at some place in the woods. A man whose wife had an affair with Fitzpiers has set a mantrap on the path which he expects his rival to follow, but it is Grace who is caught by the trap—an engine, or "gin," which looks like Freud's crocodile's mouth, for it exhibits "the combined aspects of a shark, a crocodile, and a scorpion" (*W* p. 264). A "long cry" resounds in the wood, "penetrating, but indescribable" (*W* p. 266). Fitzpiers hears it and wonders "what it could mean" (*W* p. 267). Feeling uneasy, he "reverts" to the scream and walks along the path, till he stumbles on "a confused mass of silken drapery and iron-work that conveyed absolutely no explanatory idea to

57 In the opinion of the members of Mrs Charmond's household, the "deeper sinner" is not Fitzpiers but "their mistress" (*W* p. 174). "Mistress" is not univocal here. But it is usually Grace who is said to assume in Fitzpiers's eyes "the true aspect of a mistress in her lover's regard" (*W* p. 108). The quest for the "ideal mistress" (*W* p. 95) reminds one of Pierston (whose name is phonemically close to Fitzpiers).

his mind at all"[58] (*W* p. 267). Striking a match, he sees a sight which congeals his blood:

> The man-trap was thrown; and between its jaws was part of a woman's clothing—a patterned silk skirt—gripped with such violence that the iron teeth had passed through it, skewering its tissue in a score of places. He immediately recognized the skirt as that of one of his wife's gowns—the gown that she had worn when she met him on the very last occasion.
>
> *W* pp. 267–268

So far the scene is set for a typical Hardyan tragedy: Fitzpiers believes his wife has been caught by the trap, "taken out mangled by some chance-passer, and carried home, some of her clothes being left behind in the difficulty of getting her free" (*W* p. 268). In all probability, the skirt is a close fit, with "no line of demarcation between flesh and clothes"—like Eustacia Vye's clothes. Its presence between the iron teeth of the mantrap is interpreted as a sign of Grace's death. Fitzpiers is shocked and is seen writhing with pain.

But the story is about to take a totally different turn, for a strange female figure suddenly appears gliding in the gloom: it is Grace, "white up to the waist, and figured above [...] lacking the portion of her dress which the gin retained" (*W* p. 268). She tells Edred Fitzpiers not to grieve on her account, for she is not hurt, and she proceeds to explain what happened:

> 'I was coming on to you', she said [...] 'I was trying to be as punctual as possible, and as I had started a minute late I ran along the path very swiftly—fortunately for myself. Just when I had passed between these trees I felt something clutch at my dress from behind with a noise, and the next moment I was pulled backward by it, and fell to the ground. I screamed with terror—thinking it was a man lying down there to murder me—but the next moment I discovered it was iron, and that my clothes were caught in a trap. I pulled this way and that, but the thing would not let go, drag it as I would, and I did not know what to do [...] I could think of no other plan than slipping off my skirt, meaning to run on and tell you what a strange accident had happened to me.
>
> *W* pp. 268–269

58 One is reminded of Knight being unable to put a name on the fringe of Mrs Jethway's shawl.

Soon after, husband and wife set out to break the tragic spell by working together to open the mouth of the trap and wrench the skirt from its grip:

> By their united efforts, each standing on one of the springs of the trap, they pressed them down sufficiently to insert across the jaws a billet which they dragged from a faggot near at hand; and it was then possible to extract the silk mouthful from the monster's bite, creased and pierced with many holes, but not torn.
>
> *W* p. 269

The bar (or "billet") of wood placed across the jaws of the crocodile's mouth has put a "bar" (in the Lacanian sense) on the devouring Other of tragedy: the uncontrollable enjoyment of a malevolent Other is now "barred," i.e. prohibited. The bar is also the Saussurean bar between signifier and signified, sign and referent (or between tenor and vehicle in a metaphor), for what has just been achieved is the cut between flesh and clothes: now that a line of demarcation has been drawn between bodies and textiles, Grace no longer runs the risk of being killed by an intextuation of her body. Just as a ram had been sent *in extremis* to be sacrificed *instead of* Isaac, Grace's dress only *represents* her. The metaphoric process of substitution has been initiated, and this act (which prohibits the destructive enjoyment of the Other) puts an end to the possibility of sacrifice. The "indescribable" cry has come to make sense, and the "confused mass of silken drapery," which was unreadable and unsymbolizable, is now interpreted, divided into distinguishable parts. The dress, which had been decomposed (the top remaining on Grace and the skirt being caught in the trap), has now been recomposed, an operation which cannot fail to remind us of the definition of the Greek *sumbolon*: an object broken into two parts, which are put together again to form a whole, their perfect dove-tailing being a proof of their common origin. All these are clear signs of the restoration of the Symbolic (and of the Name-of-Father). That is how we step out of tragedy in *The Woodlanders*.[59]

Most importantly, signifiers of lack and division appear in the text: Grace is "lacking the portion of her dress which the gin retained," and the "silk mouthful" *extracted* from the "monster's bite" is "creased and pierced with small holes, but not torn" (*W* p. 269). What an admirable way of saying, in poetic language, that the holes in the fabric of life are no longer unsymbolizable "crevices"—tragic wounds that cannot be healed—but *structural* holes, like the holes woven into a cloth by the interlacing threads! In far less elegant Lacanian

59 A similar life-saving operation is performed in *A Pair of Blue Eyes*: Elfride takes off part of her clothing to save Knight's life. But tragedy will not be avoided after all.

terms, I would argue that what has been restored is the blank from which the signifying chain originates—the blank which is missing in Hardy's tragic world. The primordial object of desire, the "object-cause,"[60] has been *extracted*, and the metonymy of desire can now follow its course towards an unattainable object—whether or not Fitzpiers and Grace will be able to live happily ever after is another question, which I would rather not attempt to answer. What is striking is the poetic quality of the text, for instance in the sentence about Fitzpiers's awed reaction on discovering his wife's dress caught in the man-trap: "'O my own—my darling—O cruel Heaven—it is too much this!' he cried, writhing and rocking over the sorry accessories of her he deplored" (*W* p. 268).[61] The repetition of the letters "o" and "r" (in different phonematic combinations, "r" being mute in "deplored"), the echo of "sorry" heard in "accessories," make us sense that the letter of the text tries to *contain* the horror (in both senses of the term, to constrain and to contain, to hold back and to hold as a container). The nodal point in this particular passage is the signifier "dress," around which all is irradiated: the word sends out poetic resonances that reverberate throughout the text, with words like "press" (which is recurrent), "empress," or "distress."[62] In fact the whole novel appears amazingly poetic—no wonder it was a favourite with Hardy. We have seen how "tress," "dress," "mistress," "press," "address," etc., form a paradigmatic chain that runs from the beginning of the novel to its very end (an ending in which Grace is said to be her "own mistress," *W* p. 273). We can imagine, rightly or wrongly, that after the episode where a woman's "dress" has been so effective in restoring a proper system of signification, there will be no more "false tresses," no more "mis-tresses" in Fitzpiers's life, no more "distress" in the couple formed again by Grace and Fitzpiers. But the most important thing for the reader is the "silk mouthful"[63] (*W* p. 269) which the poetic letter allows him to savour, lingeringly, lovingly, with utter relish.

---

60 In other words *Das Ding*, figured in the passage by the word "thing," and by the repetition of "it," the unknowable thing.

61 On this particular passage, see Ramel, 2013a, pp. 10–11.

62 "Dress" has been prepared by"undress" (*W* p. 266) and by "empress" ("if she had been his empress and he her thrall" *W* p. 266), then it surfaces as a replacement of "skirt" and "gown" ("the portion of her dress," "clutch at my dress" *W* p. 268, "leaving the dress behind" *W* 269), then we hear "the voice of [Fitzpiers's] distress" (*W* p. 268), and the signifier "press" becomes specially insistent (he […] pressed her to his breast" *W* p. 268, "he continued to press his face to her" *W* p. 269, "each standing on one of the springs of the trap, they pressed them down" *W* p. 269).

63 This interpretation of the "silk mouthful" does not preclude the possibility of other readings. Like for instance one that might underline the erotic implications of the phrase.

CHAPTER 2

The Feminine: Reading Hardy after Lacan's XXth Seminar

A "silk mouthful," affording exquisite pleasure to writer and reader alike: that is how a text/textile could be defined. But then, one might ask, what is the nature of that strange enjoyment that one may derive from a literary text? An interesting *mise-en-abyme* of the reading act may be found in one of Hardy's short-stories, "An Imaginative Woman," where the heroine, Ella Marchmill, a would-be poetess unhappily married to a prosperous gunmaker, falls in love with a man she has never met merely by reading his poetry. So passionate is her devotion to him, so exquisite the sensations felt as her hand follows the half-erased letters traced by the poet on her bed-room wall, that her husband believes her to have been adulterous. The male perception is faced with a total enigma here, that of a woman's desire—the "dark continent" that resisted Freud's investigation. One cannot but marvel at Hardy's insight into those mysteries, owed undoubtedly to his position as an artist—for, as Lacan reminded us, the artist always precedes the psychoanalyst.[1] This chapter will turn to what is often called the *feminine* mode of enjoyment, as Lacan attempted to figure it out in his XXth *Seminar*. But we must bear in mind when reading the following pages that there are some men, especially among artists, who are "just as good as women" (Lacan, 1975/1998, p. 76), men who too have access to that "Other" *jouissance*. This section will end with a parallel between the feminine pursuit and the artist's quest.

We will start with an interrogation on Hardy's supposedly "adulterous" heroines. Like Ella, many of Hardy's heroines are reviled for their supposed improper or "adulterous" behaviour: Tess, rejected by her husband because of her previous affair with Alec d'Urberville, is left with no choice but to become a kept woman; in *The Return of the Native*, rumour has it that Eustacia Vye is a witch and that she is attempting to elope with a former lover of hers, Wildeve. Ella's husband is so utterly convinced of his wife's infidelity that after her death he rejects their fourth child whom he thinks is not his own but the poet's.

---

1 "[…] le seul avantage qu'un psychanalyste ait le droit de prendre de sa position […] c'est de se rappeler avec Freud qu'en sa matière, l'artiste toujours le précède et qu'il n'a donc pas à faire le psychologue là où l'artiste lui fraie la voie" (Lacan, 2001a). Lacan is referring to Freud, who claimed that an author is "the precursor of science and scientific psychology" (Freud, p. 172).

 | DOI 10.1163/9789004296626_004

Yet in all these stories the heroine is unduly accused: Ella has never even seen the poet believed to have fathered her child, he is not much more than a figment of her imagination. Eustacia never commits any form of adultery, for all the gossip about her being "a voluptuous idle woman" (*Return* p. 204), for all the suspicions entertained by her husband. Critics often see her relation with Wildeve as "adulterous" (Garson, 1991, pp. 57, 58), but whatever she might eventually have done had the course of events been different, she never *intends* to run away with Wildeve, and she never does. Tess is asleep when she is raped/seduced, she is simply not there, she is elsewhere. And it is circumstances that compel her to become Alec's mistress. As Hardy puts it, she is "a pure woman." Each story is a typical case of the *diffamation* that Lacan says is the lot of woman: "On la dit-femme, on la diffâme" (Lacan, 1975, p. 79).[2] Why then are those heroines a prey to such *diffamation*? What logic underlies the insistence on their being "adulterous," despite evidence to the contrary?

2.1 An Imaginative Woman

Ella Marchmill's story is apparently simple: a jealous husband imagines his wife cheated on him, though she did not. Of course paternity is always uncertain—*pater semper incertus.* But Hardy's cryptic words in his preface to *Life's Little Ironies* have made matters rather complex: "An Imaginative Woman," he writes, is about "a trick of Nature, so to speak, a physical possibility that may attach to a wife of vivid imaginings, as is well known to medical practitioners and other observers of such manifestations" (*CSS* p. 377).[3] How can Hardy write that a woman, merely by indulging in "vivid imaginings," may be *impregnated* by a man, to the effect that the child she gives birth to is of questionable paternity? Isn't he somehow giving credit to the husband's belief in his wife's infidelity? What can be made of the hypothesis that, by reading the "half-obliterated pencillings" (*CSS* p. 389) of a poet on a bed-room wall, an expectant mother could provoke a genetic mutation[4] in her own womb, thereby causing the foetus to

---

2 In the English translation: "She is called woman (*on la dit femme*) and defamed (*diffâme*)." Lacan (1975/1998 p. 85).

3 Thomas Hardy, *Collected Short Stories*, referred to as *CSS* in this paper.

4 Rosemarie Morgan suggests that Hardy might be referring to a form of trauma-induced genetic mutation—a concept not yet available to him, but which the science of epigenetics is currently researching. For Hardy's short-story rests on his belief that the organic and the inorganic worlds are *not* mutually impenetrable (in opposition to Bergson's theory), so thin is the barrier supposed to separate them (Morgan, 2013, pp. 33–43).

assume a physical likeness to the poet whose lines she is reading? In my view, an answer is to be found in the concept of feminine *jouissance*: indeed a woman is more likely than a man to become *impregnated*, not *by* a man's semen, but *with* the enjoyment that a poetic text, a piece of music, or a work of art, may instil into her body, a *jouissance* originally felt by the creator, which his art allows him to share with a receptive reader, listener, or viewer. It is that trickle of *jouissance* from the Other, permeating her body, which makes the feminine subject *structurally* adulterous. For woman has access, according to Lacan, to an Other *jouissance*, a "supplementary" jouissance, "beyond the phallus": "There is a jouissance that is hers about which she herself perhaps knows nothing if not that she experiences it—that much she knows" (Lacan, 1975/1998, p. 74). That mode of jouissance makes porous the barrier between self and Other, as Josiane Paccaud-Huguet has shown in her reading of *The Waves*: "[Virginia Woolf] makes room for the other, feminine mode, of an *unextracted* enjoyment/jouissance, i.e. en corps, within the body, which makes it impossible to distinguish inside and outside, self and Other" (Paccaud-Huguet, p. 290). Those who experience that mode of enjoyment are indeed susceptible to *impregnation*. No wonder Ella is said to wait impatiently for "the pregnant day and hour" (*CSS* p. 394) of the poet's expected visit—a visit that will never take place.

In "An Imaginative Woman," Ella is dissatisfied with her gun-making husband, named "Will": she objects to the phallic order.[5] Ella, whose name makes her emblematic of the feminine, is *more than* a woman responding to the phallic game through feminine masquerade: "Ella was *more than* a mere multiplier of her kind" (*CSS* p. 383, my italics). Tired of the semblances of phallic discourse, she craves for *truth*, and so she finds herself a new partner (whom she never meets), a young poet, whose name is... Robert Trewe, the author of lines Ella finds "most touching and true" (*CSS* p. 389), a man "who can't stand lies" (*CSS* p. 395). On holiday in a Wessex watering-place, she and her family have found lodgings in rooms that are usually occupied by Robert Trewe. While her husband enjoys sailing without his wife, going aboard cheap steamers "where there was dancing by moonlight" (*CSS* p. 385), Ella spends most of her time in Robert Trewe's bedroom, imbibing the spirit which the poet seems to have left behind like a pervasive fragrance, deciphering the "orts, scraps, and fragments" (Woolf, 1941/1998, p. 169), still traceable on the wall, "the thoughts and spirit-strivings which had come to him in the dead of night" (*CSS* p. 390) and which he had later tried to erase. Ella has found an

5 A point made by Stéphanie Bernard, who views Ella as recalling hysterical women (Bernard, pp. 4, 9).

ally in a sympathetic landlady, who tells her all about Robert Trewe, his habits, his appearance, etc. and who reveals to her that the framed picture representing the Royal Duke and Duchess can be overturned to reveal a picture of the poet himself (after the poet's death, the landlady will give Ella that picture and a lock of his hair). Once in possession of the picture, Ella waits impatiently till she is alone, "with a serene sense of something ecstatic to come" (CSS p. 388), and then in the seclusion of her bedroom she arranges a phantasmic scenario, "first getting rid of superfluous garments and putting on her dressing-gown, then arranging a chair in front of the table and reading several pages of Trewe's tenderest utterance" (CSS p. 389). She derives exquisite enjoyment from the scene:

> There they were—phrases, couplets, *bouts-rimés*, beginnings and middles of lines, ideas in the rough, like Shelley's scraps, and the least of them so intense, so sweet, so palpitating, that it seemed as if his very breath, warm and loving, fanned her cheeks from those walls, walls that had surrounded his head times and times as they surrounded her own now. He must often have put up his hand so—with the pencil in it. Yes, the writing was sideways, as it would be if executed by one who extended his arm thus. [...] These inscribed shapes [...] had often been written up hastily by the light of the moon, the rays of the lamp, in the blue-grey dawn, in full daylight perhaps never. And now her hair was dragging where his arm had lain when he secured the fugitive fancies; she was sleeping on a poet's lips, immersed in the very essence of him, permeated by his spirit as by an ether.[6]
>
> CSS p. 390

Ella, who is also a poet, a rival of Robert Trewe in fact, is drawn to the *letter*, the Lacanian letter "still permeated with the substance of enjoyment" (Paccaud-Huguet, p. 287), retaining in its curves and arabesques some trace of the poet's *jouissance* as he wrote "sideways," allowing his hand, his arm, his body, to shape the letter and impregnate it. The physical contact with the poet's *absent* body fills Ella with ecstasy, such ecstasy that no physical contact with his real body could ever have given rise to. She becomes absent to herself, oblivious of her self as she is "immersed in the very essence of him." Yet in that very annihilation of her self, she is fully alive, her body becomes "the recipient of

6 Martin Ray draws our attention to some revisions Hardy made in his manuscript to emphasize the spiritual nature of Ella's feeling for Trewe: Ella originally described as "permeated by him" was finally said to be "permeated by his spirit" (Ray, p. 178).

burning enjoyment/*jouissance*" (Paccaud-Huguet, p. 288). Like Saint Teresa in Bernini's statue, there is no doubt that "she's coming" (Lacan, 1975/1998, p. 76). The words used all along the short-story make this very clear: everything about her, especially her eyes, grows wet (*css* p. 386), she feels "a rush of tender curiosity," her face flushes "without knowing why" (*css* p. 385), she is "possessed by an inner flame" (*css* p. 385), she is "a woman of very living ardours" (*css* p. 386), but she does not care for sex with her husband, the prospect of meeting the poet makes her feel "secret delight" (*css* p. 386), etc. Ella's *jouissance* is an enjoyment *en-corps* ("Encore"), in her body.

Yet we should not mistake that enjoyment for *sexual* enjoyment: Ella feels a strange kinship with Robert Trewe, a poet like herself—even though she envies his work, "so much stronger [...] than her own feeble lines" (*css* p. 383). To her he is not a man but "a brother poet" (*css* p. 393), she writes to him under her masculine *nom de plume*, John Ivy, as if he were some sort of double, or mirror-image, of herself, in a relation which is thoroughly narcissistic:

> No, he was not a stranger! She knew his thoughts and feelings as well as she knew her own; they were, in fact, the self-same thoughts and feelings as hers, which her husband distinctly lacked [...] 'He's nearer my real self, he's more intimate with the real me than Will is, after all, even though I've never seen him'.
>
> *css* p. 389

She even wonders why he "had never once thought of passing himself off as a woman," in exact inversion of her passing herself off as a man, ascribing this to "a man's unsusceptibility on the question of sex" (*css* pp. 382–383). In fact the question of sex is entirely out of the scene. Robert Trewe is to her a "circumambient" presence, surrounding her day and night, literally whispering to her "at every moment" (*css* p. 385). As Žižek has underlined, the feminine Other enjoyment "is not centred on the phallus" but "bombards the body from all directions" (Žižek, 1999a, p. 130). Ella's careful undressing should not be misconstrued as an erotic scene: no man is there to see her, and any way she has kept her dressing-gown on. What Ella aims at is a nudity "en-corps," that she can feel within her body.[7] It is a sort of mystical vacuity, the obliteration of

7 Of course one might well imagine Ella enjoying the male gaze in a fantasmatic scenario, even though no male is present to see her. She would then be playing the game of phallic masquerade, which should not surprise us: Other *jouissance* being defined as "beyond the phallus," it cannot exist without the phallus.

her being, like Lol in Marguerite Duras's novel, *Le Ravissement de Lol .V Stein.*[8] And she will indeed be reduced to *nothing* at the end of the story, when she becomes mere waste, "a crouching object" sprawling on the ground near the newly-made grave of Robert Trewe—such is the fate[9] of those women who reveal the insubstantiality of the feminine masquerade and allow their "ontological void" (Žižek 1999a, p. 138) to appear unmasked. "There is no feminine secret at all," exclaimed Weininger in a violent anti-feminist ourtburst, "behind the mask of the Enigma there is simply nothing!"[10] Trewe, who cannot bear the semblances of the phallic order, commits suicide with a revolver—an ironic ending, for the gun has probably been manufactured by Ella's husband! Ella, following a parallel course, allows herself to die in giving birth to her child—a child who bears such a strong resemblance to the poet she has never seen that her husband rejects him, exclaiming "you are *nothing* to me!" (*CSS* p. 400, my italics).[11] "Nothing" is the key-word here, the final point aimed at by the whole story. We are "beyond sex" (in "the Beyondsex," Lacan, 1975/1998, p. 85). As Lacan has made clear, "as long as the soul souloves the soul (*l'âme âme l'âme*), sex is not involved. Sex doesn't count here" (Lacan, 1975/1998, p. 84).

So the adultery committed by Ella is not sexual, but the "structural adultery" that Philippe Julien writes about in *L'étrange jouissance du prochain*, more specifically in his reading of a short-story by Albert Camus, "La femme adultère." Janine, the heroine, who is "unable to tear herself away from the void opening before her," feels dissatisfied with her husband. One night she leaves the conjugal bed and opens herself to the night, allowing the stars in their slow gyration to identify with "the core of her being":

> After so many years of mad, aimless fleeing from fear, she had come to a stop at last. At the same time, she seemed to recover her roots and the sap again rose in her body, which had ceased trembling. Her whole belly pressed against the parapet as she strained toward the moving sky; she was merely waiting for her fluttering heart to calm down and establish silence within her. The last stars of the constellations dropped their

8 "Lola Valérie Stein fait le vide" (Montrelay, p. 16).

9 Or perhaps the "consummation devoutly [...] wished" by those women.

10 Žižek of course reverses the meaning of that sentence to make it serve the Lacanian argument that "La Femme n'existe pas" (Žižek, 1999a, p. 134).

11 Most importantly, Ella has been unable to *tell* her husband about her experience ("I can't tell what possessed me"), and "she could get no further then for very exhaustion" (*CSS* p. 400), which leaves a blank for her husband to fill. This is a typical case of feminine *jouissance* as something woman feels but knows nothing about, except that she experiences it (Lacan, 1975/1998, p. 74). It cannot be told, but it can be written about.

> clusters a little lower on the desert horizon and became still. Then, with unbearable gentleness, the water of night began to fill Janine, drowned the cold, rose gradually from the hidden core of her being and overflowed in wave after wave, rising up even to her mouth full of moans. The next moment, the whole sky stretched out over her, fallen on her back to the cold earth.[12]

Philippe Julien concludes: "There, Camus makes himself the witness of that obscure core of a woman's being, of that part of herself which makes her adulterous to the supposed sexual complementarity."[13]

2.2 The Garden Scene in *Tess of the d'Urbervilles*

Janine in ecstatic contemplation of the starry night calls to mind another heroine, Tess, who astonishes her fellow workers at Talbothays farm by claiming that she can leave her body and attach herself to some big bright star:

> 'I don't know about ghosts,' she was saying; 'but I do know that our souls can be made to go outside our bodies when we are alive.'
> The dairyman turned to her with his mouth full, his eyes charged with serious inquiry, and his great knife and fork (breakfasts were breakfasts here) planted erect on the table, like the beginning of a gallows.
> 'What—really now? And is it so, maidy?' he said.
> 'A very easy way to feel 'em go,' continued Tess, 'is to lie on the grass at night and look straight up at some big bright star; and, by fixing your mind on it, you will soon find that you are hundreds and hundreds o' miles away from your body, which you don't seem to want at all.'
>
> *TESS* p. 124

A few pages further, Tess finds herself "on the outskirts of the garden" at Talbothays, and such an exaltation comes over her while Angel is playing the harp. This time the ecstasy is not deliberately called forth by Tess: "The exaltation which she had described as being producible at will by gazing at a star, came now without any determination of hers" (*Tess* p. 127). A beautiful passage

12 Albert Camus, "The Adulterous Woman," pp. 32–33. Translated from "La femme adultère," in *L'exil et le royaume*, Paris: Gallimard, Folio (1967, p. 34).

13 "Là, Camus se fait le témoin de ce centre obscur d'une femme, de cette part d'elle même qui la rend adultère du supposé rapport sexuel" (Julien, p. 179, my translation).

describes Tess's emotions (it is one of the few passages where Tess's sensuality is described from her own perspective) as she abandons herself to the caress of Nature:

> She went stealthily as a cat through this profusion of growth, gathering cuckoo-spittle on her skirts, cracking snails that were underfoot, staining her hands with thistle-milk and slug-slime, and rubbing off upon her naked arms sticky blights which, though snow-white on the apple-tree trunks, made madder stains on her skin.
>
> *TESS* p. 127

Strikingly, the sensations felt by Tess are "exquisite," that is to say sometimes verging on pain, as when "the tall blooming weeds" of the uncultivated garden emit "offensive smells." But most of the time she is filled with pure, unalloyed pleasure. What she experiences here is the "oceanic feeling" that Freud wrote about.[14] She becomes one with Nature, which becomes "extimate" to her, as she allows herself to be penetrated by a flux that fills her with unspeakable ecstasy, her own tears mingling with "the weeping" of the garden:

> [...] she undulated upon the thin notes of the second-hand harp, and their harmonies passed like breezes through her, bringing tears into her eyes. The floating pollen seemed to be his notes made visible, and the dampness of the garden the weeping of the garden's sensibility.
>
> *TESS* p. 127

Modern critics have read the "Garden scene" as showing a woman's lush, voluptuous sexuality. To Rosemarie Morgan, who stresses "the palpability of female sensation" in Hardy's novels (Morgan, 1991, p. IX), the scene is "an erotic scene" evoking "sexual readiness" (Morgan, 1991, p. 86), reaching a climax of "sexual ecstasy" (Morgan, 1991, p. 88). Tess responds to Angel's presence by physical reactions: she is wetted and stained by the secretions of her own body, "the mucosa and emissions of biological sex," "the generative fluids of sex," as she becomes one with the luxuriant and untamed fluidity of the garden (Morgan, 1991, pp. 87–88). I subscribe to that reading, but with a difference: I do not believe that Tess's burning sensations are a form of sexual arousal caused

---

14 The expression, used by Freud in *The Future of an Illusion* and *Civilization and its Discontents*, comes from Romain Rolland, in a letter to Freud (5 December 1927), in *Un beau visage à tous sens. Choix de lettres de Romain Rolland (1866–1944)*, Albin Michel (1967, pp. 264–266).

by proximity to Angel and a sense that the seductive moment is approaching. It is *more* than that—Rosemarie Morgan's remark that Tess is moving close to "transcendental ecstasy" (Morgan, 1991, p. 88) seems more insightful to me. For it is not phallic enjoyment that the heroine experiences here, but the Other, unspeakable, feminine *jouissance*, the enjoyment which is "Beyondsex," "beyond the phallus," and whose paradigmatic example is "The Ecstasy of Saint Teresa" (Lacan, 1975/1998, p. 76). Yet, one should never lose sight of the fact that enjoyment "beyond the phallus" has the phallus as a prerequisite: to be able to get "beyond," one must first go *through* the phallus.

One reason why I believe Tess's ecstatic experience is closer to that of Teresa of Avila (and to that of Ella) than to sexual orgasm is the narrator's comment pointing to the similarity between Tess's "exaltation" in this chapter and the experience of gazing at a bright star related by Tess in the previous chapter—a sort of "out-of-body" experience, in which the soul leaves the body to reach out for a bright star, a body "which you don't seem to want at all"[15] (*Tess* p. 124). How can sexual enjoyment be felt *outside the body*, in an Aristotelian perspective of disjunction between body and soul? The other approach, the Lacanian approach, starts from a radically different premise, from the idea that the "castle of the soul" (in Teresa of Avila's words) may be understood as the *locus* of enjoyment,[16] especially in the feminine experience of mystical *jouissance*. A look at Hardy's novel will confirm that Tess's *soul* is the most *incarnate* part of her being—a fact which may have prompted Henry James's rather caustic remark, in a letter to Robert Louis Stevenson, that Tess's "pretence of sexuality is only equalled by the absence of it" (James, I, p. 205). It is mostly the male "appropriating" gaze of the narrator that sees Tess as a sexual being, by indulging in those "erotic fantasies of penetration and engulfment" which "enact a pursuit, violation, and persecution of Tess in parallel with those she suffers at the hands of her two lovers" (Boumelha, 1993, p. 47). But perhaps the narrator is "androgynous" (Boumelha, 1993, p. 47), or at any rate divided, as this passage suggests:

> She was yawning, and he saw the red interior of her mouth as if it had been a snake's. She had stretched one arm so high above her coiled-up

15 An "ecstasy" is, etymologically, an experience that puts you "out of place" (*The New Shorter Oxford English Dictionary*).

16 Lacan underlines the fact that Master Eckhart "uses *Ding* to refer to the soul" (Lacan 1986a/2008, p. 76; Lacan, 1986a, p. 77). The soul as *Das ding* indicates that it is the *locus* of the *jouissance* of the Other, S(Ⱥ) in Lacan's formulation, the Other to which the feminine is drawn.

> cable of hair that he could see its satin delicacy above the sunburn; her face was flushed with sleep, and her eyelids hung heavy over their pupils. The brim-fulness of her nature breathed from her. It was a moment when *a woman's soul* is more *incarnate* than at any other time; when the most spiritual beauty bespeaks itself flesh; and sex takes the outside place in the presentation.
>
> *TESS* p. 172, my italics

For if the beginning of the quotation views Tess from outside, we become aware that "sex" is only a "presentation" taking the "outside place" of something far more difficult to grasp, something that eludes the male gaze because it concerns Tess's very essence, her inner being, her "soul." Which leads Penny Boumelha (after Mary Jacobus) to write: "the language of incarnation is destabilized by the physicality and interiority of 'the woman's soul', co-extensive with 'the brimfulness of her nature', that it seeks to represent" (Boumelha, 1993, p. 48). The idea of the "physicality" of an "incarnate" soul is an oxymoron, which defies interpretation. Quite logically, Boumelha admits that Tess's sexuality is "unknowable and unrepresentable" (Boumelha, 1993, p. 48).

Lacan makes it clear in his *Seminar* XX that feminine *jouissance* involves the soul: "I soulove, you soulove, he souloves" (Lacan, 1975/1998, p. 84; "J'âme, tu âmes, il âme," Lacan, 1975, p. 78). If one admits with Lacan the idea that the soul is the very *locus* of feminine enjoyment, and even further that it is in itself a *substance* of enjoyment ("the substance [Aristotle] calls the soul"[17]), then the "physicality" of Tess's soul begins to be remotely conceivable, and the "brimfulness" of her nature ceases to be incompatible with the void that she seeks to open in herself by gazing at a bright star and fleeing from her body. Paradoxically, her *jouissance* is *en-corps,*[18] lodged within her body, inasmuch as she has succeeded in ridding herself of her body. It takes a poet to express this idea (for the poet always precedes the psychoanalyst). A poem by John Donne, "The Extasie,"[19] seems to me relevant to Tess's experience of feminine

---

17 "the body is made for an activity [...] somewhere the entelechy of this body is based on the substance he calls the soul" (Lacan, 1986a/2008, p. 88).

18 Penny Boumelha asserts that "it is as if Tess's sexuality resides quite literally *within* her body, and must be wrested from her by violence" (Boumelha, 1993, p. 48) —a point to which I subscribe, provided one replaces the word "sexuality" by *jouissance*.

19 It is Lacan who draws our attention to metaphysical poetry, in particular to "The Ecstasy" (Lacan, 2013, p. 14). Hélène Cixous too commented on that poem in an interview by Marine Landrot (25 January 2007). An excellent article on the poem has been published by Josiane Paccaud-Huguet: "Le désir visé en lui-même." *Ironik!* Retrieved from: http://www.lacan-universite.fr/wp-content/uploads/2014/12/index.html (n° 3, December 2014).

jouissance here—not only because Donne's lovers "entergraft" their hands as a means to make themselves one, like Tess and Angel washing their hands in one basin.[20] One point made by Donne is that when love "interinanimates two souls," when a soul "flows" into another soul and becomes one with it, we are "unperplexed," we understand "it was not sex":

> This ecstasy doth unperplex,
> We said, and tell us what we love;
> We see by this it was not sex,
> We see we saw not what did move.
>
> "THE ECSTASY," stanza 8

A final conceit attempts to approach that sheer impossibility, an enjoyment experienced in the soul which is a *jouissance en-corps,* felt within the body:

> Love's mysteries on souls do grow,
> But yet the body is his book.
>
> Stanza 18

Indeed for Donne, our very substance, the "atomies" we are made of, are "souls":

> We then, who are this new soul, know
> Of what we are composed and made,
> For th'atomies of which we grow
> Are souls, which no change can invade.
>
> Stanza 12

What the poet wrote, the psychoanalyst tried to conceptualize. For Lacan such *jouissance* is *unextracted,*[21] that is to say not located in the missing object he calls *objet a*. It is indeed *en-corps,* not detached from the object-cause of desire, not severed from the Other, S(Ⱥ). Isnt the lesson taught by mystics that it is possible for a feminine subject to achieve a sort of vacuity of existence in order to enjoy fullness of being in the encounter with the Other? Tess, like Ella, tends towards some kind of annihilation of her being in order to reach mystical fusion with the Other—whether the Other is Angel (whom she divinizes) or

20 "'Which are my fingers and which are yours?' he said, looking up. 'They are very much mixed'" (*Tess* p. 215). One wonders whether Hardy had in mind the poem by Donne. The irony of the scene would then be all the more powerful.

21 Paccaud-Huguet, p. 290.

the cruel Other of tragedy who has had his fill at the end of the novel ("the President of the Immortals [...] had ended his sport with Tess" *Tess* p. 384). The chapter entitled "Fulfilment" may be understood in both perspectives. One already sees the part played by the death-drive in the novel.[22]

In her reading of Duras's *The Rapture of Lol V. Stein* (*Le Ravissement de Lol V. Stein*), Sophie Marret writes:

> Rapture is the conjunction of a defect in the extraction of the object and of the detachment of the image of the body. When the primordial extraction of *jouissance* has not occurred through symbolic castration, rapture is the phenomenon in which the image of the detached body carries off with itself the object of the drive, leaving the subject identified with pure vacuity.[23]

If I follow the author correctly in her analysis, "rapture" is a state in which one is "ravished," that is to say carried off (in an experience of loss of selfhood, which may also be, as in Tess's case, an experience of "rape," the word having the same etymology), and simultaneously "enraptured," filled with ecstasy, the experience being made possible by a defect in symbolic castration and the non-extraction of *objet a*. The logic is that developed by Lacan in his graph of sexuation, where it appears clearly that on the non-phallic (or "feminine") side castration is inoperative.[24] The inference regarding Tess is that the experience of mystical vacuity is concomitant with a *jouissance* felt *in the soul*, a fullness of being achieved *en-corps* in the Paradise scene at Talbothays, when Tess listens ecstatically to the music played by Angel.

In fact Tess is an oxymoron: she is ethereal and sensual, incarnate and disincarnate. She is often depicted as "ghostly," "as if she were merely a soul at large" (*Tess* p. 134). Angel sees her as "a visionary essence of a woman," calling her

22 This assertion is not a novelty. Hillis Miller writes: "Erotic desire is a mask for the death wish. Life is a detour on the journey towards death. For Hardy, as for Freud, only in death—not in any happy conjunction with my other half—can I escape the unappeasable desire for something which is missing" (Hillis Miller, p. 135).

23 My translation from the French: "Le ravissement est conjonction du défaut d'extraction de l'objet et du détachement de l'image du corps. Faute que soit advenue l'extraction primordiale de jouissance par l'opération de la castration symbolique, le ravissement est le phénomène par lequel l'image du corps détachée emporte avec elle l'objet pulsionnel, laissant le sujet identifié à une pure vacuité" (Marret, p. 28).

24 Castration operates on the phallic side, where "any speaking being" (whether male or female) "has the choice of positing itself" (see below for full quotation, Lacan, 1975/1998, p. 80).

"Artemis, Demeter, and other fanciful names," much to her distress ("'Call me Tess', she would say askance" *Tess* pp. 134–135). Ghostly, spectral, Tess is assigned a place which is that of the dead: Angel lays her down in "an empty stone-coffin" (*Tess* p. 244);[25] he tells her that her arms "are like wet marble" (*Tess* p. 187), which makes her consubstantial with those "Purbeck marble and alabaster people in Kingsbere church" who really are her lineal forefathers (*Tess* p. 131). "True d'Urberville to the bone" (*Tess* p. 131), she knows the *truth* about herself, she is nothing but bones: "The wife of Angel Clare put her hand to her brow, and felt its curve, and the edges of her eye-sockets perceptible under the soft skin, and thought as she did so that a time would come when that bone would be bare. 'I wish it were now', she said" (*Tess* p. 270). Once the masks of feminine masquerade have fallen away like the skins of an onion, once "the wife of Angel Clare" has become "bare" (note the rhyme), what appears is the "black hole" of "the Lady-Thing" (Žižek, 1999b, p. 155). Tess is revealed in her true essence: she is nothing. That she knows: "When I see what you know, what you have read, and seen, and thought, *I feel what a nothing I am*! I'm like the poor Queen of Sheba who lived in the Bible. There is no more spirit in me" (*Tess* p. 130, my italics). Tess's decision at the end of the chapter to keep quiet about her noble ancestry ("she held her tongue about the d'Urberville vault" *Tess* p. 132) is very wise indeed: not just because Angel hates old aristocratic families (a piece of information heard from dairyman Crick), but because the d'Urberville "vault" is that void, that "black hole" that had better be left unseen, and that the feminine masquerade is here to mask. In a later chapter Tess will go back on her resolve to tell Angel about her "fault" and instead she will tell him about her "family-vault"—a change of mind that will prove disastrous.

Vault and fault: the two words rhyme together, and are strangely interchangeable. Both refer to holes in the earth: "fault" in its geological sense means a crack in the earth's surface,[26] a "vault" is a subterranean cavity. But whereas "vault" connotes death and vacuity, the woman's "fault" calls to mind images of Tess's lush sexuality, like the "madder stain" on her body, the trace left by an enjoyment supposedly derived from sexual intercourse. The two words are in fact two sides of the same coin. "Fault" is the perception of the male gaze, ascribing to Tess a fullness of being, a lush sexuality fantasized as *excess*. In that view Tess's body is out of proportion with her real being. It is that very *fault* which causes Alec's eyes to rivet themselves upon her:

25 "He encoffins the sexual instinct," writes Tony Tanner (Tanner, p. 195).

26 The feminine sexual organ is also an obvious connotation.

> It was a luxuriance of aspect, a fullness of growth, which made her appear more of a woman than she really was. She had inherited the feature from her mother without the quality it denoted. It had troubled her mind occasionally, till her companions had said that it was a *fault* which time would cure.
>
> *TESS* 45, my italics

Tess as a surplus object, always "more than" normality, with a "brimful" nature that appears excessive in the eyes of men, who has to snip her eyebrows off with a pair of little scissors so as to be "insured against aggressive admiration" (*Tess* p. 272), and whose name is a truncated form of "Teresa," is perhaps emblematic of the feminine *jouissance* which is "more than" phallic *jouissance*, situated in a "Beyondsex" where she always wants *more*, "Encore," *en-corps*. Like Ella, who is "more than a mere multiplier of her kind." In fact, Tess is both a figure of radical vacuity and a surplus in the field of vision.[27] Both vault and fault. The "madder stain" is in excess of reality, an object that has to be removed for the world to be restored to normality (Ramel, 2008b). Yet the red spot as an emblem of Tess's "fault" makes manifest the *diffamation* suffered by her: for the male gaze is all too ready to *misconstrue* the spot as the stigma left by her experience of sexual enjoyment, to recognize it as her "fault" imprinted on her skin—as Philippe Julien has argued, it is reassuring to substitute a supposed *knowledge* for what is unspeakable, unrepresentable, the enigma of feminine *jouissance*.[28] Knowledge about Tess's supposed "fault" is far more acceptable, in the phallic perspective, than the unfathomable "black hole" of her Other *jouissance*, the unknowable "d'Urberville vault." Such certainties are an easy way out of an unpalatable truth: that beyond the phallus there is an indecipherable *jouissance* that a woman may enjoy. And in the *studium* of Hardy's fiction, the red stain is the *punctum* that gives figure to that radical enigma.[29]

At this stage, the question to be raised concerns Tess's desire: what does the woman want? A logical answer is that her desire is a desire for the Other.

---

27 After the accident that has killed Prince, the Durbeyfields' horse, she seem to be drained of her blood while the horse's blood is spouting from the wound and "falling with a hiss into the road": "The atmosphere turned pale [...] the lane showed all its white features, and Tess showed hers, still whiter" (*Tess* p. 37). But at the same time she herself turns into a stain when she is "splashed from head to skirt with the crimson drops" (*Tess* p. 37).

28 "Cette diffamation vient de l'homme en tant qu'il prétend résoudre par elle l'énigme de la jouissance de la femme. Comment en effet surmonter l'angoisse du *non-rapport* sexuel, sinon par un supposé *savoir* de ce qu'il en est de la jouissance de l'Autre?" (Julien, p. 188).

29 We will see later, in the chapter on the object-gaze, that the red stain is loaded with the unknowable *jouissance* at work in the scopic drive.

A desire for masculine otherness? There is nothing in the passage that indicates a *sexual* attraction to Angel. If we are to believe the narrator, what draws Tess to the garden "like a fascinated bird" is Angel's music—but his irony makes this reading uncertain: "to speak absolutely, both instrument and execution were poor" (*Tess* p. 127). Why then do those notes, which Tess had heard before in the attic above her head, appeal to her so much in the present circumstances? No doubt because "they wandered in the still air with a stark quality like that of nudity." Something of the essence of things appears in its nudity, as though the "cotton-wool" of reality (Woolf, 1976/1978, pp. 83–84) had been pierced, revealing what Virginia Woolf calls "the thing that lies beneath the semblance of the thing" (Woolf, 1931/2005, p. 138). A reading suggested by the description of the evening light shed on the scene: "the light which still shone was derived mainly from a large hole in the western bank of cloud" (*Tess* p. 128). In that perspective, Tess could be seen as indulging in exquisite contact with the Lacanian Real, her body becoming porous to its delicious and "offensive" presence, through her skin, through all the orifices of the sense organs. The sense of a dissolution of spatial and linguistic categories tends to confirm that analysis: "There was no distinction between the near and the far, and an auditor felt close to everything within the horizon. The soundlessness impressed her as a positive entity rather than as the mere negation of noise. It was broken by the strumming of strings" (*Tess* p. 127). Perhaps that "soundlessness" has more to do with Tess's emotions here than any "sexual readiness" in her—a point that will be explored later, in the chapter on voice.[30]

2.3 The Feminine Pursuit, the Artist's Quest

Death, then, is what looms on the horizon of desire. Nothingness is the point reached by Tess when she becomes absorbed in an all-devouring figure of Otherness, "the President of the Immortals," who has had his "sport" with her when the tragedy ends. But then, one might object, is that the fate that awaits a woman who does not "give in as to her desire"? One first answer is that The Woman does not exist (if she did she would be mad); a woman, by essence,

30 In the pages following this extract, Angel will insist on restoring the function of the signifier, by thrusting upon Tess a distinction between "indoor fears" and "outdoor fears" (*Tess* p. 128), and suggesting that she should take up a course in history to alleviate the pain of feeling she is "nothing" (*Tess* p. 130). In the novel there is no way out of that radical asymmetry between two opposed modes of enjoyment (phallic and Other), except in tragic death. This scene allows us to foresee all the ravages that will be caused by the lack of a sexual *rapport* between Angel and Tess (and by the failure to accept it as part of the human condition).

is "not-all,"[31] which means that a part of her subscribes to the phallic order. It is very important not to lose sight of that, especially with regard to Tess, for whom Angel is *also* a desired object, and who even lets her eyes be "dazed" (*Tess* p. 83) by Alec for a few weeks. But even so, argues Nestor Braunstein, should one fail to be precise enough on the Lacanian conception of femininity, the only space left for a woman to live *as a woman*—that is to say beyond phallic *jouissance*—would be "that unthinkable place of the Thing where silence merges with the cry, where all significations vanish and where life gives in to death" (Braunstein, p. 161). Braunstein objects to that, arguing that a woman's quest leads her to "a world of lived values which is beyond phallic imperialism and its universe of sense, a world which is the secret of those mystics (both men and women), who are not, no, there are not mad, and of those subtleties of the feminine soul which undo the arrogant certainties of phallic discourse about love."[32] The motto of that "beyond," he continues, is *encore*.

Braunstein is right to insist on the feminine pursuit after "a signifier impossible to articulate" (Braunstein, p. 162) —which is also the artist's quest. For there lies the possibility of a *mi-dire*, of an ethics that can reconcile feminine *jouissance* with life. In that space, a woman and a man can experience a strange kinship, like the kinship between Ella Marchmill and the poet Robert Trewe. For as Lacan argues, enjoyment "beyond the phallus" is not exclusively feminine: the two sides in his graph of sexuation do not represent the masculine versus the feminine, but are definitions of "the so-called man or woman portion for that which finds itself in the position of inhabiting language" (Lacan, 1975/1998, p. 80). About the side where is inscribed "the woman portion of speaking beings," Lacan writes:

> Any speaking being whatsoever, as is expressly formulated in Freudian theory, whether provided with the attributes of masculinity [...] or not, is allowed to inscribe itself in this part. If it inscribes itself there, it will not allow for any universality—it will be a not-whole, insofar as it has the choice of positing itself in Φx or of not being there.
>
> LACAN (1975/1998, p. 80)

In other words, "one is not obliged, when one is male, to situate oneself on the side of $\forall x \Phi x$. One can situate oneself on the side of the not-whole. There are men who are just as good as women. It happens. And who also feel just fine about it. Despite—I won't say their phallus—despite what encumbers them

31 Or "non-all," in Žižek's formulation.

32 Braunstein, pp. 161–162. My own translation into English, from the French translation of *El Gode, un concepto Lacaniano*.

that goes by that name, they get the idea or sense that there must be a *jouissance* that is beyond. Those are the ones we call mystics" (Lacan, 1975/1998, p. 76).

But Lacan does not stop at mystics (like Saint Teresa or Hadewijch) and their writings, for he adds:

> These mystical jaculations are not idle chatter or empty verbiage; they provide, all in all, some of the best reading one can find—at the bottom of the page drop a footnote, 'Add to that list Jacques Lacan's *Écrits*', because it's of the same order.
>
> LACAN (1975/1998, p. 76)

If the list were continued, it would also include artists—in all the fields of art, in music, painting, literature, etc.—for such is the logic at work in Lacan's definitions. "Beyond the phallus," that undiscovered country mostly inhabited by women, is also a favourite haunt with artists of either sex.[33] There, it is possible for a poet, for any writer of literature, whether male or female, to turn the "nothingness" to which she/he aspires into the "mere nothings" of poetry (or literature), like Robert Trewe's "bouts-rimés," Virginia Woolf's "orts, scraps, and fragments" (Woolf, 1941/1998, p. 169), or Marilyn Monroe's *Fragments,*[34] left-overs from a massive *jouissance* that the poetic Letter has the power to break up into minute particles, letters to be scattered abroad to the four winds, to be eventually enjoyed by a community of readers.[35] Thus the destructive *jouissance* can be both *constrained* and *contained* by the poetic use of language.[36]

---

33 "This kind of jouissance, usually experienced by women, can also be experienced by artists and male mystics" (Golan, p. 90).

34 Marily Monroe, Stanley F. Buchtal, Bernard Comment. *Fragments: Poems, Intimate Notes, Letters*, New York: Farrar, Strauss and Giroux (2010). About Marilyn's "fragmentary, poem-like texts scribbled in notebooks and on loose-leaf paper," see "Brain pickings" (2012): <http://www.brainpickings.org/index.php/2012/07/27/marilyn-monroe-fragments-poems/> (2014). An excellent article by a French psychoanalyst on the importance of *fragmentation* in Marilyn Monroe's *Fragments*: "Au plus près du dire et de l'indicible: Hannah Arendt et Marilyn Monroe," Jocelyne Huguet-Manoukian, *Par Lettre*, n° 33, février 2014.

35 For Marilyn, and for Virginia Woolf, the defence against the indomitable appeal of the death-drive only lasted a certain time, until the "mere nothings" of literary creation were powerless against the pressure of a massive *jouissance*, the craving for nothingness.

36 "The littoral state of the signifier enables it to both *contain* and *constrain* the silence of the drive towards the primordial object which is always the drive towards annihilation" (Paccaud-Huguet, p. 289).

Recent research on Joseph Conrad has foregrounded a new concept, the "textual voice" (Maisonnat, 2012, pp. 164–180), a voice which, in a literary text, "undercuts both the authorial voice and the narrative voice at the same time because [...] the authorial and the narrative voices deal with reality, whereas the textual voice deals with the Real"[37] (Maisonnat, 2012, p. 176). In other words it is connected with the unconscious at work in a text. The effect is to delay the production of ultimate meaning:

> [...] It challenges the authorial voice by destabilizing the construction of meaning. Its function is to get the upper hand on the authorial voice so that interpretation becomes open to discussion and questioning. Whereas the authorial voice is the voice of mastery based on the primacy of the signified over the signifier, the textual voice, based on the primacy of the signifier over the signified, is disruptive and opens grey areas of uncertainty.
>
> MAISONNAT (2012, p. 168)

In his article, Maisonnat argues that the frame narrator in *Heart of Darkness* puts forward a similar distinction when he opposes the simplicity of the "yarns of seamen," the "whole meaning of which lies within the shell of a cracked nut," to the diffraction of "meaning" that may be observed outside the tale, enveloping it "in the likeness of one of these misty halos that sometimes are made visible by the spectral illumination of moonshine" (Conrad, p. 138). The former, he claims, "obviously finds its source in the predominance of the authorial voice," whereas the halo "supplies a striking visual metaphor for the textual voice" (Maisonnat, 2012, p. 168). The textual voice "precludes ideological and interpretational closure and alerts the reader to his responsibility in constructing his own interpretation" (Maisonnat, 2012, p. 176). It tends towards the fragmented, the multiple, like the Lacanian Letter—the material part of the signifier, the "mere nothings" of language—which is its very substance. It is clear that the authorial voice, which promotes the illusion of a writer's authority over his text, corresponds to the phallic temptation of order, clarity and univocity. As opposed to that, the textual voice is the voice of equivocation and ambivalence, which undermines the phallic construction of meaning. The voice that does not endow words with a definite sense comes very close to "a dangerous sort of enjoyment" (Dolar, 1996, p. 20). Such a voice, Dolar argues, is "self-evidently equated with femininity, whereas the text, the instance of signification, is in this simple paradigmatic opposition on the side of

37 The Real in the Lacanian sense.

masculinity" (Dolar, 1996, p. 17). Beyond the words, beyond *logos*, and therefore "beyond the phallus," the textual voice is situated on the feminine side of Lacan's graph of sexuation, on the side of the "not-whole." One cannot but conclude that, in a literary text, there is a "feminine" voice vying with the authorial and narrative voices, subverting their phallic certainties. And making considerations on the gender of the writer partly irrelevant. For the inference of this demonstration is that *écriture* is always "feminine."

No wonder Ella Marchmill enjoys communication with a "brother poet" who, "with a man's unsusceptibility on the question of sex" (*CSS* p. 382), never even thinks of passing himself off as a woman. No wonder a male novelist can take upon himself the task of speaking for a woman when she is unwilling or unable to defend herself (Mallett, pp. 394–395, note 26). It is no surprise that "it was consistently thought that the author of *Far from the Madding Crowd* might be a woman" (Gittings, p. 291)[38] —a misapprehension that would not have astonished G.H. Lewes, for whom the novel is a feminine literary form.[39]

38 When Hardy started publishing *Far from the Madding Crowd* anonymously in *Cornhill Magazine*, "a guess hazarded that it might be from the pen of George Eliot—why, the author could never understand" (*Life* 100).

39 "The very nature of fiction calls for that predominance of sentiment which we have already attributed to the feminine mind." G.H. Lewes, "The Lady Novelists," *Westminter Review*, 58 (1852), p. 133.

CHAPTER 3

The Logic of Desire

3.1 "Much Ado about Nothing"

"Nothing" is the final point aimed at by Ella in "An Imaginative Woman," the ending towards which the whole plot drives. It is also the ultimate consummation in *The Mayor of Casterbridge*, as figured in Henchard's will:

> 'That Elizabeth-Jane Farfrae be not told of my death, or made to grieve on account of me.
> '& that I be not bury'd in consecrated ground.
> '& that no sexton be asked to toll the bell.
> '& that nobody is wished to see my dead body.
> '& that no murners walk behind me at my funeral.
> '& that no flours be planted on my grave,
> '& that no man remember me.
> 'To this I put my name.
> 'Michael Henchard'.
>
> *MC*, p. 333

Absolute silence is required—Elizabeth-Jane is not to be "told" of Henchard's death, the bells are not to be "tolled." The absolute "nothingness" reached here is beyond all limits, it is the total annihilation of being craved for by Antigone, which Lacan called "the second death," as opposed to the first death (the physical death of the body): "the second death imagined by Sade's heroes—death insofar as it is regarded as the point at which the very cycles of the transformation of nature are annihilated" (Lacan, 1986a/2008, pp. 305, 362). "I cannot bear my fate as writ, I'd have my life unbe" says Tess in the poem "Tess," hereby giving voice to the "pure and simple desire of death as such" (Lacan, 1986a/2008, p. 348), a longing for the complete erasure of her being. No traces, no ashes left on the pyre after the final destruction—such was the terrible purpose of the Holocaust, the "perfect crime" in Gérard Wajcman's words, not because it was to remain unpunished, but because nobody was ever to know that it had taken place.[1] And it is worth noting that in *The Mayor of Casterbridge*, Abel Whittle is

1 "Anéantir et l'Homme et l'Autre. Effacer des hommes de la liste des vivants et les effacer aussi de la liste des morts. Comme s'ils n'avaient jamais existé. Et puis effacer la liste elle-même,

 | DOI 10.1163/9789004296626_005

grateful to Henchard, though the Mayor was "rough" to him, because "he was kind-like to mother when she wer here below, sending her the best ship-coal, and *hardly any ashes* from it all" (*MC* p. 332, my italics).

That "zero-point" of total obliteration is never reached of course in Hardy's fiction, were it only because, paradoxically, the text is here to celebrate it, to imprint it on our memories.[2] But it is aimed at in many novels, it is the point that many tragic characters seek to identify with, thus causing the primitive signifying chain to solidify, as I have shown in the section on "the missing blank." For instance in *A Pair of Blue Eyes*, "nothing" is the final consummation reached by Elfride, Knight, and Stephen—whether or not it was "devoutly" wished for by the three protagonists. The keynote is struck with a description of Lady Luxellian, "a lady with skim-milky eyes and complexion, belonging to the 'interesting' class of women, where that class merges in the sickly, her greatest pleasure being apparently to enjoy nothing" (*APBE* p. 138). "Nothing" can be understood here as "a positive entity" (*Tess* p. 127), "the nothing" which Lacan claimed was an object (Lacan, 1994, pp. 184–185), and it cannot fail to remind us of anorexia—a condition in which the patient eats "nothing." "How do you draw the line between women with something and women with nothing in them?" (*APBE* p. 178) asks Knight, in a scene where he forces Elfride to own that she would prefer a pair of ear-rings to "the well-chosen library of the best music." The truth is unveiled: Elfride is "a girl with nothing much in her but vanity" (*APBE* pp. 178–179). In that scene, Knight's cruelty to Elfride betrays his *dread* (and perhaps also his secret desire) that might be exposed the insubstantiality of the feminine masquerade—that might be revealed, once the masks had fallen off like the skins of an onion, absolute *nothingness*. Then, in that abyss, he might be confronted to his own "ontological void" (Žižek, 1999a, p. 138). For, as Žižek argues, we should recognize "in the ontological void of the woman the very void that defines subjectivity" (Žižek, 1999a, p. 138). No wonder Knight cannot face that experience of the abyss, that "empty nothing"

---

rendre une feuille blanche, et puis faire disparaître jusqu'à la feuille, la réduire en cendres, et puis disperser ces cendres, et puis dissiper la fumée et l'odeur de brûlé" (Wajcman, 1997, p. 19). ("To annihilate Man and the Other. To obliterate men from the list of the living and then to obliterate them from the list of the dead. As if they had never existed. And then to obliterate the list itself, to give in a blank paper, and then to destroy the paper itself, to reduce it to ashes, and then to scatter the ashes, to dispel the smoke and the smell of burning," my translation).

2 Henchard's last will asks for symbolic obliteration, yet it is signed with his name. A similar paradox concerns the silence that Hardy writes about in his poems, which the poetic text makes audible. As Laurence Estanove remarks, "the unsaid—silence—haunts the poem, and yet the poem is greatly eloquent" (Estanove, p. 23).

which Hegel called "the Night of the World"[3] (Žižek, 1999a, p. 136): the blank of origin is what he *will* not face—we have seen how that subjective position threatens the emergence of the symbolic order.[4] And of course, by denying the structural hole, he precipitates himself (and others) into the tragic void, his course can only lead him to that pure negativity which he sought to avoid.[5]

An ear-ring, says Knight, is "a mere nothing" (*APBE* p. 270): indeed the earring lost and found will bring about the downfall of Elfride, and the tragic *dénouement*. The novel ends with the parallel courses of Knight and Stephen converging at a point which is exactly the "nothing" I am writing about: the hearse carrying Elfride's coffin, which is "light as vanity; full of nothing" (*APBE* p. 358). As it is raining when the two men reach Endelstow, they turn for shelter to a smithy where a hammer is "ringing." Then a fascinating scene shows the bearer of a mysterious package carefully removing its wrappings: first a sheet of brown paper, then a piece of baize, then a wrapper of tissue paper. When all the coverings have been taken off and "spread flat," Knight and Stephen, "as if animated by one soul," can read the inscription on the coffin-plate which tells them that the hearse travelling with them (and whose destination was the same as theirs, *APBE*, p. 362) contained Elfride's body (*APBE* pp. 366–367). When all the skins of the onion have been peeled off, what appears is not some attainable kernel of enjoyment, but sheer nothingness—represented here by a few letters engraved on a coffin-plate. Interestingly, this passage is a *mise en abyme* of the act of writing: the parcel, which is a "flat one," laid "flat on the anvil," is a metatextual representation of the literary text. Elaborated in the smithy[6] of literary creation, where the poetic voice can be heard ringing, any text (but especially *A Pair of Blue Eyes*) is after all but a "hear-ring," which makes resonant the silence of utter nothingness, turning the

---

3 "One catches sight of this night when one looks human beings in the eye—into a night that becomes awful." Hegel, quoted from Donald Philip Verene, *Hegel's Recollection* (Albany, New York: Sunny Press, 1985, pp. 7–8). One is reminded of Pascal Quignard's "Sexual Night."

4 "And the symbolic order, the universe of the word, *logos*, can emerge only from the experience of this abyss" (Žižek, 1999a, p. 136). See Žižek's very clear explanation of "the status of this nothing," "the pure void of subjectivity," in "Otto Weininger, or 'Woman doesn't exist'" (Žižek, 1999a, p. 135). About the uneasiness felt by men in front of the feminine "inconsistency," he writes: "behind the multiple layers of masks is nothing, or, at the most, nothing but the shapeless, mucus stuff of the life-substance" (Žižek, 1999a, p. 139).

5 But which, perhaps, he longed for. The existential choice for him is between all and nothing: "ordinary truth I *will have*, or nothing at all" (*APBE* p. 325). His desire carries him beyond any form of compromise.

6 Stephen *Smith*, a young architect who is the son of a local stonemason, is of course a figure of the author.

absolute "nothing" reached in the diegesis into the "mere nothings" of literature. What is at the core of the literary is nothingness, the unrepresentable Thing which the poetic letter seeks to approach, as closely as possible. The last section of the novel makes audible the loss felt by the two men:[7] "In a new niche of the crypt lay a rather new coffin, which had lost some of its lustre" (*APBE* p.371). "Lost" is echoed by "lustre" (in which we overhear "lost her"), and the poetic flicker of meaning produces an *effet de sens* which is also an *effet de trou* ("a sense effect," "a hole effect"[8]). As Serge André argues in *Que veut une femme*, the new signifier created by the artist "does not attempt to fill the gaping void left by S(Ⱥ), but on the contrary to reveal it and to make it operate as such."[9] Thus the "missing gap" in the diegesis of *A Pair of Blue Eyes* can find a place in the text.

In the train-journey that takes Knight and Stephen to Endelstow, what is remarkable is that the sombre van "full of nothing" is "connected" to them (*APBE* p. 358), in such a way that Stephen has to look back to see it: "Stephen's vacant eyes rested upon the operations of some porters, who were shifting a dark and curious-looking van from the *rear* of the train" (*APBE* p. 357, my italics). Curiously, the object here is *behind*. Similarly, it is by glancing "behind her back" that Elfride catches sight of the missing ear-ring lodged in a crevice in the rock (*APBE* p. 300). These considerations bring to the fore another novel by Hardy, *Far From the Madding Crowd*, and another character, Boldwood. For Boldwood too is a man who can only look back. When reading the chapter entitled "Effect of the Letter—Sunrise," we see him dressing and walking out "towards the gate of a field to the east." But, rather strangely, an inversion[10] turns the rising sun into a sunset: "the whole effect resembled a sunset as childhood resembles age" (*FFMC* p. 81). Looking to the east is a habit with Boldwood, who is "a troublesome image" to Bathsheba, "a species of Daniel in her kingdom who persisted in kneeling *eastward* when reason and common sense said that he might just as well follow suit with the rest" (*FFMC* p. 78,

7 Note that they are still "the pair," while Lord Luxellian ("a peer") has a "symmetrical build" (*APBE* p. 371).

8 Poetry, writes Lacan, is "effet de sens, mais aussi bien effet de trou" (*Ornicar?*, n° 17–18, May 1977, p. 22).

9 "Le signifiant nouveau créé par l'artiste ne cherche pas à combler le trou béant laissé par S(Ⱥ), mais au contraire à le révéler et à le faire opérer comme tel" (André, p. 264, "De la mascarade à la poésie," my translation). André refers to the potter in Lacan's 7th *Seminar* (Lacan, 1986a, pp. 144–146), who "sculptures" the void and creates the pot *ex nihilo*.

10 Boldwood's whereabouts seem to have become confused, with all distinctions annulled in fact: between east and west, indoors and outdoors, up and down, heaven and earth, light and darkness (*FFMC* p. 81). As Catherine Lanone has shown, "images of inversion pepper the novel" (Lanone, p. 106).

my emphasis).[11] Setting aside the religious connotations of the "eastward position" in the Victorian age, one must bear in mind that, in our imaginary representations, facing the east is facing the rising sun, that is to say the origin. Strikingly, the editor's textual note that tells us that "Hardy mistakenly has Daniel face east, when, in fact, Jerusalem would be west of Babylon" (*FFMC* p. 78): indeed Boldwood is *mistaken* when he is facing east, he should be facing west. Every human being should turn away from the origin and look westward, where "the land is bright"[12] —though of course death looms on the horizon of whoever looks at the "Occident."[13] The interchangeability of east and west suggests that origin and death are one and the same thing, and that for Boldwood it will not be possible to leave the origin behind and move forward on the path of life: what is behind has come to the fore-front. When he ponders on the Valentine he has just received, he sees it even when it is *behind* him: "he was conscious of its presence even when his back was turned upon it" (*FFMC* p. 80).

In fact, his whole attention is riveted on one object: the origin. When he receives the Valentine card, the signifier "origin" is repeated three times in two pages:

> [...] the letter and its dictum changed their tenor from the thoughtlessness of their *origin* to a deep solemnity, imbibed from their accessories now [...] The letter must have had an *origin* and a motive [...] She was a misty shape, and well she might be, considering that her *original* was at that moment sound asleep and oblivious of all love and letter-writing under the sky.
>
> *FFMC*, pp. 80–81, my italics

Had the letter been signed and attributable to a definite, nameable person, had it been part of the normal circuit of symbolic exchanges, Boldwood's reaction would have been totally different. Here the unsigned letter exerts on him an irresistible fascination because it seems to encapsulate the mystery of origin, the "sexual night" that Pascal Quignard writes about.[14] The "misty shape" of the woman writing/creating has an extraordinary appeal to Boldwood, comparable

---

11 Boldwood never looks in the same direction as the other characters: against "reason and common sense," he looks to the east (*FFMC* p. 78); against the general trend, when everybody is looking away from Bathsheba, he observes her, and when they all regard her, he turns aside (*FFMC* p. 124).

12 "And not by eastern windows only,/ When daylight comes, comes in the light,/ In front, the sun climbs slow, how slowly,/ But westward, look, the land is bright" (Arthur Hugh Clough, "Say not the Struggle Naught availeth").

13 From the Latin *occidere*, "to fall," from which is also derived the French *occire*, "to kill."

14 Which is the same thing as Hegel's "Night of the World."

to the fascination for the letters of Geoffrey Aspern in James's novella *The Aspern Papers*—by securing the letters, James's character fancies he might have access to the secret of creation and thus solve "the riddle of the universe." Indeed it is possible to read the Valentine scene as a "primal scene," the erotic charge being rather obvious with words that play on two registers, that of hand-writing (the "curves" of the letters), but also that of a woman's body (her "curved" mouth).[15] It is the opacity of the "sexual night" which fills Boldwood with an irrepressible longing to turn a radical mystery into an enigma that he might solve. From now on, Boldwood will be intent on following only one course, the "onward glide" (*FFMC* p. 185)[16] towards the origin, towards the east, which takes him, inexorably, paradoxically, to the setting sun. Quite logically, when he walks "towards the gate of a field to the east" (*FFMC* p. 81), his rising sun looks like a sunset: the eastbound course is the sole possible choice for him, but his orient can only be an occident.

In order to clarify what may still appear obscure in my analysis, it might be of interest to compare Boldwood to Gabriel Oak, who is not a tragic character. To him Bathsheba is a true "object," in the sense that an object is, etymologically, an *ob-jectum*, a "thing thrown before" (*OED*): something to follow in an unending quest, a bright star that remains inaccessible, on the horizon of his desire. "I've danced at your skittish heels, my beautiful Bathsheba, for many a long mile, and many a long day" (*FFMC* p. 303), are his words when he realizes she is willing to marry him. Gabriel dancing at Bathsheba's heels, in pursuit of her, means that she is to him a "thing thrown before" him, a object of desire. Here we could ponder on a question asked by Lacan: "is the object of desire *before* us?" No, answers Lacan, "the object is behind desire" (Lacan, 2004, p. 120, my translation).[17] We have seen that Lacan opposes *agalma* ("ornament" in

15 "Somebody—some *woman's* hand had travelled softly over the paper bearing his name; her unrevealed eyes had watched every curve as she formed it. Her brain had seen him in imagination the while. Why should she have imagined him? Her mouth—were the lips red or pale, plump or creased—had curved itself to a certain expression as the pen went on" (*FFMC* p. 80). "Softly," like "curve," refers to writing but has sexual undertones. If one accepts Gilbert and Gubar's assertion that the pen is a metaphorical penis in Western thought, it is possible to overhear a sexual significance in "as the pen went on." Boldwood appears as a creature born of her imagination ("why should she have imagined him?"), conceived by her ("the paper *bearing* his name," my italics).

16 Boldwood's movement gives an impression of motionlessness. Gabriel and Coggan see him sitting erect upon his horse, "his head turned to neither side, the elbows steady by the hips, the brim of the hat level and undisturbed in its onward glide" (*FFMC* p. 185).

17 "Est-ce que l'objet du désir est *en avant*? C'est là le mirage dont il s'agit [...] je dirais que l'objet *a* n'est pas à situer dans quoi que ce soit d'analogue à l'intentionnalité d'une noèse.

Greek) to *palea* ("waste" in Latin).[18] *Agalma*, the object aimed at in love, is a deceitful object. It is *before* the subject, whereas the true object-cause is *behind*.

Boldwood, with his strange capacity to see the Valentine even when his back is turned upon him, is fastened to the *true* object of desire, the *object-cause*. No wonder Bathsheba feels uneasy because she is the *cause* of Boldwood's party: "But I am *the cause* of the party, and that upsets me" (*FFMC* p. 275, italics in the text). To Boldwood, she is not an *objectum* thrown before him. She is his "one delight" (*FFMC* p. 161), his feeling for her is "a thing strong as death" (*FFMC* p. 157). "I cannot say how far above any idea and object on earth you seem to me," he says to Bathsheba, "nobody knows—God only knows—how much you are to me" (*FFMC* p. 101). No other earthly object could be substituted for her, she is *irreplaceable*—just as Polynices as Antigone's brother is irreplaceable to her. He will not deviate one inch from the course he has set his mind upon, he will not (to use a Lacanian formula) "give way as to his desire" (*céder sur son désir*).[19] It is at this point that we enter tragedy—we have seen how the impossibility of metaphoric substitution is the very essence of the tragic. Gabriel Oak, on the contrary, however strong his love for Bathsheba may be, is not tied to her by "a thing strong as death": "he had been held to her by a beautiful thread which it pained him to spoil by breaking, rather than by a chain he could not break" (*FFMC* p. 106). To understand this, one has to bear in mind that *objet petit a* may be envisaged from two angles: in one perspective, it is the "true" object-cause, the one and only object that will suffer no replacement; in the other, it is forever missing, "a vacuum, sucking other objects into its place" (Kaye, p. 56), an object whose function is to inscribe "the presence of a hollow which any object may come into" (Dor, p. 185, my translation). It is that second version of *objet a* which sets in motion the metonymy of desire. For Boldwood *objet a* is not "extracted," it is not a vacuum, his predicament is very close to psychosis. And the way is open for tragedy as far as he is concerned.

Gabriel, on the contrary, is in love with a bright star shining in the firmament of his desire, but that star is already fallen, it is but a substitute for the ideal, inaccessible one. In the second chapter, when Gabriel discovers Bathsheba on a cold wintry night, he first mistakes the artificial light of her "shed" for a star, but soon realizes his mistake:

Dans l'intentionnalité du désir, qui doit en être distinguée, cet objet est à concevoir comme la cause du désir [...] l'objet est *derrière* le désir" (Lacan, 2004, p. 120).

18 See note 9 in the introduction to this book.

19 See note 32 in chapter 1.

> Occupied thus, with eyes stretched afar, Oak gradually perceived that what he had previously taken to be a star low down behind the outskirts of the plantation was in reality no such thing. It was an artificial light, almost close at hand.
>
> *FFMC*, p. 15

The radiance that has attracted him is not a star high up in the sky, nor even a star low down on the horizon: it is but a lantern in a "shed" occupied by a cow-girl and her acolyte, the two women busying themselves with such mundane occupations as tending two cows (one of them being a new-born calf which, in striking parallel to Gabriel, mistakes the lantern for the moon!). Hardy's humour makes it plain that we are in a post-lapsarian world where the real thing-in-itself is missing. Something of the original glamour is already lost, something has had to be "shed"—the "shed" of course is part of the general downward movement of the scene, involving Gabriel's body, his gaze as well as ours. In that fallen world the object of desire comes to occupy a vacant place, as the narrator makes explicit in terms that could very well have suited Lacan:

> Having for some time known the want of a satisfactory form to fill an increasing void within him, his position moreover affording the widest scope for his fancy, he painted her a beauty.
>
> *FFMC*, p. 17

Gabriel, so we are told, draws on his fancy to invent the missing details that his position (affording but a partial view of the girl) does not allow him to enjoy. And so, continues the narrator, "we colour and *mould* according to the wants within us whatever our eyes bring in" (*FFMC* p. 17, my italics).

The word "mould" is important here, not only because it is proleptic of the scene in which the space left untouched by Troy's sword is "almost a mould of Bathsheba's figure" (*FFMC* p. 145), but also because it is a good representation of *objet a* as a vacuum, a "mould" to be filled by any object. It is worth noting that Lacan has compared *objet a* to what he calls an *en-forme*, a hat-mould, both as the form around which a hat is shaped and as the hollow thus produced: "The field of the Other is [...] enformed like *a*. This *enforme*, or mould, is inscribed in a topology where it appears as hollowing out this field."[20] In similar fashion, an analepsis in *Far From the Madding Crowd* "hollows out" the narrative: the loss of Bathsheba's hat is only related as a flash-back in

20 Lacan (2006, p. 301): "Le champ de l'Autre est [...] en forme de a. Cet *en-forme* s'inscrit dans une topologie où il se présente au niveau de ce champ comme le trouant" (my translation).

the conversation between the two women, which Gabriel overhears while he is spying on them: "Well, my hat is gone [...] It went over the hedge I think. The idea of such a slight wind catching it" (*FFMC* p. 16). No doubt the incident is of minor importance—yet it is worth noting that, unlike Stephen in *A Pair of Blue Eyes*, Oak will succeed in his search for "the missing article" and restore it to its owner. Insignificant or not, the missing scene opens a void in the text, like the *enforme* of a hat, like a mould enveloping a radical absence, revealing a "pure deficit" yet somehow giving it substance, on both the diegetic and the narrative levels (for the hat and the narrative are both absent). That vacant space is the exact representation of Lacan's *objet a*, and in the economy of the novel it is the matrix out of which desire will grow, for Gabriel in particular, but also for Bathsheba. What is delineated here is the void of the "object-cause," that may be filled temporarily by *ersatz* objects, but which for any subject entering symbolic exchange is a radical vacuity. No such hole has been delved in Boldwood's experience of reality. The Valentine card intruding into his parlour is a *surplus* object, placed on the wings of the spread eagle surmounting the time-piece above the mantel-shelf (*FFMC* pp. 79–80).

3.2 *Das Ding*

In his seventh *Seminar*, Lacan develops the idea that desire is oriented by "this object, *das Ding*, as the absolute Other of the subject, that one is supposed to find again"—though Lacan has previously made it clear that "what is supposed to be found is never found again. It is in its nature that the object as such is lost. It will never be found again" (Lacan, 1986a/2008, p. 63). Then Lacan attempts to give a topographical representation of *das Ding*, which he places "at the center" (Lacan, 1986a/2008, p. 87)—a difficult operation indeed, for *das Ding* is "extimate" to the subject, that is to say it "has to be posited as exterior, as the prehistoric Other that it is impossible to forget [...], something strange to me, although it is at the heart of me, something that on the level of the unconscious only a representation can represent" (Lacan, 1986a/2008, pp. 86–87). However, the Thing to Lacan, "as the intimate exteriority or 'extimacy'," is described as "the central place" (Lacan, 1986a/2008, p. 171), "that central emptiness which up to now has been the form in which access to *jouissance* has presented itself to us" (Lacan, 1986a/2008, pp. 248–249).

In other words, that "central emptiness" is the locus of *jouissance*, and in the context of tragedy, it is "the kingdom of death, the empire of Thanatos where eagles fear to venture, the place into which Antigone, still quivering with life, steps down to find her sepulchre, the fascinating and dangerous seat of a lethal enjoyment" (Braunstein, p. 85, my translation). Long before Freud and Lacan, Shakespeare knew what reigned in the central void of the "hollow crown":

> For within the hollow crown
> That rounds the mortal temples of a king
> Keeps Death his court.
>
> SHAKESPEARE, *Richard II*, III, 2, 156–158

It is only by going *round* it that one can avoid the tragic fall into the abyss: "the pleasure principle governs the search for the object and imposes the detours which maintain the distance in relation to its end. In French the etymology of the word—which replaced the archaic 'quérir' ('to search') — refers to *circa*, detour" (Lacan, 1986a/2008, p. 71).

In *Far from the Madding Crowd*, the precipice is there right from the start, it engulfs Oak's ewes, which will be found dead and dying by the unfortunate farmer (*FFMC* p. 33). But it is to be noted that the sacrifice offered to the gods in this scene is not a human sacrifice: one could say that the ewes are immolated *instead of* Gabriel. What happens is but "A Pastoral Tragedy" (*FFMC* p. 30). For, as I have already said, Oak is not a tragic character, and in the narrative economy of the novel he is the one who has the capacity to find ways *around* the object of desire. The whole novel, after all, is but a detour that takes him to wedlock after a first aborted attempt. One scene is particularly enlightening in this respect: the one in which Gabriel proposes to Bathsheba. Both protagonists run playfully around a holly bush, whose red berries represent the inaccessible/forbidden fruit. First Bathsheba tries to escape Gabriel: "Seeing his advance take the form of an attitude threatening a possible enclosure, if not compression, of her person, she edged off round the bush" (*FFMC* p. 27). Bathsheba continues the game, encouraging Gabriel to wait for her. He casts despairing glances at that burning bush which stands in the way between them:

> He regarded the red berries between them over and over again, to such an extent, that holly seemed in his after life to be a cypher signifying a proposal of marriage. Bathsheba decisively turned to him. 'No; 'tis no use', she said. 'I don't want to marry you'.
>
> *FFMC*, p. 28

In this play of hide-and-seek, Gabriel will not gain the Thing-in-itself, only words, words, words: "a cypher signifying a proposal of marriage." The force of his words will not be enough to transport him to the other side of the bush:

> 'Why won't you have me ?' he appealed, creeping round the holly to reach her side. 'I cannot', she said, retreating. 'But why ?' he persisted, standing still at last in despair of ever reaching her, and facing over the bush. 'Because I don't love you [...] You'd get to despise me'. 'Never', said Mr Oak, so earnestly that he seemed to be coming, by the force of his words, straight through the bush and into her arms'.
>
> *FFMC*, p. 28

Desire, as an endless metonymic quest, must beat about the bush.

Whenever Boldwood is concerned in the novel, the logic at work is totally different. The topology of the novel always places danger at the centre of diegetic space: to that arena the victims are drawn, there they are put to death. Escape is only possible away from the centre, away from that focal point where all the destructive forces converge. Chapter LII, which relates events leading to Boldwood's Christmas party, is entitled "Converging Courses." Then, in the following chapter, Boldwood tries to wrench from Bathsheba her "word" that she will marry him in six years' time, thus exerting on her an extreme form of symbolic violence.[21] But the man does not stop there: after Bathsheba has refused his present of a ring as a "token" from him, he forces the ring on to her finger ("And Boldwood slipped the ring on her finger" *FFMC* p. 287). Boldwood has thus placed Bathsheba *at the centre of the ring*—which is structurally similar to the Ring in *The Mayor of Casterbridge*, or to Stonehenge in *Tess of the d'Urbervilles*. There she is, awaiting sacrifice, trapped in the middle of the "hollow crown," where Death keeps his court.[22]

Fortunately, the course of events will take a different turn. In the scene that follows, Boldwood occupies a central position in the room, "by the fire-place."[23]

---

21 I mean that by wrenching her "word" from Bathsheba, Boldwood is trying to *silence* her: "But do give your word! [...] You owe it to me!" (*FFMC* p. 286). It is as though the woman had to pay a debt, once and for all. Unlike the "symbolic debt," which is a debt of language that can never be paid, the payment demanded here would settle all accounts, and leave Bathsheba speechless: for once she had given her "word" she could only be dumb. Give me your word, Boldwood seems to be saying, and the rest shall be silence: "Say the word, dear one, and the subject shall be dismissed" (*FFMC* p. 286). Bathsheba will escape such a perverse "business compact," she will not fall a prey to symbolic violence.

22 That should be read in parallel with the scene in Chapter XXVII ("The Hollow amid the Ferns") in which Bathsheba is encircled by the "circling gleams" of Troy's sword, "enclosed in a firmament of light, and of sharp hisses, resembling a sky-full of meteors close at hand" (*FFMC* p. 144).

23 The fire-place is a focal point in the room: the word *focus* is a Latin word which means "fire." The French word *foyer* (hearth) has the same etymology.

Bathsheba is at the bottom of the stairs, on the edge of the scene, having a last look at the gathering before passing though the hall to make her exit. Somebody raps at the door, Troy enters, standing in the doorway, then advances "into the middle of the room" (*FFMC* p. 288). Bathsheba's dread of Troy and her "quick, low scream" prompt Boldwood to seize a gun from the gun-rack just behind him, above the fire-place, and to shoot at Troy: "Troy fell. The distance apart of the two men was so small that the charge of shot did not spread in the least, but passed like a bullet into his body" (*FFMC* pp. 289–290). Boldwood has shot point-blank at his rival, both men standing in that self-same arena where all contests end in death. Significantly, escape is only possible away from the centre: "All the female guests were huddled aghast against the walls like sheep in a storm" (*FFMC* p. 290). The forces of life are centrifugal in this novel, it is the central void that one must keep away from. But a change takes place once Troy and Boldwood are gone. Boldwood now stands on the edge of diegetic space, hardly discernible by Gabriel who overtakes him when riding to Casterbridge: "he rode on [...] not discerning, when about three miles from Casterbridge, a square-figured pedestrian passing along *under the dark hedge* in the same direction as his own" (*FFMC* p. 291, my italics). The farmer is no longer part of his community, he is "suspended in the zone between life and death" (Lacan, 1986a/2008, p. 345), in other words "Between-Two-Deaths." Boldwood's elimination from the world of the living has somehow "purged" the community of its passions and restored order. For the centre is now an *agora* where symbolic exchanges will again be possible, and where the work of mourning may start at once: "Troy recumbent in his wife's lap formed now the sole spectacle in the middle of the spacious room" (*FFMC* p. 291).

Like the "charge of shot" fired by Boldwood, the stream of water spouted by the "gurgoyle" in Chapter XLVI is not in the least "spread," or fragmented, or deviated. It goes in a straight line and hits the mark, striking at the very heart of Fanny Robin's grave:

> We follow its course to the ground at this point of time. The end of the liquid parabola has come forward from the wall, has advanced over the plinth mouldings, over a heap of stones, over the marble border, into the midst of Fanny Robin's grave.
>
> *FFMC*, p. 242

The torrent from the gurgoyle's jaws directs "all its vengeance" into the grave, stirring "the rich tawny mould"[24] into motion, and causing the earth to boil

24 The polysemy of the signifier "mould" makes us sense how easily *agalma* may be reversed into *palea*: "mould" as an ornament used in architecture ("the plinth mouldings" *FFMC*,

"like chocolate" (*FFMC* p. 242). What is that shapeless and colourless mass, "pulsing [...] with inchoate life" (Žižek, 1992, p. 14), which the furious stream causes to appear in "the midst" of the grave ? Bathsheba, after discovering the devastated grave (and the inscription on the tombstone), plants again the uprooted flowers and asks Oak to fill the hole. Another request she makes deserves some attention:

> She requested Oak to get the churchwardens to turn the leadwork at the mouth of the gurgoyle that hung gaping down upon them, that by this means the stream might be directed sideways, and a repetition of the accident prevented.
>
> *FFMC*, p. 246

Why is it important to direct the stream *sideways*—beside the obvious practical reasons for such an action? Could it be because avoiding the "central emptiness" is the only way out of the tragic?

To try to answer those questions, it can be useful to examine another passage, that in which Bathsheba runs away from home after the scene around a coffin containing "Fanny Robin and child"—it may be of some interest to mention that the coffin had been placed "in the middle of a little sitting-room next the hall," according to Bathsheba's directions (*FFMC* p. 224). First Bathsheba sits by the coffin, in the room which is "silent as a tomb" (*FFMC* p. 229). Both women are somehow entombed together. Then she uncovers the coffin and discovers "the unconscious pair." Troy enters the room, sees his wife "pallid as a corpse" (*FFMC* p. 229), and there ensues a scene that ends with his "heartless" declaration to her: "You are nothing to me—nothing" (*FFMC* p. 231). Bathsheba, seized by "a vehement impulse to flee from him, to run from this place, hide, and escape his words at any price," runs out of the house. The next chapter (XLIV, "Under a Tree—Reaction") relates her flight away from home—away from the room/tomb of desolation. And the course she follows shows her resolve not to accept that place which Troy has just allotted to her: "nothing." Bathsheba *will not* plunge into "that central emptiness" which is the form assumed by *jouissance* in our representations.[25] She seeks shelter in a brake of fern, and sinks down upon "a tangled couch of fronds and stems" (*FFMC* p. 232).

---

p. 242), or as the luminous "mould of Bathsheba's figure" (produced by Troy's *aurora militaris*, *FFMC* p. 145), turns here (on the very same page) into "tawny mould," that is to say loose earth on the grave, which is also a "mouldering" substance connoting death and decay—like the "moist and poisonous coat" of the malignant swamp dotted with fungi (*FFMC* p. 233).

25 Thus she anticipates her refusal of Boldwood's ring (or any rate her resistance to the gift, since he forces the ring on to her finger).

On awakening the next morning, she realizes that the ground beneath her feet slopes downwards "to a hollow, in which was a species of swamp, dotted with fungi" (*FFMC* p. 232). The swamp contrasts with the beautiful yellowing ferns among which she has just had a night's repose:

> The hollow seemed a nursery of pestilences small and great, in the immediate neighbourhood of comfort and health. Bathsheba arose with a tremor at the thought of having passed the night on the brink of so dismal a place.
>
> *FFMC*, p. 233

Pure chance of course has led Bathsheba to "light" on that spot—but one marvels at the wisdom of such a choice, the choice of *the brink* of a swamp! The general aspect of the swamp is "malignant": "from its moist and poisonous coat seemed to be exhaled the essences of evil things in the earth, and in the waters under the earth" (*FFMC* p. 233). But it is enchanting as well as pestilential, the horror of rotting leaves and poisonous fungi appears both repellent and attractive. The seat of a lethal yet fascinating beauty, it is the locus of *das Ding*, the very "nothingness" to which Troy had condemned Bathsheba. A poetic passage describes the place in an oxymoronic way:

> A morning mist hung over it now—a noisome yet magnificent silvery veil, full of light from the sun, yet semi-opaque—the hedge behind it being in some measure hidden by its hazy luminousness.
>
> *FFMC*, pp. 232–233

The flowers that grow in this depression are "a peculiar species of flags, the blades of which glistened the emerging sun," catching the sun-rays like diamonds and treating the eye to the beauty of dawn. But the Grim Reaper is on the prowl, for the blades look "like scythes" (*FFMC* p. 233), and "flagging" is the dim prospect that awaits the new-born day. Behind the precious object, *agalma*, there looms the horror of *palea.*

Bathsheba, safe on the brink of *das Ding*, hears some birds singing, children's voices, the ordinary sounds of life. She feels hungry and thirsty, she is reborn to life, she is not "nothing." Suddenly she catches sight of a person approaching from the other side of the swamp: it is Liddy, her maid. She tries to call her name but her voice fails: "'O, Liddy!' she said, or attempted to say; but the words had only been framed by her lips; there came no sound. She had lost her voice by exposure to the clogged atmosphere all these hours of night" (*FFMC* pp. 233–234). She vainly attempts to warn her against crossing the swamp: "'You can't come across', said Bathsheba in a whisper, which she vainly endeavoured to make loud enough to reach Liddy's ears" (*FFMC* p. 234). Then she watches Liddy treading across the swamp and landing safely on her side:

> Bathsheba never forgot that transient little picture of Liddy crossing the swamp to her there in the morning light. Iridescent bubbles of dank subterranean breath rose from the sweating sod beside the waiting maid's feet as she trod, hissing as they burst and expanded away to join the vapoury firmament above. Liddy did not sink, as Bathsheba had anticipated. She landed safely on the other side.
>
> *FFMC,* p. 234

Bathsheba soon recovers her voice—her aphonia was not so much caused by exposure to the damp as by a dangerous proximity to the silent abyss of tragedy. Indeed she has come very close to "that unthinkable place of the Thing where silence merges with the cry, where all significations vanish and where life gives in to death" (Braunstein, p. 161). The passage has made it very clear that what must be avoided is *the centre,* the place where mud lies in wait for the reckless pedestrian venturing on its treacherous surface. Quite remarkably, the two women return to the house "by a circuitous route" (*FFMC* p. 235). When the pleasure principle, as opposed to *jouissance,* governs human conduct, people follow a round-about way which keeps them from harm. Comedy deals with the detours of human life, tragedy with the straight line of those who will not "give in as to their desire."[26] That is why it is essential for the stream vomited by the gurgoyle to be directed *sideways.* The comic resolution of the novel is due to Boldwood's man, Samway, *deviating* the second gunshot to the beam across the ceiling (*FFMC* p. 290).

26 Boldwood is described as a man who never lets himself be distracted from the course he has chosen: "The farmer had *never turned his head once,* but with eyes fixed on the most advanced point along the road, passed as unconsciously and abstractedly as if Bathsheba and her charms were thin air" (*FFMC* p. 75, my italics).

CHAPTER 4

The Object Gaze

4.1 Anamorphosis

The organization of diegetic space in *Far From the Madding Crowd*, with the "central emptiness" as the locus of *das Ding*, raises questions about the visual field. If it is imperative for pedestrians to take circuitous routes to avoid the "nursery of pestilences great and small" in the middle; if desire has to be directed sideways, there ensues logically that the gaze too should be deviated. Did not Perseus need to *deflect* the Gorgon's mortal gaze by means of his polished shield to approach Medusa safely and cut off her head?

"Looking awry" is the only possible way of glimpsing the horror of the Thing. In *Looking Awry*, Slavov Žižek quotes a long passage from Shakespeare's *Richard II*,[1] in which Bushy tries to comfort the Queen, who grieves over her husband's departure for the war in Ireland and has evil forebodings. He tells her that by "looking awry" on her lord's departure she sees "nought but shadows of what is not":

> Each substance of a grief hath twenty shadows,
> Which shows like grief itself, but is not so;
> For sorrow's eye, glazed with blinding tears,
> Divides one thing entire to many objects;
> Like perspectives, which rightly gazed upon
> Show nothing but confusion, eyed awry
> Distinguish form: so your sweet majesty,
> Looking awry upon your lord's departure,
> Find shapes of grief, more than himself, to wail;
> Which, look'd on as it is, is nought but shadows
> Of what it is not. Then, thrice-gracious queen,
> More than your lord's departure weep not: more's not seen;
> Or if it be, 'tis with false sorrow's eye,
> Which for things true weeps things imaginary.
>
> SHAKESPEARE, *Richard II*, 2.2.14–27

But, Žižek argues, the meaning of Bushy's words may be reversed, for it is precisely by "looking awry," that is at an angle, that the Queen can "distinguish

1 See Žižek's brilliant analysis of this passage, Žižek (1992, pp. 10–12).

 | DOI 10.1163/9789004296626_006

form," whereas the view "rightly gazed upon" shows "nothing but confusion." Bushy "entangles himself in contradiction," writes Žižek, when he passes from the metaphor of a sharpened glass surface to that of anamorphosis (Žižek, 1992, pp. 10–11). In fact the Queen is not convinced by Bushy: she finds that thinking makes her "with heavy nothing faint and shrink." As Jacques Ramel points out,

> what Bushy does not want to see is [...] the 'nothing' that the Queen sees and that makes her sad, that 'unborn sorrow' which is soon to come to life. The Queen has caught sight of that growing 'nothing', which must not be seen, and which is nevertheless about to be born—and which can only be death, the central hollow around which the whole of the play is organized.[2]

The oxymoron ("heavy nothing") tells us that "nothing" is the matter, and yet that this "nothing" is heavy with meaning, charged with an unpleasant truth that one had rather not face. The anamorphosis which Shakespeare had in mind was probably Holbein's *Ambassadors*, which, when "rightly gazed upon," shows two richly-clad young men, two French ambassadors to the Court of England, with objects in the background connoting art, wealth, and knowledge.[3] A strange ivory-coloured object across the foreground of the painting is unidentifiable, unless one looks "awry": by putting one's eye against the bottom left corner of the canvas, one is able to distinguish the form of a skull. The hidden skull turns the painting into a vanity, "that is the category of art that brought together symbols of life, of success, of greatness, of pleasure, and of human knowledge, with a *memento mori* under the form of a skull: *vanitas vanitatis, omnia vanitas*" (J. Ramel, p. 115).

Thus, by looking awry, one may discover an object which is normally not included in the field of vision. There is "more than meets the eye" in Holbein's painting, just as "more's not seen" by the Queen when her reality is "rightly gazed upon." It is possible, Jacques Ramel argues, "to hear like an echo of this *memento mori* in the repetition of the word 'more' in the passage" (J. Ramel, p. 116). Lacan, however, goes further than reading Holbein's painting as a vanity. What is made visible in the painting, he claims, is not just an image of "the subject as annihilated," it is "the gaze as such, in its pulsatile, dazzling, and

2 Jacques Ramel, "Undeaf Your Ears: What *the Tragedy of Richard II* Gives Us to Hear," B.A.S (*British and American Studies*), ed. Hortensia Parlog, Timişoara, XIV, 2008, p. 115.

3 I will not go into the symbolic of the objects displayed in the painting, which is rather complex.

spread out function" (Lacan, 1973/1986b, p. 89).[4] Indeed the skull does not merely represent death, it *looks at you* from its empty sockets. At the same time, *it does not see you*, for the onlooker is sheltered from its gaze by the necessity for him to be displaced in order to adopt a new angle of vision (just as Perseus was protected by his shield deflecting Medusa's gaze). It is not an object but a mere hollow, an empty shell enveloping a "heavy nothing" whose "objectivity" depends on its distortion ("it is nothing but the embodiment, the materialization of this very distortion" Žižek, 1992, p. 12). Like the *enforme* of a hat, that "hollow bone"[5] could well be taken as a representation of Lacan's *objet a*. In likeness to "the anamorphotic object," writes Žižek, "the object *a* is 'objectively' nothing, though, viewed from a certain perspective, it assumes the shape of 'something'" (Žižek, 1992, p. 12). In the visual field, such an object is called "the object gaze" by Lacan. "Of the Gaze as Objet Petit a" is the title of the second part of the XIth *Seminar* given by Lacan in 1964:[6] there, Lacan defines the gaze as an object, which he adds to the four drive objects listed by Freud.[7] In the light of that seminar, it becomes clear that the anamorphic blot is a figure given in our cultural representations to what Žižek translates as "the gaze *qua* object": "the *unheimlich* surplus forever missing in the mirror image, i.e., 'unspecularizable'" (Žižek, 2001, p. 126). "More's not seen" in our visual field; in Žižek's words, "there certainly is in the mirror image 'more than meets the eye', yet this surplus that eludes the eye, the point in the image that eludes my eye's grasp, is none other than *the gaze itself*" (Žižek, 2001, p. 127).

At this stage a few words are necessary to clarify Lacan's theory of the "object-gaze." Lacan, unlike Sartre who posited a reciprocity between seeing the Other and being seen by him, separates the eye, which is on the side of the subject, and the gaze, on the side of the object. The split between the eye and the gaze means that "*you never look at me from the place where I see you*," and that conversely "*what I look at is never what I wish to see*" (Lacan, 1973/1986b, p. 103).[8] When I look at you, I cannot see the point from which you look at me,

4 See Lacan, 1973, Chapter VII, "L'anamorphose," and Chapter VIII, "La ligne et la lumière," pp. 75–96.

5 The name of the painter, Holbein, *hohl Bein*, means "hollow bone" in German, and the skull could be an injoke, like some kind of signature.

6 Lacan (1973/1986b, p. 65).

7 The "object voice" is another object added by Lacan, the "object voice" and the "object gaze" being two interrelated forms of *objet a*. The "object gaze" is the object of the scopic drive.

8 The actual translation in the Penguin version is: "*you never look at me from the place from which I see you*," which does not make sense, and is erroneous—the French being "*jamais tu ne me regardes là où je te vois*" (Lacan, 1973, p. 95). I have taken the liberty of correcting the translation.

which is a blind spot in my visual field. Louis Aragon expressed the same idea in a poem quoted twice by Lacan in his XIth *Seminar*:[9]

> In vain your image comes to meet me
> And does not enter me where I am who only shows it
> Turning towards me you can find
> On the wall of my gaze only your dreamt-of shadow.
> I am that wretch comparable with mirrors
> That can reflect but cannot see
> Like them my eye is empty and like them inhabited
> By your absence which makes it blind.

Lacan's idea is that even before I start looking, I am looked at from everywhere: "I see only from one point, but in my existence I am looked at from all sides" (Lacan, 1973/1986b, p. 72). The example he gives is the sardine-tin which he remembers a fisherman pointed out to him when, as a young man, he was sailing with him in Brittany. The man exclaimed: "You see that can? Do you see it? Well, it does not see you!" (Lacan, 1973/1986b, p. 95). Lacan kept asking himself questions about those words because, he says, "if what Petit-Jean said to me, namely, that the can did not see me, had any meaning, it was because in a sense, it was looking at me all the same. It was looking at me at the level of the point of light, the point at which everything that looks at me is situated" (Lacan, 1973/1986b, p. 95). The sardine tin here presentifies that point which he calls the "object-gaze": the point from which the Other looks at me, prior to my looking back at him.

There, Lacan is indebted to Merleau-Ponty who, in his *Phenomenology of Perception*, takes the example of a floodlit stage:

---

9 Lacan quotes it as an introduction to his second chapter, "The Freudian Unconscious and ours," and to his seventh chapter on "Anamorphosis":

> Vainement ton image arrive à ma rencontre
> Et ne m'entre où je suis qui seulement la montre
> Toi te tournant vers moi tu ne saurais trouver
> Au mur de mon regard que ton ombre rêvée
> Je suis ce malheureux comparable aux miroirs
> Qui peuvent réfléchir mais ne peuvent pas voir
> Comme eux mon œil est vide et comme eux habité
> De l'absence de toi qui fait sa cécité

(Louis Aragon, *Le Fou d'Elsa*, "Contre-chant," quoted and translated in Lacan, 1973/1986b, p. 17).

> The lighting directs my gaze and causes me to see the object, so that in a sense it knows and sees the object. If I imagine a theatre with no audience in which the curtain rises upon illuminated scenery, I have the impression that the spectacle is in itself visible or ready to be seen, and that the light which probes the back and foreground, accentuating the shadows and permeating the scene through and through, realizes before us some kind of vision.
>
> MERLEAU-PONTY, p. 278

Commenting on this passage and its influence on Lacan as he developed his theory of the gaze, Jacques-Alain Miller writes:

> This is about a supplementary gaze which is always there—to take up Merleau-Ponty's example—and which is contained in visibility itself. In addition to that vision which another may have of me, there is the supplementary gaze of the Other, of the hidden Other. One may glimpse it when the light not only offers a field of visibility but also, simultaneously, focuses on a luminous spot which may figure the gaze, which incarnates for a moment the all-seeing gaze of the big Other.[10]
>
> MILLER (2008, p. 103)

What this analysis brings out is that Lacan's object-gaze is the gaze of the big Other. Should that evanescent spot, briefly illuminated and glimpsed, become a fixture in the field of vision, then the subject could be assigned only one position, that of paranoia: under the gaze of a malevolent Big Other/Brother.[11] That is why it is essential for the object gaze to be "extracted"—an operation normally effected by symbolic castration. For Žižek, the coherence of our reality depends on the exclusion of that object:

> Lacan pointed out that the consistency of our 'experience of reality' depends on the exclusion of what he calls the *objet petit a* from it: in order for us to have normal 'access to reality', something must be excluded,

---

10 "Il s'agit d'un regard supplémentaire qu'il y a toujours—pour reprendre l'exemple de Merleau-Ponty—et qui est le regard contenu dans la visibilité même. Qu'en plus de la vision qu'un autre peut avoir de moi, il y a le regard supplémentaire de l'Autre, de l'Autre caché. On peut percevoir cela quand la lumière non seulement offre un champ de visibilité mais se concentre en même temps sur un point lumineux qui peut avoir valeur de regard, qui incarne un moment le regard omnivoyant du grand Autre" (my translation).

11 As it tends to do in our modern world. See Wajcman (2010).

> 'primordially repressed'. In psychosis, this exclusion is undone: the object (in this case, the gaze or voice) is *included* in reality, the outcome of which, of course, is the disintegration of our 'sense of reality', the loss of reality.
>
> ŽIŽEK (1996, p. 91)

The effect of anamorphosis is precisely this: to give a "hollow" form to the object-gaze, to make it somehow visible, yet to "extract" it from our field of vision by placing it in a liminal position, on the edge of the painting, where it is indecipherable. The gaze of the big Other is incarnated for a moment, during the brief lapse of time when the onlooker's eye, placed against the canvas, is able to look sideways—an uncomfortable position that could not last very long. Anamorphosis makes it possible to visualize the split between the eye and the gaze: the eye that looks at the painting cannot see the Other's gaze hidden in the hollow bone; the Other's gaze cannot reach the eye of the onlooker when the picture is "rigthly gazed upon," unless the latter should move to the side of the painting and adjust his angle of vision—a proceeding which involves his body and requires *time*. The lack of reciprocity between the eye and the gaze is thus illustrated.

Similarly, in *The Return of the Native*, the tumulus known as Black barrow, from which Eustacia is looking at Wildeve's lit window through her telescope, is distinct from Mistover Knap, where her own bonfire is kept burning to attract her lover's attention. It takes her a good twenty minutes (*RN* p. 55)[12] to walk to her observation post and then back to the place where she means to be reached by the gaze of the other. As with the device of anamorphosis, time is required for the body of the onlooker to move to a new vantage-point. The split between the eye and the gaze is thus made manifest though the spatial/temporal organization of the diegetic world. Yet one little detail makes us sense that this structure is about to be disrupted: Eustacia's fire, the "quiet eye" (*RN* p. 27) burning steadily on Mistover Knap, suddenly meets the eye of the man for whom it is meant as a signal: "[...] the little bonfire on Mistover Knap again *met his eye*" (*RN* p. 49, my italics). Here the gaze and the eye coincide in perfect reflexivity. And "this quiet eye," the "moon of the whole shining throng," is an enduring fire fuelled by good cleft-wood, not a perishable bonfire burning light material gathered on the heath (*RN* p. 26). The villagers' fires scattered all over the heath are subject to "rapid flares and extinctions," the "decaying embers" left on Blackbarrow are sometimes rekindled by a gust of wind raising "a fitful

12 The insistence on time is to be noticed. Eustacia has brought an hour-glass to Blackbarrow to be able to measure time.

glow which came and went like the blush of a girl" (*RN* p. 53). But Eustacia's fire is "steady and persistent" (*RN* p. 47), a "permanent blaze" (*RN* p. 55): "[...] though some even of the wood fires had reached their decline no change was perceptible here" (*RN* p. 27). Such wood fires are "steady, unaltering eyes like planets" (*RN* p. 26). Unblinking eyes, like those of the dead. Indeed when the Other's gaze meets the eye of the onlooker in absolute *fixity*, it becomes the "evil eye," a deadly, Medusa-like gaze. As Žižek argues, "when the gaze *qua* object is no longer the elusive blind spot in the field of the visible but is included in this field, one meets one's own death" (Žižek, 1996, p. 94).

4.2 *The Return of the Native* and Anamorphosis

Looking awry is therefore a structural necessity if the Other's gaze is to be tamed. In *The Return of the Native*, as in many other novels by Hardy, the eye is indeed an "evil eye."[13] One might even argue that the main subject of the novel is the lethal power of the gaze. All along Chapters III, IV, and V, the eye is alternately threatening and threatened. When told by Diggory Venn that Thomasin is not with her husband Wildeve, Mrs Yeobright puts her hand over her eyes as if to shield them from some unbearable sight (*RN* p. 35). The reddleman's eye looks like that of a bird of prey: "His eye, which glared so strangely through his stain, was in itself attractive—keen as that of a bird of prey [...]" (*RN* p. 8). He refuses to grant a fellow traveller permission to look at the girl asleep in his van (*RN* p. 10). Venn has hung all the drapery in his possession around the girl's couch to keep her from any contact with the red material of his trade, yet the invasive light of the lantern seems to be creeping under her eye-lids, as though allowing the circumambient redness to penetrate her: "Though her eyes were closed, one could easily imagine the light shining in them as the culmination of the luminous workmanship around" (*RN* p. 36). The unseeing eye is not to be seen: the girl, we are told, "was not made to be looked at thus" (*RN* p. 36). Yet danger seems to lurk in the redness, in the potential *visibility* of the girl's eyes, in the possible intrusion of the gaze of the Other into her innermost being. The "quiet eye" which represents Eustacia for Wildeve in Chapter III ("The Custom of the Country") turns into the girl's dark eye in Timothy Fairway's talk about

13 According to Lacan, there is "some appetite of the eye on the part of the person looking." Lacan wonders about the true function of organ of the eye, "the eye filled with voracity, the evil eye." And he adds: "It is striking, when one thinks of the universality of the function of the eye, that there is no trace anywhere of a good eye, an eye that blesses" (Lacan, 1973/1986b, p. 115).

her ("the lonesome dark-eyed creature up there, that some say is a witch" *RN* p. 47), and an old man admits that if she accepted to marry him he would be "pretty glad" to "take the risk of her wild dark eyes ill-wishing [him]" (*RN* p. 48). Clym is literally *blinded* by Eustacia, as his mother prophetically warns him when he announces his intention of marrying her: "'You are blinded, Clym', she said warmly. 'It was a bad day for you when you first set eyes on her'."[14] As we will see later, it is Eustacia's wild dark eyes that kill Mrs Yeobright, in a mortal confrontation between the gaze of the mother-in-law and that of Eustacia. The eye is the root of all evil.

In *The Expressive Eye*, J.B. Bullen follows Hardy's suggestion that the rustic characters depicted on Blackbarrow are "drawn with Dureresque vigour and dash" (*RN* p. 15) and develops the idea that Hardy is indebted to Dürer in *The Return of the Native*, in strong contrast to "the quieter pictures of English and Dutch life" which had inspired the scenes of earlier novels (Bullen, p. 99). Dürer's art as perceived in the 1870s, he argues, "did not conform to classical or Renaissance standards of beauty," it appeared characterized by "wilful and deliberate distortion" (Bullen, p. 99). The stress on the grotesque, on the comic and the macabre, certainly connects the scene on the heath to Dürer's art, he claims. To add my contribution to that analysis, I would like to point out what seems most striking to me: the connection between Hardy's art and anamorphosis, as popularized by Holbein's *Ambassadors*. It may be useful here to remind the reader that Dürer (1471–1528), who was learning "the art of secret perspective,"[15] is sometimes considered as having contributed to the invention of the art of anamorphosis. Artists in the Renaissance experimented with perspective, and were thus enabled to develop techniques of stretching and distorting images, so as to have a secret image revealed from a different vantage-point.[16] The first known example of an anamorphic drawing is

---

14 *RN* p. 194. See also *RN* p. 201: "his sight grew accustomed to the first blinding halo kindled about him by love and beauty."

15 In 1506, Dürer wrote to his friend Pirkheimer that he was going to Bologna to learn *die Kunst in geheimner Perspektive* ("the art of secret perspective"). See Anamorphose (2001): <http://people.via.ecp.fr/~jm/TTLanamorphose/historique.htm> (2014).

16 Cf Lacan (1973/1986b, p. 87): "It was Dürer himself who invented the apparatus to establish perspective [...] It was to establish a correct perspective image [...] that the *lucinda* was introduced. If I reverse its use, I will have the pleasure of obtaining not the restoration of the world that lies at the end, but the distortion, on another surface, of the image that I would have obtained on the first, and I will dwell, as on some delicious game, on this method that makes anything appear at will in a particular stretching." The method is of course anamorphosis, which is the subject of Chapter VII in *The Four Fundamental Concepts of Psychoanalysis*.

Leonardo's *Eye* (1485). Then Erhard Schön (circa 1491–1542), a Nuremberg engraver and pupil of Albrecht Dürer, created a woodcut he called *Vexierbilder* ("Secret Images"), another example of anamorphosis, where distortion serves the purpose of hiding political messages. Holbein's *Ambassadors*, the masterpiece of perspectival anamorphosis, was painted in 1533. So all these artists were contemporaries, who shared a common interest in perspective and its applications. Therefore, if one compares Hardy's art to the paintings of Dürer (as Hardy himself suggested), it is not far-fetched to extend the comparison to the art of anamorphosis, in particular to Holbein's *Ambassadors*.

The organization of the scene on the heath invites the comparison with *The Ambassadors*. As a preliminary to this study, I wish to make a few theoretical remarks on my choice of studying the narrated scene as a "picture"—with special attention paid to the relation between frame and picture. Some readers might rightly object that we are reading a text, not looking at a picture. One first answer lies in J.B. Bullen's study of Hardy, which has put to the fore the "pictorial" quality of his fiction (Bullen, p. 6). Reference should also be made to a recent publication by Liliane Louvel, *Poetics of the Iconotext*, more particularly to her concept of the "painting-effect" in texts, "an illusionistic effect so powerful that painting seems to haunt the text despite the absence of any direct reference to painting in general or to a particular painting" (Louvel, 2011, p. 90). Louvel lists the textual markers of pictoriality, among which are for instance explicit references to the visual arts, the use of framing effects, the staging of focalization, etc. The following development on the Egdon Heath scene focuses on framing effects—framing effects found within the diegesis itself.[17] As Chapter III ("The Custom of the Country") opens, the narrator's first task is to frame the scene, to surround the illuminated space where the action takes place by an area of darkness:

> It was as if the bonfire makers were standing in some radiant upper storey of the world, detached from and independent of the dark stretches below. The heath down there was now a vast abyss, and no longer a

17 I am not referring here to the narrative as a "frame" containing within itself another narrative (as in *Heart of Darkness* for instance), but to any kind of frame surrounding a scene in the diegesis of a novel, which makes it clear that the text is an "iconotext." As Liliane Louvel has noted, a window delineating a character (or a scene) often works as a frame (she says we should remember Alberti's famous prescription: "to make a picture one has to draw a *quadrangolo* which is like a window open onto composition [*la storia*]"), Liliane Louvel, "Telling 'by' Pictures: Virginia Woolf's Shorter Fiction," *Journal of the Short Story in English*, 50, 2008, p. 20, <http://jsse.revues.org/699?lang=en>. A typical example is the window within which Bathsheba is sitting during the shearers' supper in *Far from the Madding Crowd* (FFMC p. 120).

> continuation of what they stood on; for their eyes, adapted to the blaze, could see nothing of the deeps beyond its influence.
>
> *RN* p. 14

However porous the barrier between the "the human circle" and the "dark turf around" may be (for an occasional darting light from the fire may temporarily kindle some part or other of the "deeps"), darkness here works as a frame edging the picture. A line is drawn between the visible world and an external void, which is "off camera."[18] The text as a "picture" does not exist autonomously of course, it is produced by a narrative act, which implies someone who sees the picture (as well as a narrative voice). In the passage just quoted, it is the villagers' view which delineates the scene. We see the importance of focalization in its relation to the "iconotext."[19]

This being specified, it is now possible to turn to the "picture" itself: in the middle is a party of villagers, jolly rustics who discuss the marriage that has just been celebrated (so they believe) and rejoice over Clym's return home. An old man sunning himself in the heat with "a cumulative cheerfulness" is singing a popular ballad ("The Jovial Crew") and starts "a private minuet" (*RN* p. 16); later a "very audible concert" (*RN* p. 28) is heard when Susan Nunsuch and Timothy Fairways begin dancing on the site of the nearly extinguished fire, soon followed by the rest of the party. "The Custom of the Country" appears like a joyful celebration binding together the members of a tight-knit community, the atmosphere seems genial and convivial. Yet a few uncanny details jar with that impression and foreshadow the tragedy to come: the talk is on marriage as a "mess" (*RN* p. 21), on failing to get married (Thomasin and Wildeve are getting married at last, after their first attempt was stopped by Mrs Yeobright forbidding

---

18 I deliberately use vocabulary borrowed from film theory because Hardy has been said to be "a cinematic novelist," who makes use of visual effects similar to those used in film-making. The idea was first put forward by David Lodge. See Terry Wright, "Hardy as a Cinematic Novelist: Three Aspects of Narrative Technique," in *Thomas Hardy on Screen*, T.R. Wright ed. Cambridge: C.U.P., 2005, 8–19.

19 I will not dwell on the question of focalization, but a few examples may be given here: the end of Chapter II is focalized by the reddleman ("the scene before the reddleman's eyes…" RN p. 11), the beginning of Chapter III shifts to focalization by a hypothetical viewer ("Had a looker-on been posted in the immediate vicinity of the barrow he would have learnt…" *RN* p. 13), who is in fact a figure of the omniscient narrator. Soon the panoptic gaze of the narrator is replaced by the partial vision of the bonfire makers in the passage just quoted, and later the "quiet eye" of Eustacia's fire attracts their attention away from their own circle (*RN* p. 27). The gaze produced by multiple focalization is fragmented, as opposed to the object-gaze, the gaze of an all-seeing Other.

the banns). And though a centripetal force seems to be taking the different actors towards a centre (Thomasin carried back home from Southerton, the old man walking back home, Clym returning to his native place), our attention, along with that of the travellers, is directed towards objects on the periphery of the diegetic world. One man apparently belonging to the group, but so far unnoticed by his pals, Christian Cantle, confesses to being an exception to the general rule ("I'm the man [...] the man no woman will marry" *RN* p. 23)—in fact hardly a man at all since he was born on a night when there was no moon and, as the saying goes, "no moon, no man" (*RN* p. 24). He is tragically unique, not one man among others but excluded, elected by Fate. The theme of exclusion becomes insistent with "the figure against the sky," the woman who is displaced from her position on the summit of Blackbarrow by the arrival of the party of villagers, a woman who too is solitary, unique, alien to her community, an anomaly in the landscape. She keeps burning a fire that is an exception ("a little fire [...] that nobody else may enjoy" *RN* p. 27), and the red blaze which represents her metonymically makes us sense that she too is ear-marked by Fate.

Our gaze is driven further away from the centre of the picture when another solitary figure makes its appearance on the edge of the scene, intruding upon the party of villagers. The newcomer is "a long, slim, indistinct figure approaching the barrow" (*RN* p. 29): a strange unidentifiable creature, a devil or perhaps a ghost, but no ordinary ghost (for "most ghosts be white"), in fact a "red ghost" which seems to have been "dipped in blood" (*RN* p. 25). The figure has been seen "not exactly here; but in this same heath" (*RN* p. 25). Its liminal position, on the edge of the diegetic world, not within the frame but *on the frame*, cannot fail to remind us of the enigmatic "hollow bone" at the bottom of Holbein's painting—a similar long, slim, stretched-out object that cannot be deciphered by the frontal gaze looking at the picture. And we should bear in mind that this joyful celebration is a "bonfire," a word which etymologically means a "*bone*-fire," bones being the chief material formerly used. Diggory Venn as exterior to the Egdon circle celebrating "the custom of the country" is gradually drawn into it: first as a subject of the conversation, then as a voice rising from the surrounding darkness—a floating, spectral voice, totally untraceable, impossible to attribute to a speaker. That "voice from the darkness," which is "behind" Christian Cantle (*RN* p. 29) is a correlate of what Michel Chion calls the "acousmatic voice":

> The voice which transgresses the boundary outside/inside, since it belongs neither to diegetic reality nor to the external vocal accompaniment, but lurks in the in-between space, like a mysterious foreign body which disintegrates from within the consistency of 'reality'.
>
> ŽIŽEK (2001, p. 120)

The voice does exactly this here: it transgresses the boundary inside/outside, it introduces into the picture a foreign element which so far was off-camera. Venn as an elongated form is the "anamorphic ghost" (Lacan, 1973/1986b, p. 89) recognizable by its "particular stretching" (Lacan, 1973/1986b, p. 87).

The idea of Diggory Venn as an anamorphic object appearing on the edge of the picture is confirmed if one looks back to the pages that precede the scene on the heath. The reference to Dürer is explicit there:

> The brilliant lights and sooty shades which struggled upon the skin and clothes of the persons standing round caused their lineaments and general contours to be drawn with Dureresque vigour and dash.
>
> *RN* p. 15

Because the flames are constantly moving ("the nimble flames towered, nodded, and swooped through the surrounding air" *RN* p. 15), it is impossible for the looker-on to discover any "permanence" in the faces of the individuals composing the scene:[20]

> All was unstable; quivering as leaves, evanescent as lightning. Shadowy eye-sockets, deep as those of a death's head, suddenly turned into pits of lustre: a lantern-jaw was cavernous, then it was shining; wrinkles were emphasized to ravines, or obliterated entirely by a changed ray. Nostrils were dark wells; sinews in old necks were gilt mouldings; things with no particular polish on them were glazed; bright objects, such as the tip of a furze-hook one of the men carried, were as glass; eyeballs glowed like little lanterns. Those whom Nature had depicted as merely quaint became grotesque, the grotesque became preternatural; for all was in extremity.
>
> *RN* p. 15

The lines which follow make us understand that so far we have been looking awry and that reality, when "rightly gazed upon," is different. The narrator proceeds to redress the angle of vision:

---

20 Visual instability is paralleled by instability in *what we hear*. As in *Far from the Madding Crowd*, the polysemy of the signifier "mould" ("gilt mouldings") allows a flicker of meaning between "mould" as an architectural ornament and "mould" as the "tawny mould" wherein dead bodies moulder. "Guilt" may also be overheard in "gilt." The equivocal nature of language produces poetic effects similar to those of anamorphosis.

> Hence it may be that the face of an old man, who had like others been called to the heights by the rising flames, was not really the mere nose and chin that it appeared to be, but an appreciable quantity of human countenance.
>
> *RN* pp. 15–16

It is at this point that the scene depicting the joyful celebration begins, and the rest of the chapter gives us a frontal view of the villagers—until our attention is gradually drawn towards the edge of the picture, as I have shown. When "eyed awry," the world appears uncanny, foreign to our normal representations. The ceaseless movement of the flames causes variations in the lighting: a "changed ray" may bring out a detail, while the disappearance of light reveals objects so far hidden from our sight. It is impossible to view things "rightly" because of those constant changes in the modalities of the gaze. As with anamorphosis, the effect produced is a distortion of reality. It is therefore no surprise when one particular shift introduces the *vanitas* theme: "Shadowy eye-sockets as deep as a death's head suddenly turned into pits of lustre." That theme is present all along the chapter, with Christopher Cantle, the "man of no moon," asserting that he is nothing but bones ("'Tis said I be only the rames of a man, and no good in the world at all" *RN* p. 24); then Susan Nunsuch threatens to "crack" Fairway's "numskull" (*RN* p. 28), and the apparition of the red ghost reminds her of a dream she had the night before of "a death's head" (*RN* p. 30). Quite significantly, the skeleton theme is connected to Diggory Venn and Christopher Cantle, two characters who occupy liminal positions. In a later chapter (Chapter VI), Eustacia's fire is kept burning at the junction of two banks which are bare of a hedge, "save such as was formed by disconnected tufts of furze, standing upon stems along the top, like impaled heads above a city wall" (*RN* p. 54). The insistence on the *memento mori* theme in its relation to the frame or the edge makes it clear that anamorphosis is certainly a genre that influenced Hardy in this novel.

A little detail bears out this analysis: the presence in the diegesis of the novel of a strange object, both incongruous and familiar, in excess of reality, yet included in the field of vision: the funerary "urns" dug out from nearby barrows, which the Egdon inhabitants use as flower-pots on their window-sills. The function of each urn is that of a *memento mori* placed on the frame of the picture; therefore, structurally speaking, the urns are skulls. One is reminded of an engraving by Dürer, "Saint Jerome in his Study," where a skull is laid on the window-ledge. In the description of Eustacia's house such an urn arrests the gaze like the hollow bone in Holbein's painting:

> The only visible articles in the room were those on the window-sill, which showed their shapes against the low sky, the middle article being the old hourglass,[21] and the other two a pair of ancient British urns which had been dug from a barrow near, and were used as flowerpots for two razor-leaved cactuses.
>
> *RN* p. 121

In another passage Christian Cantle tells Mrs Yeobright about a barrow that has just been opened, while Clym attended the operation:

> They have dug a hole, and they have found things like flowerpots upside down, Mis'ess Yeobright; and inside these be real charnel bones. They have carried 'em off to men's houses [...] Mr Yeobright had got one pot of the bones, and was going to bring 'em home—real skellington bones—but'twas ordered otherwise.
>
> *RN* p. 191

Mrs Yeobright speaks sharp words of reproach to her son because, instead of bringing home the urn as a present to her, he has given it to Eustacia, who is said to have "a cannibal taste for such churchyard furniture" (*RN* p. 191). A little further, Mrs Yeobright is sitting alone in her room while Thomasin is getting married. As Mrs Yeobright's eyes are "directed towards the open door," a sparrow enters through the door, and endeavours to go out by the window. But the bird flutters among the flower-pots (which we assume must be "flowerpots" dug from ancient graves), and it has to be released by Mrs Yeobright (*RN* p. 217). The urns are no ordinary objects: they are in excess of reality, and therefore they bar the view and prevent escape. Whereas the parts within the frame of a *jeu de taquin* can move freely about because there is a hole somewhere, all movement is blocked here by the spectral presence of a surplus object.

4.3 The Object-Gaze in *The Return of the Native*

Again we must go further than viewing those obtrusive objects as part of the *vanitas* theme. Indeed there is much more in them than mere reminders of the transiency of human life. As Lacan has argued, the anamorphic "ghost" is the gaze itself, the "object-gaze." In the celebration on the heath, this is made

21 The "old hour-glass," which is that used by Eustacia's in the chapter "The Figure Against the Sky," serves as a *memento mori*, of course.

particularly clear, for it is eyes that are brought into view by the *chiaroscuro* effects of the "bone-fires." The "shadowy eye-sockets" are the first term of a paradigm involving the eye, soon followed by "eyeballs glowing like little lanterns" (*RN* p. 15), wood-fires described as "steady unaltering eyes like planets" (*RN* p. 26), the "quiet eye" of Eustacia's fire, the perishing fire on Blackbarrow greeting Eustacia "like living eyes in the corpse of day" (*RN* p. 50). Diggory Venn, the anamorphic ghost appearing on the edge of the bonfire scene, is not only a figure associated with a death's head, he is first and foremost an eye that sees everything: "his eye, which glared so strangely through his stain, was in itself attractive—keen as that of a bird of prey" (*RN* p. 8). Venn's "keen eye" can discern what Yeobright's "feeble vision" cannot (*RN* p. 267). He keeps watch on every one (*RN* pp. 271–272), knows everything, and so can manipulate people to serve Thomasin's interest—or rather his own, as Rosemarie Morgan has argued (Morgan, 1991, p. 67). He in fact materializes the gaze of an all-seeing Other, and the position he occupies in the diegesis is exactly that of the "object-gaze": not the "elusive blind spot" in the field of the visible, but a permanent gaze embracing the whole of reality, the "evil eye" which, far from operating as a "benign regulating force," reveals "a malevolent underside" (Morgan, 1991, pp. 68–69).

As I have already argued, the bonfire on Mistover Knap meant as a signal to Wildeve represents Eustacia metonymically. Fire is the distinctive mark of Eustacia: "You could fancy the colour of Eustacia's soul to be flame-like. The sparks from it that rose into her dark pupils gave the same impression" (*RN* pp. 63–64). Dressed in her best attire, "she blazes with dazzling splendour" (*RN* p. 88). But fire is part of a larger series, the "chain of red things" associated with her all along the novel—whether they be the "red ribbon round her neck," the blood oozing on her skin when she and Clym try to draw water from a well, the "scarlet puncture" caused by Susan Nunsuch's needle, etc. Then a question arises: if the colour red is what characterizes Eustacia, how does one explain its being *also* the hallmark of Diggory Venn? Why should the reddleman be seen as "a sinister redness [...] dull and lurid, like a flame in sunlight" (*RN* p. 149)? What relation exists between those two "flame-like" characters, and why does the exclusion of Eustacia at the end purge the community of its redness?[22] One possible answer could be that Eustacia is the intruder on Egdon and the agent of disorder,[23] and that the red stain logically disappears once Egdon has been

22 About the "whitewashing" of Venn at the end of the novel and the reasons which prompted Hardy to meet "readers' expectations of marriage-and-happy-endings," see Morgan (1991, p. 71).

23 Morgan (1991, pp. 73, 179). Rosemarie Morgan here refers to *The Return of the Repressed* by Perry Meisel (Newhaven and London, 1972, p. 76). However Meisel hastens to add that "the

rid of her presence. But then other critics have convincingly argued that Venn as "intruder and moral watchdog [...] does not operate as a benign regulating force" (Morgan, 1991, pp. 66–69). Hardy, by ascribing to a reddleman a "punitive role," "craftily brings together three significant elements: the colour scarlet, the compound used for branding the female, the sexually active woman as outcast"; Venn, continues Rosemarie Morgan, "unlike most Hardy characters, would not seem completely out of place in Nathaniel Hawthorne's world of *The Scarlet Letter*" (Morgan, 1991, p. 179). Are we to understand that the man branding the female as fallen is given a taste of his own medicine? My own view is that the red stain is much more than a sign conveying meaning and loaded with ideology. Its value can neither be reduced to the "Grundyist" view of Eustacia as marked by a scarlet stain because of her "improper" behaviour, nor to the opposite view of Venn the moralist as bearing the very same mark in an ironical reversal. The question should not be addressed in the binary terms of axiology (good/bad, pure/sinful, etc.),[24] because the madder stain is to me a radical enigma. Like Barthes's *punctum*, it is "poignant," it affects the reader (with pleasure, or pain, or both), it is not part of the *studium* of the text, it cannot be invested by the reader's "sovereign consciousness." In Lacanian terms it does not pertain to reality, it is a point of contact with the unsymbolizable Real.[25]

But then all those "red things" have common points which could perhaps help us approach the unknowable kernel manifested in them, or at any rate

---

forces of nature are in secret alliance with her" (Meisel, p. 77), and he admits that "Hardy's artistic sympathy lies secretly with Eustacia" (Meisel, p. 86). He argues that in this novel "the potential for the destruction of the community no longer lies with en external interference; it is latent within the society itself" (Meisel, p. 78). Another critic, John Paterson, in *The Making of 'The Return of the Native* (California, 1960), views Eustacia as thoroughly evil. From his reading of the Ur-text of the novel, Paterson infers that Eustacia's behaviour denotes "satanic pride and wilfulness." Quoted in Morgan (1991, p. 180).

24 Venn is not a thorough villain, nor is Eustacia a witch.

25 The significance of the madder stain is as elusive as that of the "blighted" star in *Tess of the d'Urbervilles*, which turns into the "big bright star" stared at by Tess in her efforts to escape from her body, then is changed into the "sticky blights" making madder stains on her arms ("though snow-white on the appletree-trunks"), often read (or misread) as a sign of her "corporeal blight" (*Tess* pp. 127–129). The "red thing" in Hardy's fiction is as impenetrable as the cavernous eye-sockets transformed into "pits of lustre" on Egdon Heath by a whimsical ray of light. It can only be rendered poetically, or through the visual device of anamorphosis. Similarly, the "gilt-mouldings" brought into view on Egdon Heath by a flame throwing its light on "sinews in old necks" are indecipherable: they can be read as prefiguring the "encrustations of gilding" (*RN*, p. 198) in the Louvre which Clym will depict to Eustacia, or as a foreboding of the guilt that will harrow them both.

draw a line around it: one of them is the gaze. A key-word in the text is "glare,"[26] which in English refers both to a particular way of looking and to some dazzling brilliance. In *The Return of the Native*, the crimson "glare" is simultaneously what sees and what is seen. Venn, an embodiment of the Other's gaze, has a keen eye "which glared so strangely through his stain" (*RN* p. 8): he actually *sees through his stain*, while Eustacia *beholds* (*RN* p. 149) his "sinister redness" and Wildeve "stares" at his "tall crimson form" (*RN* pp. 229–230). The first bonfire lit on Mistover Knap, by which Eustacia presents herself to the gaze of her lover, is a "quiet eye";[27] the second fire lit by Charley the following year faces Eustacia and sends "a ruddy glare" into the room (*RN* p. 343). When she first appears to Clym without her disguise, after the mummers' performance, she is "gazing down" from an upper window "whose panes blazed in the ruddy glare from the west" (*RN* p. 184). The sparks rising from her "flame-like" soul are visible in her eyes (*RN* p. 64). The "ruddy glare" as *both gaze and stain* is the object of desire and also the very thing that kills. The scopic drive, which is predominant in this novel,[28] carries human desire to an extreme point which lies beyond the pleasure principle, in the forbidden realm to which Lacan has given the name of *jouissance*. Thus the red stain is an "evil eye" as well as an object endowed with an irresistible power of attraction. We have seen that Venn and Eustacia are figures of the evil eye: Eustacia's "ill-wishing" eyes fascinate the Egdon rustics, and dazzle Clym to such an extent that he becomes nearly blind; she kills Clym's mother by her Medusa-like gaze. If we bear in mind that for Lacan the stain is "the first model of the gaze,"[29] it now becomes clear that the red "glare" (personified in the novel by Eustacia and Diggory

26 See pp. 106, 116, 184, 343. In *Tess of the d'Urbervilles*, on the wedding night, "a steady glare" (*Tess* p. 220) from the flameless embers paints every object and Tess's face with its colours, and the "red-coated glow" from the fire falls on Tess and Angel, "*peering* into the loose hair about her brow" (*Tess* p. 222, my italics). There is no doubt whatsoever that the glare is a gaze, in *Tess of the d'Urbervilles* as in *The Return of the Native*.

27 An insistent metaphor compares several fires to "eyes" (*RN* pp. 26, 50).

28 Indeed the scopic drive predominates over the sexual drive. Venn betrays his tendency to voyeurism in Chapter 2 by frequently stepping behind the van and looking at the sleeping girl though a small window (*RN* p. 8). Eustacia uses a telescope (like her grandfather). "O that I had seen his face!" are the words she exclaims on awaking from her dream (*RN* p. 118). Wildeve claims that *seeing* Eustacia has satisfied him: "A sight of you. Upon my eternal honour, I came for no more" (*RN* p. 287). The consummation devoutly to be wished is the sight of a person—the sight of a *dead* woman: "you shall see her" is the promise made by Clym to both Charley and Diggory Venn (*RN* p. 380).

29 For Lacan has argued that the spot (or stain) is "the first model of the gaze" (Lacan, 2001b: "J'enseigne que la vision se scinde entre l'image et le regard, que le premier modèle du

Venn) is a figure of the object-gaze. More precisely, those two characters occupy a *place* which is that of the scopic object—such a reading does not imply any moral judgment on them, for neither of them is evil or demonic. That is my hypothesis: the red stain in this novel (and in many others by Hardy) is loaded with the unknowable *jouissance* at work in the scopic drive; it therefore presentifies what is normally "unspecularizable" (Žižek, 2001, p. 126), the gaze *qua* object.

In support of this assertion, I wish to draw attention to the *reflexivity* that always operates when the red stain exerts its fascinating power. Clym, on the way to his mother's home after meeting Eustacia on the heath, feels that he is marked by a crimson stain:

> The light which shone forth on him from the window revealed that his face was flushed and his eye bright. What it did not show was something which lingered upon his lips like a seal set there. The abiding presence of this impress was so real that he hardly dared to enter the house, for it seemed as if his mother might say, 'What red spot is that glowing upon your mouth so vividly?'.
>
> *RN* p. 192

He is now caught in a mirror-relation with Eustacia: the fiery red stain which represents her has been impressed on his body. But the key-scene is that in which Mrs Yeobright is literally killed by Eustacia's gaze. Clym's mother, after knocking at her son's door, has seen "a bad sight": "I have seen [...] a woman's face looking at me through a window-pane" (*RN* p. 288). Eustacia indeed has seen Mrs Yeobright and has not opened the door.[30] Getting no answer to her repeated knocks, the old lady believes her son has cast her off and walks away from his house in the scorching heat of a fiery August afternoon.[31] She meets her death on the heath after an adder stings her. Carried by her son to a hut, she is tended by a party of villagers who use an old remedy in a desperate attempt to cure her: an adder is caught, killed, fried; Clym dips his handkerchief into

---

regard est la tache [...]" p. 194, "I teach that vision is split between the image and the gaze, and that the first model of the gaze is the spot," my translation).

30 Mrs. Yeobright has come to try to be reconciled with Clym and her, but Eustacia thinks she means harm, and fears Wildeve's presence may compromise her. Meanwhile Clym is asleep and hears nothing.

31 "In her anxiety to get out of the direct view of the house" (*RN* p. 288), she has diverged from the straightest path, so that Eustacia will not find her when she attempts to do so. Indeed what is unbearable is being exposed to the gaze of the Other.

the liquid fat and anoints the wound. While the live adder is held in a cleft stick, the eye of the creature meets Mrs Yeobright's eye:

> The live adder regarded the assembled group with a sinister look in its small black eye, and the beautiful brown and jet pattern on its back seemed to intensify with indignation. Mrs Yeobright saw the creature, and the creature saw her: she quivered throughout, and averted her eyes.
>
> *RN* p. 297

Averting her eyes will not save Mrs Yeobright. What is repeated here is the deadly face-to-face relation between her and Eustacia through the window-pane: the "small black eye" of the adder, "like a villainous sort of black currant" (*RN* p. 297), which the villagers fear might "ill-wish" them (*RN* p. 298), is of course a duplicate of Eustacia's "wild dark eyes" known for their "ill-wishing" power (*RN* p. 48). A "scarlet speck" is visible on Mrs Yeobright's foot:

> The foot [...] was swollen and red. Even as they watched the red began to assume a more livid colour, in the midst of which appeared a scarlet speck, smaller than a pea, and it was found to consist of a drop of blood, which rose above the smooth flesh of her ankle in a hemisphere.
>
> *RN* pp. 296–297

It turns the dying woman into a mirror-image of Eustacia, who in an earlier scene showed to Clym "a bright red spot" on her round white arm (*RN* p. 186).[32] The fearful symmetry of eye and gaze is a mortal encounter: Mrs Yeobright has been stung to death not by an adder but by the "darting light" sent like arrows from Eustacia's eyes (*RN* p. 245)—by the Medusa-like gaze of her daughter-in-law.[33]

---

32 The red stain is a motif associated with Eustacia. When Eustacia and Clym are drawing water from a well, one of Eustacia's hands is scratched by the rope and is bleeding. So she tells Clym it is the second time she has been wounded this very day: Susan Nunsuch has pricked her arm with a long stocking-needle. Strikingly, Clym's reaction on being told about the injury is to say: "I blush for my native Egdon" (*RN* p. 186). Eustacia draws up her sleeve and discloses the "scarlet little puncture": "A bright red spot appeared on its smooth surface, like a ruby on Parian marble" (*RN* pp. 186–187). Susan Nunsuch will finally destroy Eustacia by thrusting pins into her image, a wax figure with a red ribbon tied around its neck.

33 The words exchanged between Mrs Yeobright and Charley on the heath just before she dies are about a "bad sight" they both had. Charley tells her he once saw his own image reflected in a pond: "Once when I went to Throope Great Pond to catch effets I seed myself looking up at myself, and I was frightened and jumped back like anything" (*RN* p. 288).

In another scene Eustacia is standing before a looking-glass when Clym arrives behind her:

> [...] when he opened the door she was standing before the looking glass in her nightdress, the ends of her hair gathered into one hand, with which she was coiling the whole mass round her head, previous to beginning toilette operations. She was not a woman given to speaking first at a meeting, and she allowed Clym to walk across in silence, without turning her head. He came behind her, and she saw his face in the glass. It was ashy, haggard, and terrible. Instead of starting towards him in sorrowful surprise [...] she remained motionless, looking at him in the glass. And while she looked the carmine flush with which warmth and sound sleep had suffused her cheeks and neck dissolved from view, and the death-like pallor in his face flew across into hers. He was close enough to see this, and the sight instigated his tongue. 'You know what is the matter', he said huskily. 'I see it in your face'.
>
> *RN* p. 328

"There certainly is in the mirror image 'more than meets the eye'," writes Žižek (Žižek, 2001, p. 127). Not so in this exchange of looks: the "something more" which normally eludes the eye's grasp is included in the mirror-image. Clym sees "it." He has caught "it."[34] There is no blind spot in this very particular looking-glass: Clym's gaze enters Eustacia and reaches her at the secret point from which she sees him. He knows that she knows that he knows that she knows, etc. Specularity is flawless when Clym's death-like pallor impresses itself on Eustacia's face—for only death can join together the eye and the gaze. Absolute fixity is another characteristic of the scene: Eustacia does not turn her head, and remains motionless. Both are immobilized, as if turned to stone.

This climactic scene has been prepared by a series of passages involving the eye's *pupil*, where it seems that some exterior gaze is entering the inmost recess of the eye. First, the pool on Mistover Knap is compared to "the white of an eye

---

34 A similar analysis could be made of the passage in *A Pair of Blue Eyes* where Knight's gaze "rakes" the room in which Elfride is looking at herself in a mirror, his sight being able to pass through the two windows placed at an angle in the corner of the house (*APBE* p. 322). An even more striking scene in the same novel is the encounter between Knight's eyes and those of a dead Trilobite: "opposite Knight's eyes was an imbedded fossil, standing forth in low relief from the rock. It was a creature with eyes. The eyes, dead and turned to stone, were even now regarding him." Knight is petrified by the Medusean gaze of the fossil; such an encounter can only take place in death: "Separated by millions of years in their lives, Knight and this underling seemed to have met in their place of death" (*APBE* p. 209).

without its pupil" (*RN* p. 185), that is to say an unseeing eye, an eye *without the hole* through which the subject can see. The theme of blindness is introduced here, a major theme in the novel, closely connected to the question of the object-gaze: for "the exemplary case of the gaze *qua* object is a blind man's eyes, i.e. eyes which do not see (we experience the gaze *qua* object when a partner in conversation suddenly takes off his black glasses, exposing us to the uneasy depthless white of his eyes)" (Žižek, 2001, p. 117).[35] The eye with no pupil is a blind eye, but also, paradoxically, an eye exposed to the gaze of the Other. For the pupil works as a *screen* behind which the subject is safe. As Lacan argues,

> [...] there is something whose absence can always be observed in a picture [...] This is the central field [...] In every picture, this central field cannot but be absent, and replaced by a hole—a reflection, in short, of the pupil behind which is situated the gaze. Consequently, and inasmuch as the picture enters into a relation to desire, the place of a central screen is always marked, which is precisely that by which, in front of the picture, I am elided as subject of the geometral plane.
>
> LACAN (1973/1986B, p. 108)

The "pupil" in *The Return of the Native* is the missing hole of the structure, the point where the intrusive gaze of the Other may enter the subject's consciousness. While waiting for Eustacia on the night when an eclipse of the moon is to take place, Clym flings himself down upon the barrow, "his face towards the moon, which depicted a small image of herself in each of his eyes" (*RN* p. 195). Whether or not the feminine personal pronoun referring to the moon ("herself") carries some ambiguity (for in the novel Eustacia is repeatedly connected to the moon,[36]) one thing is certain: Clym's pupils are no longer his own inviolable sanctuary, for something exterior to him threatens to penetrate his eye. "Let me look right into your moon-lit face" (*RN* p. 19) are Clym's words of love to Eustacia—whereby he who was being pried into becomes the inquisitive eye. The theme of ocular violation was introduced in the very first chapter, with the lurid light of Venn's lantern nearly creeping under Thomasin's closed eye-lids,[37]

35 See Lacan (2004, p. 293): "Qu'est-ce qui nous regarde? Le blanc de l'oeil de l'aveugle, par exemple."

36 Her fire is "the moon of the whole shining throng" (*RN* p. 26). She is compared to Artemis (*RN* p. 64), the Greek goddess whose symbol is the moon. See also p. 381: "Eustacia, who as she lay there still in death, eclipsed all her living phases."

37 Thomasin, who is no tragic character, is protected from the object-gaze by objects which function as veils: the reddleman's drapery hung around her (*RN* p. 35), the "intervening

then it is recurrent all along the novel, involving different characters: when Venn and Wildeve are throwing the dice by candle-light, "a diminutive candle-flame [is] mirrored in each pupil" (*RN* p. 232); Wildeve, who has been watched by Venn while sending a signal to Eustacia, passes by "a knot of stunted hollies, which in the general darkness of the scene stood as the pupil in a black eye" (*RN* p. 272, the pupil here is non-existent, exactly like "the white of an eye without its pupil"). Whether glazed by an icy shine or burnt by a consuming fire, Clym's pupils are gradually being destroyed: "In the bed lay Clym, pale, haggard, wide awake, tossing to one side and to the other, his eyes lit by a hot light, as if the fire in their pupils were burning up their substance" (*RN* p. 311); "the pupils of his eyes, fixed steadfastly on blankness, were vaguely lit with an icy shine" (*RN* p. 327). As in other Hardy novels, it is the lack of a *hole* which threatens life.

Because the object-gaze is included in the field of vision, in absolute fixity, the destinies of some characters follow a tragic course. The anomaly affecting the gaze in *Return of the Native* is in fact a general disorder, which afflicts the whole community. The heath, described as "full of a watchful intentness" (*RN* p. 4), is a human figure[38] endowed with eye-sight. Whoever ventures there takes the risk of being spied upon by a great many creatures: "several keen round eyes were always ready on such a wintry morning as this to converge upon a passer-by" (*RN* p. 84); human activities "attracted the attention of every bird within eyeshot, every reptile not yet asleep and set the surrounding rabbits curiously watching" (*RN* p. 105); Clym "walked forward, eyed by every rabbit and fieldfare around" (*RN* p. 182). Even Venn, the man forever watching others, finds himself being eyed by an inquisitive gaze: "the encircling figures were heath-croppers, their heads all towards the players, at whom they gazed intently" (*RN* p. 233). No wonder Clym develops an acute form of ophtalmia—one might even argue that his symptom is what *protects* him against the object-gaze. In such a world the eye-lid no longer fulfils its protective role: Eustacia has "pagan eyes" which never seem to close, for she has "oppressive lids and lashes": "and of these the under lid was much fuller than it usually is with English women. This enabled her to indulge in reverie without seeming to do so—she might have been believed capable of sleeping without closing them up" (*RN* p. 63). Clym covers his eyes with his hand (*RN* p. 250), like his mother (*RN* p. 35), but that is of no avail: one day he awakes with a sharp pain,

---

gauze of raindrops" screening her from the lurid sight of the reddleman with his lantern (*RN* p. 368).

38 Cf Meisel p. 73: "In *The Return of the Native*, Hardy's landscape becomes personalized to a much greater degree than at any point in his earlier novels."

has to close his eye-lids, and then tie a bandage around his brow (*RN* p. 250). Eyes have lost the capacity to blink, they are either wide open or totally obscured. Veils, goggles, "strips of ribbon" used to cover the face in mumming, "representing the barred visor of the medieval helmet" (*RN* p. 128), blinds, bandages, shades worn over the eyes, are the only remedies.

4.4 "Aftercourses": Revisiting Ancient Theory

The restoration of order at the end of the novel means that the evil eye is pacified. "In the words of Job, I have made a covenant with mine eyes" (*RN* p. 402), says Clym. The whole community has in fact made a "covenant" with the eye: the red stain is erased, Venn is "whitewashed"—he is now wearing the colours of life, "the altered hues of an ordinary Christian countenance," "white shirt-front, light flowered waistcoat, blue spotted neckerchief, and bottle-green coat" (*RN* p. 388). Windows are no longer a means of prying into people's houses, they also function as screens keeping the gaze at bay:

> The window, being screened from general observation by the bushes, had been left unblinded, so that a person in this private nook could see all that was going on within the room which contained the wedding guests, *except in so far as vision was hindered by the green antiquity of the panes.*
> 'Charley, what are they doing?' said Clym. 'My sight is weaker again tonight, and *the glass of this window is not good*'.
> Charley wiped his own eyes, which were rather *blurred with moisture.*
> *RN* p. 409, my italics

No pain can now be caused by looking through a window-pane: the gaze has been "tamed"—to use Lacan's phrase, the "green antiquity of the panes" works as a *dompte-regard.*[39]

Perhaps the most important detail in this final comic re-integration is the presence of a spectral form on the *edge* of the picture. As in the initial scene on the heath, where Venn was the liminal figure emerging out of the surrounding darkness, Clym's presence is first manifested as a voice (an "acousmatic" voice from nowhere); then he appears as an "anamorphic ghost":

39 See Lacan (1973/1986b, p. 105), and note 1. "Dompte-regard" is not translated in the English version. "Dompter" means "to tame."

> 'You shall', said a low voice behind; and starting round they beheld by the dim light a thin, pallid, almost spectral form, wrapped in a blanket, and looking like Lazarus coming from the tomb.
>
> *RN* p. 380

This should be contrasted with the "mirror-scene" where Eustacia does not turn round to look at Clym approaching from behind. Here, the eye and the gaze no longer coincide, one is no longer exposed *frontally* to a "ruddy glare" shining full face into the eye. It is now possible to look awry, to *turn round*[40] so as to glimpse the "long, slim, indistinct figure" (*RN* p. 29), or the "thin, pallid, almost spectral form" placed on the outer limit of the picture. As with anamorphosis, it is possible for the gaze to move from one place to another, to glimpse the horror in an oblique way, without being confronted to it. Clym now occupies the position which was Diggory Venn's at the beginning (or Boldwood's position at the end of *Far from the Madding Crowd*). And as Žižek argues, the real "serves as a support of our symbolic reality" (Žižek, 1992, p. 32); the real (figured in the present instance by the anamorphic blot) functions "not as something that resists symbolization, as a meaningless leftover that cannot be integrated into the symbolic universe, but on the contrary as its last support" (Žižek, 1992, p. 31). Like the hollow bone at the bottom of *The Ambassadors*, without which the organized cosmos in the central field could not exist, the anamorphic ghost in *The Return of the Native* is what gives consistency to the Egdon world. The coherence of our reality depends on the *extraction* of the object-gaze.

The *unextracted* object-gaze was then the surplus object whose inclusion in reality was the cause of disorder in the Egdon community. The early chapters of the novel make it very clear that Eustacia is an anomaly in the landscape, a protrusion coming in excess of reality:

> As the resting man looked at the barrow he became aware that its summit, hitherto the highest object in the whole prospect round, was surmounted by something higher. It rose from the semiglobular mound like a spike from a helmet […] There the form stood, motionless as the hill beneath. Above the plain rose the hill, above the hill rose the barrow, and above the barrow rose the figure. Above the figure was nothing that could be mapped elsewhere than on a celestial globe.
>
> *RN* p. 11

40 Strikingly, when Thomasin asks Venn how he managed to become white again, he answers: "I *turned* so by degrees" (*RN* p. 388, my italics).

Eustacia stands on the edge of the terrestrial world, on that limit where the unmapped universe begins. She has to drop out of sight to enable the newcomers to take her place and light their bonfire. The passage at the end of the novel which shows Clym preaching from the top of Blackbarrow bears a striking resemblance to the opening scene, the two scenes being clearly meant to frame the novel:

> From a distance there simply appeared to be a motionless figure standing on the top of the tumulus, just as Eustacia had stood on that lonely summit some two years and a half before. But now it was fine warm weather, with only a summer breeze blowing, and early afternoon instead of dull twilight. Those who ascended to the immediate neighbourhood of the Barrow perceived that the erect form in the centre, piercing the sky, was not really alone.
>
> *RN* p. 411

It is now Clym, not Eustacia or Venn, who occupies the position of the anamorphic object on the periphery of the world. But his presence is not permanent, he wears a shade over his eyes (a wise precaution), the heath has been purged of its redness. And, as we shall see later, he makes his *voice* heard. In *Far From the Madding Crowd*, the description of the valentine card in Boldwood's parlour is constructed in exactly the same way as the two framing scenes in *The Return of the Native*:

> At dusk, on the evening of St. Valentine's Day, Boldwood sat down to supper as usual, by a beaming fire of aged logs. Upon the mantel-shelf before him was a time-piece, surmounted by a spread eagle, and upon the eagle's wings was the letter Bathsheba had sent.
>
> *FFMC* pp. 79–80

The surplus object, whose presence will spell disaster, is shown as *surmounting* reality. In *The Return of the Native*, Blackbarrow itself is already a "spot" in the twofold sense of the term (a place, and "a wart on the Atlantean brow" *RN* p. 11); it is already "a *bossy* projection of earth above its natural level" (*RN* p. 11, my italics), even before Eustacia appears as an "object" rising above the semi-globular mound.

A similar object is brought into focus in *The Return of the Native*. At the Quiet Woman Inn, Diggory Venn is sitting in a dark recess in the chimney-corner, totally unobserved, until he speaks and suddenly makes his "stain" audible/visible. He too is an uncanny "protrusion" in reality:

> From the niche a single object protruded into the light from the candles on the table. It was a clay pipe, and its colour was reddish. The men had been attracted to this object by a voice behind the pipe asking for a light.
>
> *RN* pp. 224–225

A most remarkable passage is that in which an eclipse of the moon is the setting for a love scene between Eustacia and Clym. Surprisingly, the eclipse is described not as a phenomenon obscuring a part of the moon, but as the appearance of a stain, a surplus object: "While he watched […] a tawny stain grew into being on the lower verge" (*RN* p. 196). Something has been added to the moon rather than subtracted from it.

The traditional conception of tragedy, as inherited from Aristotle's *Poetics*, is one in which the tragic hero serves as a scapegoat (or *pharmakos*) whose exclusion purges the community of its passions and thereby achieves *catharsis*. In *The Return of the Native* Eustacia fulfils that function—not because she is an intruder bringing sin, or evil, or witchcraft, into Egdon, for she is simply "one of us," to use Conrad's phrase. In the light of Lacanian psychoanalysis, what appears clearly now is that the cleansing effect of catharsis in Hardy's novels consists in erasing the madder stain, that is to say in *extracting the object-gaze from the field of the visible*. For as long as a someone (whoever that may be) occupies that place, as long as the gaze is included in reality, disorder is rife in the diegetic world. Extracting the surplus object, the object-gaze, excludes what must be "primordially repressed" (Žižek, 1996, p. 91) if symbolic castration is to be effective. What the operation restores is *objet petit a* as a hollow, a vacuum that any object may come into.

The exclusion of the tragic scapegoat has not only removed the stain from the field of the visible (the surrounding air at Bloom's End is now "free from every taint" *RN* p. 390), it has made it possible for objects to be *missing*: Diggory Venn waits till the moon rises to look for Thomasin's glove which was dropped under the maypole. Objects can now be lost, or given as presents: a bed is offered to the newly-married couple by the Egdon community, a lock of Eustacia's hair is wrapped up by Clym and offered to Charley (*RN* p. 409). Only one person has "his object in his pocket"[41] (in fact he is found with a bundle of banknotes in his pocket): quite logically, that person, Wildeve, dies tragically. A sign of the comic reintegration being achieved is Diggory Venn knocking his head against a beam and Thomasin checking that he has no *bump*: "she's put her hand to his head to feel is there's a lump. And now they be all laughing

41 Lacan said that the psychotic "has his object in his pocket" (unpublished seminar of 10 November 1967).

again as if nothing had happened" (*RN* pp. 409–410). When Thomasin moves back to Blooms-End, the ceilings are so low that the rooms necessitate "a sinking in the floor under the new clock-case she brought from the inn, and *the removal of the handsome brass knobs on its head*" (*RN* p. 386, my italics). What has been removed is the surplus object, the "bossy projection of earth" of the initial scene on the heath, the figure surmounting the mound "like a spike from a helmet" (*RN* p. 11).

4.5 *Far from the Madding Crowd* and Anamorphosis

In *Far From the Madding Crowd* too the gaze can be destructive. The uncanny presence of an evil eye is felt from the very beginning, with the "oval pond" on the scene of the "pastoral tragedy" glittering "like a dead man's eye" (*FFMC* p. 33), and the circular basin of the sheep-washing pool described as "a glistening Cyclops' eye in a green face" (*FFMC* p. 99). Could that unblinking eye be "full of voracity" like Lacan's "evil eye"? The eye in the novel is often an *unseeing* eye, like Boldwood's vacant gaze at Bathsheba: "Boldwood looked at her, not slily, critically, or understandingly, but blankly at gaze" (*FFMC* p. 93). Raging over Bathsheba's words about Troy, he is struck blind and deaf: "the impending night appeared to concentrate in his eye. He did not hear her at all now" (*FFMC* p. 161). During the journey home from Casterbridge Union-house, the waggon carrying Fanny Robin's coffin is enveloped by a thick fog and the air is "as an eye suddenly struck blind" (*FFMC* p. 217). No wonder the driver, Joseph Poorgrass, made ill-at-ease by that blind, enigmatic eye, seeks solace in ale at the Buck's Head and in the "multiplying eye" of intoxication[42] (*FFMC* p. 222). The scopic drive is of prime importance in a novel where voyeurism is a central theme: Bathsheba is named after a biblical character, "the daughter of Eliam and the wife of Uriah the Hittite," who is seen by King David from the roof of the palace while she is bathing.[43] In Hardy's novel the plot is triggered by Farmer Oak climbing over the roof of a shed and "putting his eye close to a hole" so as to watch the beautiful girl inside (*FFMC* p. 15). But as we have seen in the previous section ("The Logic of Desire"), Gabriel Oak is not a tragic character: to him the "bright star" shining in the night is a true "object" ("a thing thrown before"), which sets him moving along the path of life. Oak will find ways *around* the object of his desire. So we must be aware that in a novel where

42 Joseph's "multiplying eye" is the comic side of a tragic disorder affecting the gaze.

43 *II Samuel* 11: 2. David finds her beautiful, covets her, gets rid of her husband (by means which "displeased the Lord"), and finally makes her his wife.

tragic and pastoral elements are intermingled, the scopic drive is not always the destructive force that we have seen at work in *The Return of the Native*. To address the question of the gaze, our first task will be to study the frame[44] within which visual space is constructed, with a special attention paid to the relation between frame and picture.

At the beginning of the novel, a clearly-marked limit separates Norcombe Hill, the down where Oak's sheep are grazing, from the abyss into which they will be precipitated:

> The hill was covered on its northern side by an ancient and decaying plantation of beeches, whose upper verge formed a line over the crest, fringing its arched curve against the sky, like a mane. To-night these trees sheltered the southern slope from the keenest blasts, which smote the wood and floundered through it with a sound as of grumbling.
>
> *FFMC* p. 11

Beyond the limit is chaos, suggested by the grumbling of the wind struggling through the plantation. The text insists on various kinds of limits, which seem to hold back the threat: "the rim of the landscape" (*FFMC* p. 15), "two hedges," "a rough railing" (*FFMC* p. 31), "the ridge of the hill" (*FFMC* p. 32), "the outer margin" (*FFMC* p. 33). Within the "rim" is an inner space, a well-organized cosmos, structured to serve the needs of a pastoral existence ("detached hurdles thatched with straw were stuck into the ground at various scattered points, amid and under which the whitish forms of his meek ewes moved and rustled" *FFMC* p. 14). There can be heard the music of Oak's flute, and the clear ring of the sheep-bells. After Oak's sheep have broken through the railing, Oak surveys the scene:

44 The framing of the scenes, due to the pen of a man whose first trade was architecture, is subtly and skilfully done. The frame may be the window, as in Chapter XXXV ("At an upper window"), or in Chapter XXXIII ("Eventide—A Second Declaration") where Bathsheba, "enthroned inside the window" (*FFMC* p. 120), presides over the shearing-supper. The short portrait that follows ("[…] Bathsheba was unusually excited, her red cheeks and lips contrasting lustrously with the mazy skeins of her shadowy hair" *FFMC* p. 120), framed by the window, is a typical "iconotext." Dinner is served on a long table "placed on the grass-plot beside the house, the end of the table being thrust over the sill of the wide parlour window and a foot or two into the room." Thus Bathsheba sits inside the window, facing down the table: "she was thus at the head without mingling with the men" (*FFMC* p. 120). She occupies a liminal position which tends to weaken the distinction inside/outside. The frame which delineates the scene is already under threat.

> By the outer margin of the pit was an oval pond, and over it hung the attenuated skeleton of a chrome-yellow moon which had only a few days to last—the morning star dogging her on the left hand. The pool glittered like a dead man's eye, and as the world awoke a breeze blew, shaking and elongating the reflection of the moon without breaking it, and turning the image of the star to a phosphoric streak upon the water.
>
> *FFMC* p. 33

Oak's gaze is now directed towards the "outer margin" of the scene, and by looking at an angle the farmer discovers an uncanny object, a strange, distorted, elongated form, in all points similar to the ivory-coloured bone at the bottom of Holbein's *Ambassadors*. A "phosphoric streak" conveys the image of some will-o'-the-wisp exhaled from the phosphorus of skeletons. More is seen of the death's head when the oval pond turns into "a dead man's eye." The picture is meant as a *memento mori*, reminding Oak of the vanity of human enterprise. As in *The Return of the Native*, the anamorphic ghost is also an eye looking at Oak from its empty socket. All the characteristics of anamorphosis are present here. We note that so far, the death's head is confined to the edge of the picture, and its reality is produced by "a particular stretching" (Lacan, 1973/1986b, p. 87), it is "pulsatile," "spread out" (Lacan, 1973/1986b, p. 89), uncertain. It does not stare Oak in the face.

Something quite different happens when Boldwood receives the valentine card. At first the letter is a surplus object, balanced on the wings of "a spread eagle" which surmounts a "time-piece" placed upon the mantel-shelf—the reference to a spread eagle already makes us sense that *the eye* is going to play a major part in the story. An intuition soon confirmed by the fact that the red seal affixed on the letter *becomes* the eye that is staring at it: "Here the bachelor's gaze was continually fastening itself till the large red seal became as a blot of blood on the retina of his eye" (*FFMC* p. 80). The gaze of the unknown Other has entered Boldwood and reached him at the very point from which he sees. The red wax and the blood on Boldwood's retina are now one and the same substance. At the beginning the letter is placed "in the corner of the looking-glass." Then Boldwood opens again the envelope, searches it, finds nothing more in it than what he had already withdrawn, sticks back the valentine in the frame of the mirror. Suddenly the eye is no longer on the frame, enjoining Boldwood to marry him. It has migrated to the centre of the mirror:

> The solemn and reserved yeoman again closed the letter, and stuck it in the frame of the glass. In doing so he caught sight of his reflected features,

> wan in expression, and insubstantial in form. He saw how closely compressed was his mouth, and that his eyes were wide-spread and vacant.
>
> *FFMC* p. 81

It is Boldwood's death's head which now appears in the looking-glass. His own death, staring him in the face: the vacant and wide-spread eyes are those of a dead man, who has lost his substance ("insubstantial in form"), his life-blood ("wan in expression"). And the mirror sends him back his own gaze, in perfect reflexivity—the blind spot that normally eludes the eye's grasp is included in the image. The eye and the gaze coincide. The death's head is not an anamorphic ghost that can be viewed by looking awry, an uncanny object placed at some distance on the edge of the looking-glass, or "a dead man's eye" visible on the "outer margin" of the picture: it is right in front of him. The gaze is not oblique, but frontal. What is normally off-camera has invaded the centre of the visual field. The spatial organization of anamorphosis no longer prevails. The frame, which served as a barrier against the unsymbolizable Real, has disappeared, along with all the limits that gave reality its coherence.[45] It is at this point that we enter tragedy.[46]

A series of inversions shows that now the world is "out of joint." The distinction between up and down, light and darkness, is cancelled:

> The moon shone to-night, and its light was not of a customary kind. His window admitted only a reflection of its rays, and the pale sheen had that *reversed direction* which snow gives, coming upward and lighting up his ceiling in an unnatural way, casting shadows in strange places, and putting lights where shadows had used to be.
>
> *FFMC* p. 81, my italics

Then Boldwood rises, walks out, and stares at the rising sun:

> It was one of the usual slow sunrises of this time of the year [...] apparently resting upon the ridge, the only half of the sun yet visible burnt rayless, like a red and flameless fire shining over a white hearthstone. The whole effect resembled a sunset as childhood resembles age.
>
> *FFMC* p. 81

45 The problematic is exactly the same as the one I have analyzed in the section on "the littoral" in *A Pair of Blue Eyes*.

46 And psychosis, as far as Boldwood is concerned.

We discover an uncanny landscape, where spatio-temporal distinctions have been annulled: between morning and evening, childhood and old age, east and west, inside and outside, etc. Because of the snow covering the whole country, an inversion of light and shade creates the illusion that earth and sky have changed places. The horizon no longer separates them clearly:

> In other directions, the fields and sky were so much of one colour by the snow, that it was difficult in a hasty glance to tell whereabouts the horizon occurred; and in general there was here, too, that before-mentioned preternatural *inversion* of light and shade which attends the prospect when the garish brightness commonly in the sky is found on the earth, and the shades of earth are in the sky.
>
> FFMC p. 81, my italics

In fact the world outdoors is the exact repetition of the world indoors, with the red sun as a mirror image of the "large red seal"[47] which has become a "blot of blood" on the retina of Boldwood's eye. Microcosm and macrocosm are perfectly analogical. A gradual process has disintegrated Boldwood's reality: at first the sun appears on the outer limit of the scene: only half of it is visible, "resting upon the ridge," when Boldwood leans over "the gate of a field." Then the colour red spreads over the whole snowy surface, until it becomes a sort of generalized stain: "Boldwood was listlessly noting how the frost had hardened and glazed the surface of the snow, till it shone in the red eastern light with the polish of marble" (FFMC p. 82). A strange inversion has moved the red blot from the periphery to the centre of the visual space—the movement is strictly parallel to what has just happened indoors, with the eye displaced from the edge of the mirror to its centre. In fact, the "madder stain" now occupies the whole visible surface.

Some kind of frame seems to be restored when Boldwood (who is the focalizer) directs his gaze towards the edge of the scene:

> At this moment, on the ridge, up against the blazing sky, a figure was visible, like the black snuff in the midst of a candle-flame. Then it moved and began to bustle about vigorously from place to place, carrying square skeleton masses, which were riddled by the same rays. A small figure on all fours followed behind. The tall form was that of Gabriel Oak; the small one that of George; the articles in course of transit were hurdles.
>
> FFMC p. 82

---

47 The red sun, compared to "a red and flameless fire shining over a white hearthstone," occupies the same position as that of the valentine, placed above the mantelshelf.

The spatial organization bears some resemblance to that of Holbein's *Ambassadors*, with the enigmatic "skeleton masses" appearing on the edge of the picture, and the tall, bar-like figure of "the man on the hill," likened to "the snuff of a candle." Oak begins to descend the hill towards the right. At this moment, "the glow *stretched down* in this direction now, and touched the distant roof of Warren's malthouse" (*FFMC* p. 82). Is that "particular stretching" to be taken as a sign that the economy of the gaze characteristic of anamorphosis is about to be restored? We soon realize that it is not the case. For the following chapter takes us, along with Oak and Boldwood, to Warren's malthouse. And there we realize that the very same fire is burning inside, and that the whole diegetic world is now ablaze. No need for the red glare to penetrate the malthouse, it is already there, as if waiting to be joined to its outdoor counterpart—a logical consequence of the erasure of all limits:

> The scarlet and orange light outside the malthouse did not penetrate to its interior, which was, as usual, lighted by a rival glow of similar hue, radiating from the hearth.
>
> *FFMC* p. 83

Inside the building, the maltster keeps his eyes riveted to the fire, as if fascinated by the ruddy glow from the kiln. Exposure to that perpetual blaze has consumed his eyes, and turned them into a mirror-image of the fire. In fact his eyes *are* the fire:

> 'Come shepherd and drink [...]' said the maltster, removing from the fire his eyes, which were vermilion-red and bleared by gazing into it for so many years.
>
> *FFMC* p. 46

It is important to understand that in the malthouse, as in Boldwood's parlour, and as in the outdoor scene focalized by Boldwood, the "madder stain" is an eye. More precisely, to use strictly Lacanian terms, it is the gaze of the Other as identified with the subject's eye. There will be no choice for Boldwood but to obey the Other's "pert injunction" inscribed on the valentine, silently signified to him by the large red seal glaring at him: "Marry Me" (*FFMC* p. 80). Boldwood here is clearly entering a psychotic process. As far as he is concerned, the Eye is now everywhere, an all-seeing gaze that encompasses the whole of his reality.

One may wonder about Warren's malthouse, which in the general economy of the novel is the very locus of conviviality, where Gabriel Oak is welcomed by the Weatherbury community, "greeted by an atmosphere laden with the sweet smell of new malt" (*FFMC* p. 45). The "aged man," the malster, is a genial father-figure, who recognizes in the newcomer "Gable's Oak's grandson over at Norcombe"—in fact he is the only father-figure in the novel. How then can such a place harbour in its secret recesses the "evil eye" that will wreak havoc on the lives of some of the characters? One first answer is that the malt-house described in Chapter XV ("A Morning Meeting—The Letter Again") is Boldwood's view of the malthouse, for Boldwood is the focalizer here. It is in Boldwood's sense of reality that limits are erased. In Chapter VIII, the malt-house is described as "enclosed by an old wall inwrapped with ivy." Entering the building is a complicated operation, which requires groping for a leather string that has to be pulled if the door is to be unlatched. In the absence of windows "a square hole in the door was glazed with a single pane, through which red, comfortable rays now stretched out upon the ivied wall in front" (*FFMC* pp. 43–44)—a small aperture offering a partial view to any common Peeping Tom. So the place is enclosed within strict limits—no doubt a necessity if the fire contained in the furnace is to be kept from spreading around and setting the whole neighbourhood ablaze (an event which does happen in Chapter VI, with Gabriel Oak opportunely intervening and saving Bathsheba's barn). But that answer is not sufficient, for it does not take into consideration the central issue of *jouissance*: something is being *consumed* by the maltster's fire, but the action of burning is also a *consummation* (were it only because ale is consumed on the premises). It takes a vigilant guardian to watch over the fire, to keep it pent up within limits, just as it takes a function called the Name-of-the-Father to prevent *jouissance* from running out of control. Such is the function of the paternal figure here: to see to it that *jouissance* is properly restrained, within the limits of a well organized cosmos. The aged man's vermilion-red eyes, bleared by gazing into the fire, work as a sort of *dompte-regard*: for the fire is also an eye that has to be "tamed."[48] It is another manifestation of the object-gaze, which is both a "ruddy glow" (*FFMC* p. 45) and a "brazen glare" (*FFMC* p. 187), both a desired object that may bring comfort and the glare that kills. Troy will finally be killed after peeping though the "square hole" in the door of Warren Malthouse, and catching on his face a reflection of the illuminated "pane of glass." The three men who have decided to look into the malt-house are arrested by a strange sight: "The light from the pane was now perceived to be shining not upon the ivied wall as usual, but upon some object close to the glass. It was a human face [...] Troy's face was almost close to the

48 One must also bear in mind that the "extraction" of the object-gaze in the experience of symbolic castration is effected in most cases by the Name-of-the-Father. The "aged man" whose function is to "tame" the fire therefore clearly appears as the agent of symbolic castration.

pane, and he was looking in" (*FFMC* p. 284). The encounter between Troy and the illuminated pane will prove deadly—for Hardy seldom spares those of his characters who are confronted to "a window-pane." His fate is sealed from this moment, as though he had seen the Gorgon herself: he will be shot by Boldwood "before the fire-place" (*FFMC* p. 289), a perfectly suitable place if one considers the logic at work in the novel.

A clear sign indicating that order has been restored after the elimination of Boldwood and Troy is the dialogue between Poorgrass and Coggan, about the judge who is to rule on Boldwood's case. If we are to believe the villagers, the "evil eye" is no longer to be dreaded, for everybody seems to have "made a covenant" with their eyes:

> 'Did ye notice my lord judge's face ?' [said Coggan]
> 'I did', said Poorgrass. 'I looked hard at en, as if I would read his very soul; and there was mercy in his eyes—or to speak with the exact truth required of us at this solemn time, in the eye that was towards me'.
> 'Well, I hope for the best', said Coggan, 'though bad that must be. However, I shan't go to the trial, and I'd advise the rest of ye that bain't wanted to bide away. 'Twill disturb his mind more than anything to see us there staring at him as if he were a show'.
>
> *FFMC* p. 294

Earlier in the story, in Chapter XLIV ("Under a Tree—Reaction"), when Bathsheba tells Liddy she has "chosen her course" (which is to allow "youth and hope" to reassert themselves), she asks her confidante to suggest ways of "passing the heavy time away." Interestingly, one suggestion is "hemming handkerchiefs," another is finishing her sampler so that "it could be framed and glazed" (*FFMC* pp. 235–236). With remarkable wisdom, Liddy advises Bathsheba to set her life within a *frame*, to restore the border that went missing when tragedy broke into her life.

Indeed the final resolution, which places Boldwood in a liminal position, on a fringe where he is neither included within his community nor excluded,[49] is very similar to the ending of *The Return of the Native*. Just as Venn and Charley turn round to gaze obliquely at the anamorphic ghost on the edge of the scene (Clym Yeobright "looking like Lazarus coming from the tomb" *RN* p. 380), Gabriel Oak, riding to Casterbrige for a surgeon "after the shock," fails to

49 It could be said that he now lingers in that area which Lacan has called "between-two-deaths," where he is neither a living man nor a dead man ("he walked the world no more" *FFMC* p. 290).

discern "a square-figured pedestrian passing along under the dark hedge in the same direction as his own" (*FFMC* p. 291). Gabriel has not seen the man who from now on will "[walk] the world no more" (*FFMC* p. 290), but the figure is there, on the edge of the picture, an anamorphic blot that can only be glimpsed by whoever attempts to look awry. And, as Žižek has argued, the spectral form appearing on the frame is what gives consistency to the reality depicted within.

4.6 The Red Glare and Hardy's Aesthetics

One difficult question arises: what is the "madder stain" to Hardy the author? The concept of the "death of the author," introduced by Barthes in the late sixties, has ever since been widely accepted by literary critics, so that attempting to investigate the relation between a literary text and its author has become a rather perilous task. Unless one resorts to Barthes's own view of the "style" of a writer, defined as "an imagery, delivery, vocabulary [which] spring from the *body* and the past of the writer," something that "rises from the myth-laden depths of the writer and unfolds beyond his area of control" (Barthes, 1977, p. 10, my italics). If one renounces the traditional practice of connecting a text to its author's intentions or biography, and if one turns to a form of criticism that seeks in literature some reference to the writer's "biology"[50] (Barthes, 1977, p. 10), then we begin to perceive that the "madder stain" as Hardy's signature[51]—the recurrent *punctum* riddling the text—bears some relevance to the writer's inmost life, his very flesh, his own relation to the unsymbolizable Real.

A look at *The Life and Works of Thomas Hardy* confirms this intuition. Hardy's fascination with sunsets and the colour red is traceable in this reminiscence from his childhood:

> In those days the staircase at Bockhampton had its walls coloured Venitian red by his father, and was so situated that the evening sun shone into it, adding to its colour a great intensity for a quarter of an hour or more. Tommy used to wait for this chromatic effect, and, sitting alone there, would recite to himself 'And now another day is gone' from Dr Watts's Hymns [...].
>
> *LIFE* p. 20

---

50 "Zoography," instead of "biography," is a term coined by Josiane Paccaud-Huguet (used in a book yet unpublished), based on Agamben's distinction between *bios*, "qualified life" in the city, and *zoe*, "bare life." "Zoography" would be particularly relevant here.

51 Like the "hollow bone" at the bottom of *The Ambassadors*, Holbein's signature.

Much later in his life, fascination turns into anxiety when Hardy and Emma stay at a gloomy hotel at Le Havre where the waiters' manners seem "queer" and the chambermaid speaks "in a foreboding voice": "The floor of the bedroom was painted a bloody red, and the wall beside the bed was a little battered, as if struggles had taken place there" (*Life* pp. 142–143). But the most striking passage is about a note in which Hardy recalls a sleepless night at Upper Tooting:

> The following note on London at dawn occurs on May 19th [1880], a night in which he could not sleep, partly on account of an eerie feeling which sometimes haunted him, a horror at lying down in close proximity to 'a monster whose body had four million heads and eight million eyes':
>
> 'In upper back bedroom at daybreak: just past three. A golden light behind the horizon; within it are the Four Millions. The roofs are damp gray: the streets are still filled with night as with a dark stagnant flood whose surface brims to the tops of the houses. Above the air is light. A fire or two *glares* within the mass [...]'.
>
> *LIFE* p. 141, my italics

What is particularly important here is Hardy's sense of "a fancied gaze" (*Tess* p. 298) that might be *glaring* at him, a panoptic gaze reaching him from eight-million eyes and therefore embracing the whole of his reality—just as Tess feels her back "endowed with a sensitiveness to ocular beams"[52] as she leaves the barn where she has seen Alec preaching. In another scene she makes that strange confession to Angel: "The trees have inquisitive eyes, haven't they?—that is, seem as if they had" (*Tess* p. 128).[53] The modalisation in Tess's speech rules out the possibility of psychosis of course, just as Hardy's experience is but "an eerie feeling" bred by sleeplessness—a state half-way between wakefulness and sleep. However the object-gaze in both cases is a vacillating near-presence. No doubt Hardy was acutely affected by the gaze of others, and painfully resented any disparaging views of himself and his writings. It is no coincidence if the passage I have just quoted comes immediately after some lines where Hardy recalls his displeasure "when only the bad lines were quoted from his verses by certain critics, and only the careless sentences and doubtful opinions

---

52 Cf *Tess* p. 298: "She went on without turning her head. Her back seemed to be endowed with a sensitiveness to ocular beams—even her clothing—so alive was she to a fancied gaze which might be resting upon her from the outside of that barn."

53 Tess's assertion is modalized of course ("that is, seem as if they had"), but any reader of Lacan will not fail to draw a parallel between these words and the drawing by Isabella, an Italian patient at St Anne's hospital (Lacan, 2004, pp. 90, 200).

from his prose" (*Life* p. 141). His pained reaction to the reception of *Jude the Obscure* shows how vulnerable his self-image was.

But what is even more interesting is the passage that follows the lines on the "eight million eyes," for it gives an idea of the poetic use which Hardy made of his capacity to glimpse the unspecularizable object-gaze:

> Two days later they were sitting in the chairs by Rotten Row and the Park Drive, and the chief thing he noticed against the sun in the west was that 'a sparrow descends from the tree amid the stream of vehicles, and drinks from the little pool left by the watering cart'—the same sunlight causing 'a glitter from carriage lamp-glasses, from Coachmen's and footmen's buttons, from silver carriage handles and harness mountings, from a matron's bracelet, from four parasols of four young ladies in a landau, their parasol-hems touching like four mushrooms growing close together'.
>
> *Life* p. 141

The position of the artist is always liminal: he stands on the uncertain "margin of the unexpressed," on the "outer limit" that Julie Kristeva writes about, "the place where order shades into chaos, light into darkness" (Burgin, pp. 115–116), a place where both writer and reader "abdicate their usual modes of perception [...] to recreate another, in a more intense type of apprehension of the surrounding world" (Gadoin-Ramel, p. 6). From that singular position, Hardy invents his own way of deflecting the threatening gaze of a malevolent Other—a means which is not only a defence against the glaring eye, but also a positive act turning it to good account. Indeed "against" in the passage quoted above ("against the sun") means both "in opposition to" and "having as a background" for "the Four Millions" may stare at Hardy from "the golden light" of the sun, yet it is "the same sunlight" which conjures up the poetic vision of the carriage lamp-glasses, the footmen's buttons, the silver carriage-handles, and the matron's bracelet catching on their facets some brief illumination, a *fragmented* radiance which is a pleasure to the eye. Hardy's *style* achieves precisely this: it breaks up the massive *jouissance* lodged in the object-gaze into a myriad of minute particles of light, to be gathered within the reticulations of the literary text—like the "minute diamonds of moisture from the mist" hanging from Tess's eyelashes, which scintillate in the sunbeams of daybreak (*Tess* p. 135), or the "spots of froth" travelling over the swift stream where Tess hopes to be drowned with Angel (*Tess* p. 244). Those "minute diamonds" are essential to Hardy's aesthetics; like the red stain, they can be read as his signature. Scattered about to the four winds, the "spots of froth" are emblematic of the loss of a primordial *jouissance*, but they also capture something of it, some left-overs that may be shared and enjoyed by a multiplicity of readers. It is those fragments of a lost *jouissance* that turn the literary text into a *plus-de-jouir*.[54]

The minute luminous spot focused on by the narrator is therefore both a transient incarnation of the gaze of the Other, and a sign of its being *tamed*—an indication that the literary text, like a painting, works as a *dompte-regard*. It is everywhere to be found in Hardy's fiction. J.B. Bullen draws a parallel between what Tess sees as she descends for the first time into the valley of the Froom and "what Hardy had perceived in Turner's water-colours—light as modified by objects" (Bullen, p. 198).[55] He quotes this passage, which bears a strong resemblance to the extract from Hardy's *Life* quoted above:

> Those of [the cows] that were spotted with white reflected the sunshine in dazzling brilliancy, and the polished brass knobs on their horns glittered with something of military display.
>
> *TESS* p. 111

What gives Hardy's prose its "strongly pictorial" quality (Bullen, p. 6) is precisely this, for which Hardy may have found his inspiration in Turner: an object is interposed between a source of light and a reflecting surface, deviating the beam, or breaking it up into a myriad of fragments; the object may also capture some of the light and cause a brief illumination. For instance in *Tess of the d'Urbervilles* again, while the women are searching the meadow for the blade of garlic[56] which is spoiling the milk, the crude rays of the sun at noon are twice reflected, first on the buttercups, and then on the shaded faces of the girls:

> As they crept along, stooping low to discern the plant, a soft yellow gleam was reflected from the buttercups into their shaded faces, giving them an elfish, moonlit aspect, though the sun was pouring upon their backs in all the strength of noon.
>
> *TESS* p. 143

Thus the fiery light of a merciless sun is appeased, in a beautiful poetic passage. After the accident that has killed Prince, the horror is both shown and

---

54 Cf Lacan (2006), "De la plus-value au plus-de-jouir," pp. 11–25. Žižek translates *plus-de-jouir* by "surplus-enjoyment" (Žižek, 1989, p. 52).

55 Bullen here draws on a letter from Hardy: "Jan. 9 [1889]. At the Old Masters, Royal Academy. Turner's watercolours: each is a landscape *plus* a man's soul... What he paints chiefly is *light as modified by objects*" (*Life* p. 225).

56 The blade of garlic spoiling the milk is another surplus-object that ought to be "extracted."

veiled by the "hundred prismatic hues" reflected from the huge pool of blood. Beauty is there too, an effect of the diffraction of sunlight through the prism of coagulated, iridescent blood (*Tess* p. 37).

A profusion of such examples, where a visual effect is produced by "*light as modified by objects*," may also be found in *Far from the Madding Crowd*.[57] On the sides of the malignant swamp near which Bathsheba has slept, there grows a peculiar species of flag, "the blades of which glistened in the emerging sun, like scythes" (*FFMC* p. 233). The young boys playing a game of Prisoner's ball capture the evening light on their shirt-sleeves: "She could see the brown and black heads of the young lads darting about right and left, their white shirt-sleeves gleaming in the sun" (*FFMC* p. 237). The "bountiful light," admitted obliquely into the barn through the large doors open towards the sun, reaches the shearers and is reflected on their instruments: "Here the shearers knelt, the sun slanting in upon their bleached shirts, tanned arms, and the polished shears they flourished, causing these to bristle with a thousand rays strong enough to blind a weak-eyed man" (*FFMC* p. 114). The verb "to bristle" is used in another beautiful passage:

> Boldwood was listlessly noting how the frost had hardened and glazed the surface of the snow, till it shone in the red eastern light with the polish of marble; how, in some portions of the slope, withered grass-bents, encased in icicles, bristled through the smooth wan coverlet in the twisted and curved shapes of old Venetian glass.
>
> *FFMC* p. 82

In the fire episode, the blaze of the burning ricks is reflected on Gabriel's face, and only reaches his body through an intervening screen, which filters the beams:

> His weary face now began to be painted over with a rich orange glow, and the whole front of his smock-frock and gaiters was covered with a dancing shadow-pattern of thorn-twigs—the light reaching him through a leafless intervening hedge—and the metallic curve of his sheep-crook shone silver-bright in the same abounding rays.
>
> *FFMC* p. 38

This raises a crucial issue: why should sunlight have to be broken up, diffracted, deflected or deviated, if the sun "in its benevolent form" is "the source of life

---

57 I could also quote examples from *The Return of the Native*, or from *A Pair of Blue Eyes*.

and light [...] the heart of 'the great passionate pulse of existence'" (Bullen, pp. 204–205)? J.B. Bullen admits that sun and sunlight have "strong emotional connotations," connotations that vary throughout *Tess of the d'Urbervilles* ("sometimes sunlight is cheering, sometimes it is cruel or indifferent" Bullen, p. 201); he concedes that the power of the sun can be both "creative and destructive" (Bullen, p. 204). Taking issue with Hillis Miller, who argued that the red objects "are all incarnated in one form in the sun," he claims that "Hardy's allusions to redness are just one aspect of his much more extensive employment of the themes, the patterns, and the imagery associated with solar myth" (Bullen, p. 204). That approach leads him to emphasize the benign aspect of the sun, which "rises as a God in the August dawn—a 'golden-haired, beaming, mild-eyed' creature [...] the deity presiding over the 'aesthetic, sensuous, pagan pleasure in natural life'." In Hillis Miller's view the emphasis is noticeably different:

> The sun is in this novel, as in tradition generally, the fecundating male source, a principle of life, but also a dangerous energy able to pierce and destroy as Tess, at the end of the novel, lying on the stone of sacrifice at Stonehenge after her brief period of happiness with Angel, is wakened, just before her capture, by the first rays of the morning sun which penetrate under her eye-lids.
>
> HILLIS MILLER, p. 122

Whatever the cultural ramifications of the solar myth in *Tess of the d'Urbervilles*, magisterially explored by J.B. Bullen, it seems to me that the sun as understood by Hillis Miller, in its association with the "chain of red things," is always a *punctum*, a point of contact with the unsymbolizable Real. It is therefore permeated with enjoyment—a *jouissance* which is always, in its Lacanian definition, "a paradoxical pleasure produced by displeasure itself" (Žižek, 1989, p. 202), an *exquisite* sensation verging on pain and carrying the subject beyond Freud's "pleasure principle." Seen in that perspective, as a concentration of the deadly energies of *jouissance*, the sun (or the madder stain) can appear quite logically as both a source of pleasure and a force of destruction. In *The Return of the Native*, the paradox is made noticeable in the scene where Mrs Yeobright rests on the heath before she dies. The sun is clearly presented here as the agent that causes her death:[58] "The sun had now got far to the west of south and stood directly in her face, like some merciless incendiary, brand in hand,

58 In that, it is a duplicate of the red stain incarnated by Eustacia, which will be imprinted as a "scarlet speck" on Mrs. Yeobright's ankle.

waiting to consume her" (*RN* p. 290). But as she sits on the "perfumed mat" formed by "a little patch of shepherd's thyme," we feel that her pleasure is not just produced by a sense of relief from the heat and the glaring light. She seems to derive exquisite pleasure from that pause, from the sight of the ants bustling about beneath her ("to look down upon them was like observing a city from the top of a tower"), and from the resplendent vision of a heron flying towards the sun:

> While she looked a heron arose on that side of the sky and flew on with his face towards the sun. He had come dripping wet from some pool in the valleys, and as he flew the edges and lining of his wings, his thighs and his breast were so caught by the bright sunbeams that he appeared as if formed of burnished silver.
>
> *RN* p. 291

It is as though the fate that awaits her, being consumed by "a merciless incendiary," were a "consummation devoutly to be wished." We almost feel that *to burn* is her secret desire, for "burnished" contains "burn," undeniably, even though the etymology of the word connects it to "brown"[59] and not to "burn." The pain felt at the approach of death is strangely transmuted here into some kind of exquisite joy. "The burning of the sun" (*RN* p. 283) on the heath may kill on a fiery Summer afternoon, but it is also a source of enjoyment, beyond the pleasure principle.

In the diegesis, the sun (or the madder stain) may bring destruction upon the characters, but in the narrative it produces effects that are quite the opposite. It is "the source of life and light" from which the reader may draw his pleasure, because in the text its offensive glare is "modified by objects" that have the status of "sublime objects," in the Lacanian sense of "an object raised to the level of the (impossible-real) Thing."[60] The resplendent heron in the passage quoted above is exactly this: an object that enables the reader to approach the very *limit* beyond which lies the impossible Thing, without being blinded by its

59 "Brown" connects "burnished" to Mrs. Yeobright's son (sun?): Clym cutting furze on the heath is "a brown spot in the midst of olive-green gorse, and nothing more" (*RN* p. 253). He appears to his mother "of a russet hue" (*RN* p. 279), Eustacia speaks of "the rusty look he has now" (*RN* p. 283). Clym as a "brown spot" is another *punctum*, a point of contact with the Real, loaded with *jouissance*.

60 Lacan (1986a/2008). Quoted here (and commented upon) by Žižek (Žižek, 1989, pp. 202–203). Žižek's translation ("raised to the level of the Thing") is slightly different from Dennis Porter's in the Routledge edition ("raised to the dignity of the Thing," Lacan, 1986a/2008, p. 138).

absolute negativity. Thanks to the heron, we are against the threshold (*limen*) that bars access to it, etymologically just beneath it (*sub-limen*), yet filled with whatever joy may be irradiated by the core of an unattainable, transcendent, transphenomenal reality. It is on "the edge and lining" of the heron that we find beauty; it is on that limit, where the visible breaks down and gives way to the invisible, that we are brought close, so close to the Thing—and "lining" here must also be understood as a reference to the writer's *lines*, which make it possible to approach "the margin of the unexpressed."

For Kant the Sublime may be defined in this way:

> It is an object (of nature) the representation of which determines the mind to regard the elevation of nature beyond our reach as equivalent to a presentation of ideas.[61]

Žižek points out that this definition anticipates Lacan's determination of the sublime object (Žižek, 1989, pp. 202–203): raising an object to the level (or "dignity") of the Thing means turning "an empirical, sensuous object" into something that pertains to the Thing—the suprasensible essence.[62] But such an operation is a paradox:

> The Sublime is the paradox of an object which, in the very field of representation, provides a view, in a negative way, of the dimension of what is unrepresentable. It is a unique point in Kant's system, a point at which the fissure, the gap between phenomenon and Thing-in-itself, is abolished in a negative way, because in it the phenomenon's very inability to represent the Thing adequately *is inscribed in the phenomenon itself.*
>
> ŽIŽEK (1989, p. 203)

How does this relate to the vision of the resplendent heron? In my view the heron is a sublime object because it masks the Thing (it works as a blot in our field of representation, it diverts our gaze from the unbearable object-gaze

61 Kant, Immanuel. *Critique of Judgment*, Oxford, 1964, p. 119. Quoted in Žižek (1989, p. 202).

62 It is important to note that in the Lacanian perspective (as different from the traditional one), the Thing-in-itself is sheer negativity. Behind the object masking/showing the Thing, there is nothing: "The Sublime is no longer an (empirical) object indicating through its very inadequacy the dimension of a *transcendent* Thing-in-itself (Idea) but an object which occupies the place, replaces, fills out the empty place of the Thing as the void, as the pure Nothing of absolute negativity—the Sublime is an object whose positive body is just an embodiment of Nothing" (Žižek, 1989, p. 206).

figured by the sun, it embodies the failure to represent the Thing), while at the same time it gives us a "negative" picture of the Thing-in-itself, by softening the unbearable glare, sifting it, reducing it to "burnished silver," a subdued radiance that can please the eye. Sarah Kaye, in her reading of Žižek's delineation of the Sublime, gives a definition which is perfectly suited to Hardy's style of writing—an aesthetics based on "light as modified by objects":

> The possibility of positioning an object relative to the drives arises because of what Lacan terms 'The Thing'. The Thing is a pressure-point that lies just outside the symbolic and imaginary orders, where the weight of the real is sensed. It is a place of menace, because it is where the deadly impulses of the drives are gathered […] An object aligned with this point is said to be raised 'to the dignity of the Thing'. Rather like an eclipse, when a heavenly body becomes positioned between us and the sun, and appears surrounded by an aura of light so intense that we could never look directly at it, an object located in this way between us and the unsymbolizable Thing becomes as though irradiated by the drive, bathed in jouissance, transfigured, spiritualized and resplendent. Objects positioned in this way are referred to as 'sublime'.
>
> KAYE, pp. 53–54

One of course cannot fail to be reminded of Conrad's words about the true meaning of a tale:

> "[…] to [Marlow] the meaning of an episode was not inside like a kernel, but outside, enveloping the tale which brought it out only as a glow brings out a haze, in the likeness of one of these misty halos that sometimes are made visible by the spectral illumination of moonshine".
>
> CONRAD, p. 138

The spectral effects sent abroad by an object aligned with the unsymbolizable Thing is the very hallmark of Hardy's style of fiction, which could be called "sublimatory." In *Far From the Madding Crowd*, another type of mediation veils the crude light of the sun while allowing us to enjoy some diffracted brilliance from an unapproachable source of light:

> A morning mist hung over [the swamp] now—a fulsome yet magnificent silvery veil, full of light from the sun, yet semi-opaque—the hedge behind it being in some measure hidden by its hazy luminousness.
>
> *FFMC* pp. 232–233

In *The Return of the Native*, Eustacia is a "sublime object" in Sarah Kaye's acceptation of the concept: an object positioned between the unsymbolizable Thing and the onlookers (characters in the diegesis or readers),[63] which masks the Thing yet is "surrounded by an aura of light, [...] irradiated by the drive, bathed in jouissance, transfigured, spiritualized and resplendent." Clym's sight has to get accustomed to "the first blinding halo" (*FFMC* p. 210) kindled by Eustacia's beauty and his love. That halo has the power to "blind," but it can also be softened, "sublimated":

> Yeobright and Eustacia looked at each other for one instant, as if each had in mind those few moments during which a certain moonlight scene was common to both. With the glance the calm fixity of her features *sublimated* itself to an expression of refinement and warmth; it was like garish noon *rising to the dignity* of sunset in a couple of seconds.
> *RN* p. 185, my italics

Here we are not blinded by the "halo" of Eustacia's beauty, we derive exquisite enjoyment from it, because the object-gaze ("garish noon") is not viewed frontally but obliquely, deflected by a particular glance, mediated by the act of remembering "a certain moonlit scene [...] common to both." The diegetic situation here is the exact opposite of the one I have described previously (the mortal face-to-face encounter between Mrs Yeobright and Eustacia/the adder, or between Clym and Eustacia). It is particularly interesting in this perspective to note that Eustacia is consistently associated with *the moon* in the novel:[64] a planet which reflects the sunlight in an attenuated form, giving us an *indirect* access to it; an object interposed between us and the sun, which modifies light and makes it bearable and enjoyable.[65] That is perhaps why an eclipse of the moon is perceived as a threat in the novel: because it allows the intrusion of "a tawny stain" (*RN* p. 196), a surplus object which in the economy of the novel works like a point of contact with the Thing. When Eustacia lies dead in her

63 An important inference that can be made from this is that Hardy's sublime characters (Eustacia, Tess) merely *occupy* a certain place: all is a question of positions, of alignment with the void of the Thing. Neither Eustacia nor Tess is intrinsically linked to evil (the "evil" eye), to redness, or to any quality redness might connote.

64 See above, note 36.

65 In *Tess of* the *d'Urbervilles*, a soft yellow gleam is reflected from the buttercups into the shaded faces of the working girls, "giving them an elfish, *moonlit* aspect" (*Tess* p. 143, my italics).

husband's house, she is a sublime object for both the reader and the surviving characters:

> They stood silently looking upon Eustacia, who as she lay there still in death eclipsed all her living phases. Pallor did not include all the quality of her complexion, which seemed more than whiteness; it was almost light.
>
> *RN* p. 381

Eustacia as the embodiment of brightness outshines "all her living phases." But her radiance, though "more than whiteness," comes short of the absolute of pure light. It reaches a degree which is just beneath the limit (*sub-limen*), on the threshold beyond which lies a transcendent reality. Bathed in light, irradiated, spiritualized, Eustacia reflects/deflects an unbearable brilliance. Another object interposed between the eye and the unrepresentable Thing is the narrative, which works through the mediation of language, yet proves inadequate—for the word "pallor" fails to render the quality of Eustacia's complexion. The sublime here works exactly as in the definition given by Žižek: it approaches the unsymbolizable Thing, and inscribes in the text its very inability to represent it.

The object modifying light and causing *a failure in representation* is therefore essential to Hardy's aesthetics. This scene from his early life gives us an idea of the style[66] that will be his:

> He was lying on his back in the sun, thinking how useless he was, and covered his face with his straw hat. The sun's rays streamed through the interstices of the straw, the lining having disappeared. Reflecting on his experiences of the world so far as he had got, he came to the conclusion that he did not wish to grow up.
>
> *Life* p. 20

Here, as in the description of the sublime heron, "lining" is a key-word. The inadequate lining of the old hat, which allows the sunbeams to filter through the interstices of the straw, will later turn into the interlacing of the writer's lines. The straw hat as a metatextual representation of Hardy's style is so

66 I am limiting "style" here to its visual dimension, but a writer's "style" is not reducible to that. Style makes you see *and hear*. It is "an imagery, delivery, vocabulary" (Barthes, 1977, p. 10). It involves the question of voice, which will be the subject of the following chapter.

central an image that it is reappears in *Jude the Obscure* (where, curiously, the same conclusion is reached):

> He pulled his straw hat over his face, and peered through the interstices of the plaiting at the white brightness, vaguely reflecting. Growing up brought responsibilities, he found [...] All around you there seemed to be something glaring, garish, rattling, and the noises and glares hit upon the little cell called your life, and shook it, and warped it.
>
> If he could only prevent himself growing up! He did not want to be a man.
>
> *JUDE* p. 13

CHAPTER 5

The Object-Voice

5.1 Gaze and Voice

The quotation from *Jude the Obscure* in the concluding lines of the previous chapter binds together gaze and voice: "something glaring, garish, rattling" surrounds the young boy, and causes him to fear the responsibilities of adulthood. Peering at the "white brightness" through the plaiting of his straw hat, the boy feels threatened by "noises and glares" hitting upon "the little cell called your life" (*Jude* p. 13). It is as though the texture of the hat (which may be understood as a metatextual representation of the literary text) served the double purpose of filtering the sunlight through its interstices, and of dampening the unbearable noises of existence. The final chapter of this book will dwell on the relationship between gaze and voice, with a special interest given to a recurrent pattern in Hardy's fiction, especially in *Tess of the d'Urbervilles*: hearing with one's eyes, or seeing with one's ears.

To begin with, I will draw a couple of examples from *The Return of the Native*. One is the first encounter between Eustacia and Clym Yeobright, which takes place at night, on the heath. It is to a *voice* that Eustacia is irresistibly attracted: "There came to her ears in a masculine voice, 'Good-night'" (*RN* p. 115). Clym bidding her "good-night" seals her fate: whatever the obstacles, she *will* contrive to "behold face to face the owner of the awakening voice" (*RN* p. 120). And the "good night" will turn out to be the night of death. Could that alluring voice be as dangerous as the Sirens' voice? Could it be the exact counterpart in the sound register of the "evil eye" whose destructive power I have studied in the previous chapter? Eustacia strains her eyes to see the dusky forms of Clym, Mrs Yeobright, and Thomasin, but is unable to discern them. All she can do is see with her ears (a faculty which the narrator soon reverses into hearing with one's "body"):

> She strained her eyes to see them, but was unable. Such was her intentness, however, that it seemed as if her ears were performing the functions of seeing as well as hearing. This extension of power can almost be believed in at such moments. The deaf Dr Kitto was probably under the influence of a parallel fancy when he described his body as having become, by long endeavour, so sensitive to vibrations that he had gained the power of perceiving by it as by ears.
>
> *RN* p. 115

 | DOI 10.1163/9789004296626_007

The passage is soon followed by Eustacia's dream, in which she dances ecstatically with an armoured man whose face she cannot see, but whose voice fills her with delight:

> She was dancing to wondrous music, and her partner was the man in silver armour who had accompanied her through the previous fantastic changes, the visor of his helmet being closed. The mazes of the dance were ecstatic. Soft whispering came into her ear from under the radiant helmet, and she felt like a woman in Paradise.
>
> *RN* pp. 117–118

At this stage voice is but an "object" in the Lacanian sense, that is to say a mere "hollow" that any real object may come into. The "casque" (like the *enforme* of a hat) is the form assumed here by *objet petit a*, because it contains *nothing*:

> Suddenly these two wheeled out from the mass of dancers, dived into one of the pools of the heath, and came out somewhere into an iridescent *hollow*, arched with rainbows. 'It must be here', said the voice by her side, and blushingly looking up she saw him removing his casque to kiss her. At that moment there was a cracking noise, and his figure fell into fragments like a pack of cards.
> She cried aloud, 'O that I had seen his face'.
>
> *RN* p. 118, my italics

So far Eustacia is just an ordinary young girl who dreams of meeting her Prince Charming some day. We are clearly in the realm of fantasy. What is at work is the scopic drive: to see her partner is what Eustacia really wants—but her desire remains unfulfilled. For the object-gaze is prohibited, invisible, outside the visual field—in that sense it is the *cause* of desire. As long as Eustacia sees with her ears, she is safe. Things will be reversed much later, in the scene where she dances with Wildeve in the moonlight. Very little is said of the "lusty notes" played by the East Egdon band. Instead, we have visual notations (the blue waggon with its red wheels), and it is *the sound of silence* that makes itself heard as the brass instruments turn into huge eyes gleaming in darkness:

> The air became quite still, the flag above the wagon which held the musicians clung to the pole, and the players appeared only in outline against the sky; except when the circular mouths of the trombone, ophicleide, and French horn gleamed out like huge eyes from the shade of their figures.
>
> *RN* p. 263

The eye is now included in the field of vision, while sound is replaced by sight—we now *hear with our eyes*. The effect produced by such a substitution is utter silence. The logic of "the voice that gives body to what we can never see, to what eludes our gaze" has been reversed into "an image that renders present the failure of the voice—an image can emerge as a placeholder for a sound that does not yet resonate but remains stuck in the throat" (Žižek, 1996, p. 93). Hardy's text places its reader in exactly the same position as that of the person looking at Munch's *Scream*:[1] "Munch's *Scream*," argues Žižek, "is by definition silent: in front of this painting, we 'hear (the scream) with our eyes'" (Žižek, 1996, pp. 93–94). However, to see what one cannot hear is not the same as to hear what one cannot see, for "voice vivifies, whereas gaze mortifies" (Žižek, 1996, p. 94). Therefore hearing with one's eyes always has an uncanny dimension, it is the sign of an impending doom:

> Far more horrifying than to see with our ears—to hear the vibrating life substance beyond visual representations, this blind spot in the field of the visible—is to hear with our eyes, that is, to hear the absolute silence that marks the suspension of life, as in Caravaggio's *Testa di Medusa*: is not the scream of Medusa by definition silent, 'stuck in the throat'? Does this painting not provide an image of the moment at which the voice fails?
>
> ŽIŽEK (1996, p. 94)

The reason for this is structural: we can only hear a sound resonate because there is a void somewhere (after all it stands to reason that resonance can only take place in a vacuum): voice, writes Žižek, "points toward a gap in the field of the visible, toward the dimension of what eludes our gaze" (Žižek, 1996, p. 93). Therefore, if nothing eludes our gaze, if no gap hollows out the visual field, if we can see everything, sound cannot reverberate: "*ultimately, we hear things because we cannot see everything*" (Žižek, 1996, p. 93). Then we are left with only one possibility: to hear with our eyes, to hear the "absolute, deadly silence, supreme fascination and horror" (Poizat, 1986/1992, p. 92). And what this absolute silence of death makes us hear is the inaudible object-voice:

> The voice qua object is precisely what is 'stuck in the throat', what cannot burst out, unchain itself and thus enter the dimension of subjectivity. It is by no accident that, in his *Four Fundamental Concepts*, Lacan determines the *object small a* as the bone which got stuck in the subject's

1 The issue is further complicated by the fact that we use our eyes to read the text, and that the text is by defintion a silent text—unless the reader should lend it his voice.

> throat: if the exemplary case of the gaze *qua* object is a blind man's eyes, i.e. eyes which do not see (we experience the gaze *qua* object when a partner in conversation suddenly takes off his black glasses, exposing us to the uneasy depthless white of his eyes), then the exemplary case of the voice *qua* object is a voice which remains silent, i.e., which we do not hear.
>
> ŽIŽEK (2001, p. 117)

Michel Poizat makes a similar point when, In *L'Opéra ou le cri de lange*, he takes up Lacan's assertion that "the cry is the abyss for silence to rush into" (Poizat, 1986/1992, p. 90[2]) and goes on to argue that silence is what best makes present the object-voice:

> Just as the empty socket in the skull is what best makes immediate, or 'makes present', what Lacan called the seeing object [*l'objet-regard*], so the silence we are given to hear by the cry—the cry that by 'rending the silence' also lets it be heard—is what best gives presence to the vocal object, paradoxical though this may seem.
>
> POIZAT (1986/1992, p. 85)

We have seen that, in Hardy's novels, what is missing is "a gap in the field of the visible." It is the lack of a lack which causes anxiety in real life, ruin and devastation in the diegesis of the tragic novels. In *The Return of the Native*, the object-gaze is a near presence, a surplus-object which often assumes the form of a red stain. In *Tess of the d'Urbervilles*, the "madder stain" is in excess of reality, a "spot" that fills the structural void, giving presence to what should remain absent. This is made clear in the passage that shows Angel walking away from Sandbourne after leaving Tess. He unconsciously looks back:

> Why he did so he could not say, but something impelled him to the act. The tape-like surface of the road diminished in his rear as far as he could see, and as he gazed a moving spot intruded on the white vacuity of its perspective.
>
> *TESS* p. 371

Angel's gaze is arrested by an object that forms a stain on a particular point of his visual field, the vanishing point of perspective. And of course the choice of the word "spot" is significant, for indeed it is Tess who is running behind him

2 "Le cri fait gouffre ou le silence se rue," Lacan, "Problèmes cruciaux de psychanalyse," unpublished seminar of 17 March 1965.

after murdering Alec—and in Polanski's film, she wears a beautiful crimson dress, as though the "murderess" had become an incarnation of the "scarlet blot" formed on Mrs Brooks's ceiling, as though she herself *were* the stain. The "spot" comes as a surplus, it occupies "the white vacuity" of the perspective. It is therefore no other than a figure of the object-gaze, the object that should be "extracted" from the field of vision. The intrusion of the red stain into the field of the gaze indicates that Angel is now entering "a sphere where death encroaches on life" (Lacan, 1986a/2008, p. 351). The question which arises then concerns voice: the logical inference that should be drawn from this analysis is that voice in the diegesis of *Tess of the d'Urbervilles* should be muted, "stuck in the throat." When the gap in the field of the visible is missing, when no blind spot eludes our gaze, voice cannot be resonant.[3] Will our reading of the text confirm a hypothesis which, in Lacan's logic, appears as a structural necessity? Is hearing with one's eyes a recurrent pattern in *Tess of the d'Urbervilles*?

5.2 Tess's Silent Cry

The question of voice, especially Tess's voice, has been broached by several outstanding critics. Tess as a "muted" heroine is the subject of Margaret R. Higonnet's "A Woman's Story: Tess and the Problem of Voice." Starting from the feminist debate on whether it is possible for a male writer's narrative to "translate the language of women, a 'muted' group, into that of his own dominant group" (Higonnet, p. 14[4]), Higonnet focuses on the ways in which voice is "gendered," on "the complexity—even inconsistency—of the narrative voice" (Higonnet, p. 25), and finally wonders "whether silence expresses the ineffable, or more simply records the unspeakable, and the most pervasive form of violence against women" (Higonnet, p. 28). Penny Boumelha argues that "Tess is most herself—and that is, most woman—at points when she is dumb and semi-conscious." For within Hardy's ideological system, she claims, "sex and nature are assigned to the female, intellect and culture to the male" (Boumelha, 1985, p. 122). Jennifer Gribble draws attention to Eustacia as "The Quiet Woman of Egdon Heath," to the crucial importance of "withheld speech" (Gribble, p. 526), and argues that "it is when she is quietest that Eustacia is most

3 I deliberately set aside for the moment the question of the literary voice, which will be studied in a later section.

4 Higonnet gives a reference to Elaine Showalter, "Feminist Criticism in the Wilderness," in *The New Feminist Criticism: Essays on Women, Literature, and Theory*, ed. Elaine Showalter, New York: Pantheon, 1985, p. 262.

interesting" (Gribble, p. 530). It then appears that Tess (or Eustacia) as a muted heroine has attracted the notice of major critics. There is no doubt that the muted feminine voice is a central issue in Hardy's novels—one might even go as far as reading *Tess of the d'Urbervilles* as "a metanarrative about voice" (Higonnet, p. 26).

Indeed, as has often been remarked, Tess proves unable to speak when it would be vital for her to do so. So does Eustacia, so does Elfride Swancourt, and so does Henchard. But there is something more in Tess's silence—to paraphrase *Richard II* one might say that "more's heard" in her silence than in a voice muted by social constraint. For Tess's voice has a strange quality, as though it were choked, throttled, stuck in her throat. For instance when she leaves Marlott: "'Good bye, father', said Tess with a lumpy throat [...] Tess's eyes were too full and her voice too choked to utter the sentiments that were in her" (*Tess* p. 53). After receiving her mother's letter, she resolves to keep silent about "that haunting incident of bygone days" ("silence seemed, on the face of it, best for her adored one's happiness: silence it should be" *Tess* p. 192); but then she finds herself struggling "with the sob in her throat" as she tells Angel he should have loved her when she was sixteen (*Tess* p. 195). At Wellbridge, "her voice grew husky" (*Tess* p. 235). Later, in a discussion with Alec, she can neither speak fluently ("her fluency failed her" *Tess* p. 319) nor swallow her food ("she could not get her morsels of food down her throat; her lips were dry, and she was ready to choke" *Tess* p. 320). The same sensation is experienced on another of Alec's visits: "Tess again shook her head; her throat swelling with complicated emotion" (*Tess* p. 342). Margaret Higonnet comments on the "stopt-diapason note" acquired by Tess's voice when her heart "was in her speech" (*Tess* p. 99), which "reminds us of the 'stops' in Tess's speech, the breaks that mark the muffling of her story" (Higonnet, p. 20). Tess will eventually write a letter to Angel (and that letter will reach its addressee), but to *voice* her feelings is what she cannot do. Tess's voice is muffled sound, suppressed (or "withheld") speech, and her silences are not like the pauses that can punctuate speech in a system of signifying oppositions. The failure of her voice is not a form of "linguistic silence,"[5] it does not contribute to the emergence of meaning. Like the "soundlessness" of the garden at Talbothays, it impresses the reader "as a positive entity rather than as the mere negation of noise" (*Tess* p. 127). It could be described by an oxymoron, "silence audible," or by another formula, "the sound of silence." Michel Poizat distinguishes between two kinds of silences:

---

5 See Lecercle, 2013. Also Ramel, 2013b.

> There is the silence, that cuts the phonic continuum with its presence, that, through repetition, rhythmic pulsation, sets off the scansion of presence and absence and brings forth the signifier, the Word. But it may also cease to work away at the sonorous material; it may cease to beat, may yield its place entirely to the sonorous real in all its continuity without cutting it apart. The drive to effacement, this death instinct—for it is indeed a matter of the death instinct—will itself disappear and become silent—the silence of the drives—abandoning the field, after experiencing the emptiness of its object, to the continuous 'real', which, escaping all symbolizing processes as well as all naming, is cast out forever into absolute, deadly silence, supreme fascination and horror.
>
> POIZAT (1986/1992, p. 92)

Tess's silence definitely belongs to the second category, in which voice jettisons sense and becomes pure vibratory substance, "continuous material," some kind of "sonorous real."[6] Impelled by the "drive to effacement" (so strong in *Tess of the d'Urbervilles*), such a voice aspires to the condition of silence—a deadly silence which both fascinates and repels, because it gives presence to the inaudible vocal object.

In *Tess of the d'Urbervilles,* all sound aspires to the condition of silence. For instance, in the May-day dance scene at Marlott, nothing is said of the music to which the girls are dancing. For all we know, the club-walkers could be dancing *in silence*—and yet there is a band, whose "faint notes" are "the only human sounds audible within the rim of blue hill," as briefly mentioned in the previous chapter (*Tess* p.17). In the dance-scene itself, the band is not mentioned again, we are left to imagine it, to assume that some tune is being played while the girls are whirling about on the pasture. The schema here is exactly the same as in the scene where Eustacia dances with Wildeve: *we hear with our eyes*. The only notations of sound are Durbeyfield's recitative about his "gr't-family-vault-at-Kingsbere," the titter of the clubbists and Tess's reaction, then a narratorial aside about Tess's characteristic intonation (*Tess* p. 21). The general

6 The failure of *logos* in Tess's speech is conspicuous in the sentences where she endlessly repeats "yes" or "no." Tess was unable to say "no" to Alec the seducer: "I don't know—I wish—how can I say yes or no when—" (*Tess* p. 74). Pressed by Angel to accept him as a husband, she can say neither "yes" nor "no." Her answers are pure sonorous continuum, with dashes that cut into it without producing any meaning: "'Do you say no? Surely you love me?' 'O yes, yes!' […] 'You are engaged to marry some one else!' 'No, no!' 'Then why do you refuse me?' 'I don't want to marry […] I feel I cannot—never, never'" (*Tess* p. 173; see also pp. 175, 182, 188, 190, 198).

tendency of the narrative is to displace *pronouncing* and *eloquence* from the register of hearing to that of seeing: Tess is said to be the only one of the white company "who could boast of such a *pronounced* adornment" (*Tess* p. 20, my italics); "her mobile peony mouth and large innocent eyes added *eloquence* to colour and shape" (*Tess* p. 20, my italics[7]). Quite remarkably, all the dance-scenes in *Tess of the d'Urbervilles* and *The Return of the Native* take place in complete silence—a surprising fact when one remembers that Hardy was a musician who played in village-bands when he was a boy. During the dance at Chaseborough, all sounds are dampened by the carpet of *debris* of peat and hay tramped over by the dancers: "no sound of dancing was audible, an exceptional state of things for those parts, where as a rule the stamping drowned the music" (*Tess* p. 66). The fiddles are inaudible: "the muted fiddles feebly pushed their notes" (*Tess* p. 66). Instead of hearing the music, we see the "mist of yellow radiance" stirred by the feet of the dancers. It would be hazardous to deduce from these examples that Hardy's writing relies on sight rather than sound as a privileged mode of perception—for Hardy the novelist was also a poet (as well as a musician). The passage I am writing about is remarkable for the obsessive repetition of the consonant /f/ ("forms," "figure," "footfalls," "scroff," "floating fusty debris," "fiddles," "feebly," "failing," etc. *Tess* pp. 66–67), which gives to the text a poetic quality. Provided we lend our voice to the *silent* literary text, we can hear "the sound of silence," the muted music raised by the turbulent feet of the dancers and its transposition in words (*Tess* p. 127). And this "sonorous silence" has a special appeal for us. Again, what we hear is muted sound—very different from the crystal-clear sound of the pony's shoes "which clashed like cymbals at every tread" (*RN* p. 410) when Thomasin and Venn are travelling home in the final chapter of *The Return of the Native*, once Clym has found his "vocation." No one has found his "vocation" here, resonance cannot take place, voice remains "stuck in the throat." We hear with our eyes the silence of the object-voice.

The most characteristic passage is that in which Tess, after making her confession to Angel,[8] is struck dumb when Angel tells her that she is a different person from the woman he loved. No cry resonates, but a silent cry forms on her lips, soundlessly:

> She perceived in his words the realization of her own apprehensive forebodings in former times. He looked upon her as a species of impostor, a

7 Elsewhere, we are told that "her eyes grew larger and more eloquent" (*Tess* p. 103).

8 The confession itself is a narrative gap, one of the much debated narrative gaps in the novel. See Higonnet, pp. 26–27.

> guilty woman in the guise of an innocent one. Terror was upon her white face as she saw it; her cheek was flaccid, and her mouth had almost the aspect of a round little hole.[9]
>
> *TESS* p. 227

The effect produced by Tess's silent cry is all the more striking as we read this a few lines further down:

> 'Angel', she said suddenly in her natural tones, *the insane dry voice of terror* having left her now, 'Angel, am I too wicked for you and me to live together?'.
>
> *TESS* p. 227, my italics

What does that "insane dry voice of terror" refer to? Tess has just uttered two sentences mechanically, automatically, as an echo to Angel's speech: "'I don't belong to you any more, then; do I Angel?' she asked helplessly. 'It is not me, but another woman like me that he loved, he says'" (*Tess* p. 227). One might aptly apply the adjective "dry" to Tess's unemotional voice[10] here, but insanity and terror are noticeably absent from Tess's speech. "Terror" is visible on Tess's face, not audible. In fact it is her *eyes* that appear insane, "eyes such as to make his flesh creep"—again we find that sound has been displaced from the register of hearing to that of seeing. The "insane dry voice of terror" refers to Tess's silent cry, to her mouth which looks "like a round little hole." We have been made *to hear with our eyes*, exactly as in Munch's *Scream*, or in Caravaggio's *Testa di Medusa*. What the two paintings and this scene have in common is that they make the failure of voice visible, they show a sound that does not resonate but remains "stuck in the throat."

Another striking similarity between Munch's painting and *Tess of the d'Urbervilles* is the association between the silent cry and redness. Red is present in the blood-red sky above the homunculus, a fact which is underlined by the prose poem Munch wrote to go with his picture: "I walked along the road with two friends—/ and the sun went down / The sky suddenly became blood—and I felt / as if a breath of sadness / I stopped—leaned against the

9 Cf Mladen Dolar's commentary on Munch's *The Scream*, which is quite relevant to the "round little hole" of Tess's mouth: "The painted scream is by definition mute, stuck in the throat; the black opening is without the voice which would mollify it, fill it, endow it with sense, hence its resonance is all the greater" (Dolar, 2006, p. 69).

10 "a dry voice" is "a voice showing no emotion" (*Longman Dictionary of Contemporary English*).

railing / Tired to death."[11] In another text, Munch claimed that he painted the clouds "as actual blood," and that "the colour shrieked."[12] Now in Hardy's novel, we also sense that the red stain is a silent cry: Tess does not speak, she cannot voice her feelings, but the madder stain that ear-marks her somehow speaks *instead of her*. It works like a silent cry. Hardy's text says this unambiguously in the passage about the "vermilion words" painted on a stile by a religious fanatic: "these staring vermilion words shone forth. They seemed to shout themselves out, and to make the atmosphere ring" (*Tess* p. 85). The passage is remarkable in that the red mark here functions like an object-gaze, exactly like the red seal affixed on the Valentine card received by Boldwood, which becomes "a blot of blood on the retina of his eye" (*FFMC* p. 80). It is as though an omniscient Other knew about Tess and her misfortune, as if his gaze entered her and reached her at the very point from which she sees. The split between the eye and the gaze is annulled here, for Tess is in a relation of perfect reflexivity with the writing, which sends back to her an image of herself as a "fallen" woman. One might argue that the red letters impose upon Tess a vision of herself as sinful, the view of a patriarchal society which Tess rejects as untrue, as alien to her own intimate conviction. That is partly true, but there is something more in this passage, something uncanny in the fact that the red letters *see* Tess, while it is Tess who is looking at them. The vermilion words function like an omnivoyant eye "staring" at her. The stile, which has undergone "hideous defacement" (*Tess* p. 85), turns into a mirror-image of Tess—for it is Tess who has a "face" and is being "de-faced," or disfigured, by the crushing, killing words. Tess turns red like the scarlet letters when "a sudden flush" appears on her face, and the "nice bit of blank wall" has a "strange and unwonted mien" (*Tess* p. 86)—a "mien" usually refers to a person's expression, and the adjective "blank" cannot fail to remind the reader of the "feminine tissue," "practically *blank* as snow as yet," on which a "coarse pattern" has just been traced (*Tess* p. 77, my italics). The wall (or the stile) functions like Tess's double, in a perfect mirror-relation where no blind spot eludes the eye's grasp. As Žižek argues, "the horror of coming face to face with my double is that this encounter reduces me

11 Bente Torjusen, *Words and Images of Edvard Munch*, London: Thames and Hudson, 1989, p. 136.

12 "One evening I was walking along a path, the city was on one side and the fjord below. I felt tired and ill. I stopped and looked out over the fjord—the sun was setting, and the clouds turning blood red. I sensed a scream passing through nature; it seemed to me that I heard the scream. I painted this picture, painted the clouds as actual blood. The color shrieked. This became *The Scream*." "Quick Facts: Munch's *The Scream*." In *Becoming Edvard Munch* (2013). <http://www.artic.edu/aic/collections/exhibitions/Munch/resource/171> (10 November 2014).

to the object-gaze."[13] The red mark makes present the gaze of the Other, in a horrible confusion that annuls the discordance between the gaze and the (subject's) eye.

Even more remarkable is the fact that the "staring vermilion words" seem to "shout themselves out, and to make the atmosphere ring": for what we hear is a silent cry, some kind of "silence audible," the clamour sent abroad by those silent red letters painted on a stile. That pattern is characteristic of the novel as a whole—a novel whose heroine can never voice her complaint or her lament, but who is marked by a "madder stain" endowed with a vocal quality. Just as a colour in English can be said to be "loud" or "clamorous," the red stain catches the eye with an irresistible power, and makes us hear the sound of silence. Giving presence to the object-gaze, it also makes audible the inaudible vocal object, in a perfectly logical way: for we only hear things because we cannot see everything, and we are here in the (impossible) situation where no gap hollows out the visual field. Therefore we can only hear with our eyes. Only silence can be resonant. The red stain is what makes present the failure of the voice, it is "a placeholder for a sound that does not yet resonate but remain stuck in the throat" (Žižek, 1996, p. 93). The stain may occasionally assume a different colour: for instance the turnip-slicing machine at Flintcomb Ash has been painted in blue, and the colour rings out like a voice: "On the sheltered side was a turnip-slicing machine, whose bright blue hue of new paint seemed almost vocal in the otherwise subdued scene" (*Tess* p. 305). The idea of an image that can serve as "a placeholder" for a sound that does not resonate is essential to my argument, which is that the "madder stain" is a silent cry: something which is shown in the field of the gaze in *lieu* of the voice. Tess's voice cannot be heard, and *instead* we see "a spot like a paint-mark set upon her" (*Tess* p. 215). Tess's silence and the "chain of red things" are interconnected, if we follow Lacan's logic. Tess cannot make her voice resonant because of the presence of a surplus object in the visual field—but conversely a red stain ear-marks Tess because her voice is "stuck in the throat." A passage which makes this interrelation clear is the one where Tess and Angel discover that the chimney-corner has been renovated overnight by Farmer Crick as a preparation for their wedding: "At some unnatural hour of the morning the dairyman had caused

---

13 "In other words, the part missing in the mirror image of myself (the "" of the axis aa') is my own gaze, the object-gaze which sees me out there... As a rule one focuses on the horror of being the object of some inivisible, panoptical gaze (the 'someone-is-watching-me' motif)—yet it is a far more unbearable experience to find oneself at the very point of this pure gaze" (Žižek, 2001, p. 126).

the yawning chimney corner to be whitened, and the brick hearth reddened" (*Tess* p. 208). The red hearth now stands out against the white background of the chimney corner, exactly as the red ribbon in Tess's hair contrasts with her white gown in the Mayday dance. And the explanation given by the dairyman is remarkable:

> I was determined to do summat in honour o't', said the dairyman. 'And as you wouldn't hear of my gieing a rattling good randy wi' fiddles and bass-viols complete, as we should ha' done in old times, this was all I could think o' as a noiseless thing.
>
> *TESS* p. 208

This new decoration, "a noiseless thing," has been chosen *as a substitute* for the noisy wedding ceremony that the farmer would have preferred, but that Angel would not "hear of."

The same motif is found in the passage where "madder stains" appear on Tess's arms: Tess is drawn "like a fascinated bird" towards the "spot" whence come the notes played by Angel in the garden at Talbothays. Here too, sound is displaced from its own register to the visual field, we (and Tess) *hear with our eyes* the music which is supposed to fill Tess with exquisite joy:

> She undulated upon the thin notes of the second-hand harp, and their harmonies passed like breezes through her, bringing tears into her eyes. The floating pollen seemed to be his notes made visible, and the dampness of the garden the weeping of the garden's sensibility. Though near nightfall, the rank-smelling weed-flowers glowed as if they would not close for intentness, and the waves of colour mixed with the waves of sound.
>
> *TESS* p. 127–128

What causes Tess's ecstasy, then? Certainly not Angel's poor playing on a second-hand harp. I wish to argue that, rather than music, what Tess enjoys is the "soundlessness" which impresses her "as a positive entity rather than as the mere negation of noise" (*Tess* p. 127). This soundlessness, we are told, is "broken by the strumming of strings." Should we consider, then, that silence here is the backdrop against which the music is heard? No, that traditional conception must be reversed: for music in this scene is the backdrop against which the "positive entity" of soundlessness is audible. Michel Poizat, quoting from Vladimir Jankelevitch's *Music and the Ineffable*, shows that there are two ways of conceiving the relation between silence and music:

> A moment ago, living diversity broke through the uniform oceanography of ennui—that is, troubled a pre-existent and underlying continuum: silence was the resonant backdrop beneath being: and now noise is the resonant backdrop that stretches beneath silence.[14]

In the garden scene, what can be heard against the backdrop of Angel's poor performance is the pure silence of the object-voice, a sort of "silence audible" which exists in a delicately-poised state of quasi-audibility—like Tess's voice. Like Tess's silent cry which the "chain of red things" makes manifest all along the novel.

There is one single instance where a sonorous cry actually rises from Tess's lips: it is the "dirge" heard by Mrs Brooks when she is eavesdropping at the door of the d'Urbervilles' apartment. Mrs Brooks is the focalizer and, rather curiously, she does not see what is happening (she only has a partial view of Tess when she looks through the keyhole). But she sees with her ears. What she hears is a "murmur of unspeakable despair," "a dirge rather than a soliloquy" (*Tess* p. 368). Here the narrative is interspersed with dashes and suspension marks, while the numerous "O's" form "round little holes" on the page, which cannot fail to remind us of Tess's dumb mouth:

> All that she [Mrs Brooks] could at first distinguish [...] was one syllable, continually repeated, in a low tone of moaning, as if it came from a soul bound to some Ixonian wheel:
> 'Oh—oh—oh!'
> Then a silence, then a heavy sigh; and again,
> 'Oh—oh—oh!' [...]
> 'O yes, I have lost him now [...] O you have torn my life all in pieces. ... made me be what I prayed you in pity not to make me be again! ...My own true husband will never never—O God—I can't bear this! I cannot!'.
>
> *TESS* p. 368

Mrs Brooks has to retreat to her own parlour below, and from now on she hears nothing (apart from the rustle of Tess's clothes): "she could hear nothing through the floor, though she listened intently" (*Tess* p. 369). No cry is released

14 Vladimir Jankelevitch, *Music and the Ineffable*, quoted in Poizat, 1986/1992, p. 125. Poizat deduces from this that music is "a way of silence" because its "noise" silences the other noises which form the "backcloth" against which it is heard.

by the dying man[15] —at any rate no cry reaches the householder's ears. A "dead silence" prevails, soon broken by a regular beat, "drip, drip, drip." Instead of a cry, we have a "spot" in the middle of the white surface of the ceiling, which Mrs Brooks had never seen before. It is a red spot, a "scarlet blot" which rapidly grows into "a gigantic ace of hearts." Seeing with one's ears has been replaced by hearing with one's eyes. The red stain here has the same function as in the rest of the novel: it resonates like a silent cry.

5.3 The Vocal Object: Feminine or Masculine?

Viewing the "madder stain" as a silent cry is a radical shift from the visual field to the register of sound. Such a shift may remind one of the process described by Poizat in opera, when "all that is visual and all that tends toward signification fails and falls." It may be paradoxical, argues Poizat, to speak of a "falling away," or "failure," of the visual order, because "no stage presentation draws more heavily on its visual elements than opera" (Poizat, 1986/1992, p. 32). Yet what happens in certain musical passages, *most particularly when a woman is singing*, is "an acute, irrepressible irruption" of *jouissance* that makes the audience oblivious of the words, forgetful of all the elaborate visual elements that compose the set of a scene. Then the spectator closes his eyes and allows himself to be ravished, penetrated by the voice of the *Diva*, whose singing becomes "pure music free of all ties to speech," a music that "literally destroys speech in favor of a purely musical melody, a melody that develops little by little until it verges on the cry" (Poizat, 1986/1992, p. 37). Such is the power of the visual *punctum* represented by the madder stain in *Tess of the d'Urbervilles*: it "shoots out" of the *studium* like an arrow, it pierces us, but its poignancy reaches a paroxysm when we ultimately lose sight of it and become only conscious of the pure silence that it makes audible—and after all a literary text is first of all *a voice* that makes you hear the silence. The shift from gaze to voice carries us further away from the "phallic" economy (as schematized by Lacan's matheme for fantasy $ *a*), into a "beyond" where may be enjoyed a moment of unspeakable ecstasy, comparable to the ecstasy of Saint Teresa when she is pierced by an arrow from an angel: when the visual *punctum* piercing us turns into a silent cry, we too are pierced by a composite emotion which is both pleasure and pain; and whether we are a man or a woman we abandon our

---

15 "Pourquoi ne crie-t-il pas cet homme?" (*Salomé*, Richard Strauss, quoted in Poizat, 1986/2001, p. 192; Poizat, 1986/1992, p. 137).

"phallic" position[16] to surrender ourselves to the "Other" *jouissance* drawing us towards the "barred" Other, noted by Lacan's matheme S(Ⱥ). If "the voice is the flesh of the soul, its ineradicable materiality, by which the soul can never be rid of the body" (Dolar, 2006, p. 71), it clearly inhabits that "Beyondsex" where the *soul* is involved (as I have shown in my chapter on the feminine[17]), the "feminine" side of Lacan's graph of sexuation.

Malden Dolar makes this very point when he shows that "*there is a dichotomy of the voice and the signifier,*" and that the voice is "a cast-off of sense" (Dolar, 2006, p. 16). Voice, he writes, is "*what does not contribute to making sense.* It is the material element recalcitrant to meaning" (Dolar, 2006, p. 15), "a non-signifying remainder resistant to the signifying operation, a leftover heterogeneous to structural logic" (Dolar, 2006, p. 36). And in that dichotomy, he concludes, voice is on the side of femininity:

> The voice beyond sense is self-evidently equated with femininity, whereas the text, the instance of signification, is in this simple paradigmatic opposition on the side of masculinity. (Some four thousand years later, Wagner will write in a famous letter to Liszt: '*Die Musik ist ein Weib*', music is a woman). The voice beyond the words is a sensuous play of sensuality, it is a dangerous attractive force, although in itself empty and frivolous. The dichotomy of voice and *logos* is already in place.
>
> DOLAR (2006, p. 43)

"The voice that sets itself loose from the word, the voice beyond logos, the lawless voice" (Dolar, 2006, p. 45) is obviously feminine: "the voice is boundless, warrantless, and—no coincidence—on the side of woman" (Dolar, 2006, p. 51). No wonder if the flute is an instrument deemed fit for women, for "one cannot

16 If we look at Lacan's graph of sexuation, we see that on the masculine side *jouissance* "is not related to the Other as such" (Lacan, 1975/1998, p. 9) but to *objet a*, the cause of desire. Of course the object has two sides, *agalma* and *palea*, and the "bright" side of the object, whether visual or vocal, may be overturned to reveal *palea*, the horror, the abyss of S(Ⱥ). Such a reversal gives access to a certain mode of *jouissance* where the death-drive plays a prominent part and which should be inscribed on the "feminine" side of the graph of sexuation. Yet Lacan makes a subtle distinction between "making oneself heard" and "making oneself seen": "Whereas making oneself seen is indicated by an arrow that really comes back towards the subject, making oneself heard goes towards the other. The reason for this is a structural one" (Lacan, 1973/1986b, p. 195). Could one deduce from that a natural propensity for voice to tend towards S(Ⱥ)?

17 See Chapter 2 of this book. Cf "the soul souloves the soul (*l'âme âme l'âme*)" (Lacan, 1975/1998, p. 84).

utter words while playing the flute" (Dolar, 2006, p. 45). So the flute as an "impediment" to the use of the voice was considered improper for men ("the impediment which the flute presents to the use of the voice detracts from its educational value. The ancients therefore were right in forbidding the flute to youths and freemen"[18]). And therefore the flute was better suited to women—or to whoever indulged in forms of enjoyment beyond the signifier ("Bacchic frenzy and all similar emotions are most suitably expressed by the flute," Aristotle, quoted in Dolar, 2006, p. 46). It is therefore no surprise for us when Tess's voice is described as "fluty" ("what a fluty voice one of those milkmaids has" *Tess* p. 124, "her tones suddenly resuming their own fluty pathos" *Tess* p. 365). For a "fluty" voice has a musicality which is an impediment to communication and a challenge to *logos* (as the saying goes, *prima la musica e dopo le parole*).[19] The voice beyond the signifier, writes Dolar, "opens the perspective of the Lacanian problem of feminine *jouissance* (which Lacan himself tackled precisely through the women mystics)" (Dolar, 1991, p. 22). Michel Poizat has underlined the ecstatic dimension of the *jouissance* involved in a woman's voice, especially in opera—and especially in the "pure" cry of a woman.[20]

But then, argues Poizat, we should not be deluded by the fantasy of "pure" voice as feminine, a fantasy which ascribes *logos* to men and voice to women. We should not be taken in by a male fantasy based on gender roles. However, he argues, that fantasy is anchored in structural reality. For there is a "similarity" between "the structure of the object, resulting from the way it is constituted" and the structure of some masculine fantasies about the feminine, one being "superimposed" upon the other, as a certain image of woman takes on the same contours as the vocal object. This "encounter" (*rencontre au sommet*) between Woman and the Voice is beautifully formulated by Poizat:

> Elusive and inaccessible, evanescent or non-existent, the cause of desire, the locus of lack, and the nullification of lack, locus of jouissance both infinite and impossible, alluring and forbidden, death-ridden and deadly, trans-sensual and trans-sexual,[21] heavenly voice or hellish cry, angel or

18 Aristotle (2001). *The Basic Writings of Aristotle, Politics* VIII, 1341a, pp. 23–27. New York: Modern Library. Quoted in Dolar, 2006, p. 46.

19 Fanny's voice, in *Far from the Madding Crowd*, is such a voice: "The voice was unexpectedly attractive; it was the low and dulcet note suggestive of romance, common in descriptions, rare in experience. 'I'll thank you to tell me if I'm in the way for Warren's Malthouse?' Gabriel resumed, primarily to gain the information, indirectly to get more of the music" (*FFMC* p. 43). Fanny too will remain silent and will bind Gabriel to silence.

20 Cf the chapter of *The Angel's Cry* entitled "Woman's Cry, Man's Word," pp. 137–140.

21 "Beyond sense and beyond sex" would have been a better translation, in my opinion.

> demon, The Voice and The Woman come together in these tightly woven fantasies.
>
> POIZAT (1986/1992, p. 156)

If we are to dissociate fantasies about woman from the structure of the vocal object, we must bear in mind that Lacan's graph of sexuation distinguishes between two modes of *jouissance*, supposedly "masculine" and "feminine," but any speaking being may choose to situate himself/herself on either side of the graph. Any one, whether or not "provided with the attributes of masculinity," may position himself/herself on the side where is inscribed "the woman portion of speaking beings": "one is not obliged, when one is male, to situate oneself on the side of $\forall x \phi x$. One can situate oneself on the side of the not-whole. There are men who are just as good as women" (Lacan, 1975/1998, p. 76). And among such men, of course, we find artists—musicians, painters, but also poets and novelists like Hardy. It is important to make that point, because if we fail to do so we miss an essential element: the intimate connection between the voice of Hardy's heroines and the voice of the text—the "textual voice" that Claude Maisonnat writes about (Maisonnat, pp. 164–180). Saying that the *jouissance* involved in the voice is the "Other" *jouissance* (and not simply a woman's enjoyment in a "simple paradigmatic opposition," Dolar, 2006, p. 43) opens up perspectives where the literary text may be studied as a (silent) voice—that will be the task undertaken in the final section of this book.

Another question is raised and discussed by Dolar: a "simple paradigm" has been drawn so far he says, an opposition between *logos* and voice as an instrument of enjoyment; but that division is not exhaustive for "there is another kind of voice, the voice of the Father, the voice that inherently sticks to *logos* itself, the voice that commands and binds, the voice of God" (Dolar, 2006, p. 52). And he reminds us that when Lacan introduces the question of the vocal object in his seminar on anxiety, his reference is to Yahweh's voice and to *schofar*, a primitive instrument used in Jewish religious rituals.[22] The strange thing about *schofar* is that it is a voice "that commands total compliance" ("by hearing this voice, the community of believers establishes its covenant, its alliance with God; they assert their submission and obedience to the law" Dolar, 2006, p. 53), yet it is "senseless in itself," for it is just "the prolonged sound reminiscent of a bull roaring" (Dolar, 2006, p. 53). It is mimetic of the roaring of a "stunned bull":[23] it makes us hear the voice of the dying Father (as being

22 Cf "La voix de Yahvé," Chapter XVIII, pp. 281–295, in Lacan, 2004.

23 "C'est son beuglement de taureau assommé qui se fait entendre encore dans le son du schofar" (Lacan, 2004, p. 295).

murdered in the *Totem and Taboo* myth of the murder of the Father). On what side of the graph of sexuation is the voice of *schofar* to be inscribed, then? On the "phallic" side, the side of the Law that achieves symbolic castration? Or on the "feminine" side, where voice is but a senseless left-over, a remainder of the *jouissance* prohibited by the Law? Is the voice of *schofar* a vehicle for imposing the *Letter* of the Law, or does it make audible the Lacanian *letter* as "litter,"[24] the useless object that comes in excess of meaning? A possible answer could be that *schofar*, exactly like the "decadent" feminine voice detaining in its inflexions some remnant of the lost object-voice, bears witness to the "not-all" of castration: a part of the voice escapes the totalizing action of the phallic function (it will not be inscribed on the side of $\forall x \phi x$); there is indeed an irreducible *jouissance*, a surplus object, in excess of the signifier, which remains unextracted, "stuck in the throat," in defiance of the Law and its commands. Dolar comes to wonder whether those two voices (the voice that bears the Word and the voice that bears feminine enjoyment) are not after all two sides of the same coin:

> Is the voice of the Father of an altogether different species from the feminine voice? Does the voice of the persecutor differ sharply from the voice of the persecuted?
>
> DOLAR (2006, p. 56)

He comes to the conclusion that "there are not two voices, but only the object voice which cleaves and bars the other in an ineradicable 'extimacy'" (Dolar, 2006, p. 55). That "bar" placed on the Other, which Lacan has designated by S(Ⱥ), is "the point of the always-missing ultimate signifier which would totalize the Other, the point of the absent foundation of the Law, and also the point which has an intrinsic relation with femininity and the non-existence of the Woman" (Dolar, 2006, p. 56). For after all, as Lacan has noted, "why not interpret one face of the Other, the God face, as supported by feminine *jouissance*?" (Lacan, 1975/1998, p. 77)

Indeed the question of voice is essential to *The Mayor of Casterbridge*. Henchard, faced with the vital necessity of explaining his acts, remains dumb: "Henchard's lips half-parted, to begin an explanation; but he shut them up like a vice, and uttered not a sound" (*MC* p. 327). Yet at the beginning of the novel, his voice is "commanding" (*MC* p. 34), "thunderous" (*MC* p. 168), such a loud voice as "might have been heard as far as the town pump expressing his

24 "A litter, a litter, une lettre, une ordure" ("Le séminaire sur la lettre volée," Lacan, 1966, p. 25).

feelings to his fellow councilmen" (*MC* p. 113). It is often referred to as a "roar":[25] "'why didn't she know better, than bring me into this disgrace', he roared out" (*MC* p. 13); "'I don't want to hear it' roared Henchard" (*MC* p. 98); "'I tell ye to sing the Hundred-and-Ninth to Wiltshire, and sing it you shall!' roared Henchard" (*MC* p. 233). Henchard as "the masterful, coercive mayor of the town" (*MC* p. 83), who "overpowers" Susan (*MC* p. 35), appears like some kind of divine master, comparable to the Freudian father of the primitive horde, an uncastrated father whose enjoyment is boundless: he and the well-to-do enjoy sumptuous meals in boisterous feasts while the poor hardly have a crust to eat ("they can blare their trumpets and thump their drums, and have their roaring dinners [...] but we must needs be put-to for want of a wholesome crust" *MC* p. 32). The "trumpets," associated with the word "roar," inevitably call to mind the voice of Yahweh and the trumpets of the Last Judgement ("a great voice, as of a trumpet," *Revelation*, I, 10),[26] as well as the divine voice heard on Mount Sinai when the ten commandments are pronounced ("And when the voice of the trumpet sounded long, and waxed louder and louder, Moses spake, and God answered him by a voice" *Exodus*, IX, 19). Henchard's voice at this stage reverberates like a loud trumpeting sound, like the primeval voice of God which creates the world through a performative act and is the source of all enunciation (his voice resonates at the town-pump, "that original fount" where water is purer than in the other wells, *MC* p. 120). Henchard as a "corn-factor" is the maker of "corn," i.e. the origin of the seed of life—even though he is but a parodic father-figure because the bread made from his corn is "unprincipled" (he is parodic precisely inasmuch as he is not castrated, he is not a "barred" Other). A beautiful passage makes use of poetics (the play on homophony and textual proximity) to interconnect different signifiers and thus produce a "rhizomatic" effect:

> I glory in the woman's sperrit. I'd ha' done it myself—Od send if I wouldn't, if a husband had behaved so to me! I'd go, and a' might call, and call, till his keacorn was raw; but I'd never come back—no, not till the great trumpet, would I.
>
> *MC* p. 16

25 A fact which should not surprise us, since Henchard is repeatedly compared to a bull, a lion, or a tiger: "he drove me back as if I were a bull breaking fence" (*MC* p. 269), "a netted lion" (*MC* p. 303), "a fangless lion" (*MC* p. 309), "Henchard's tigerish affection" (*MC* p. 91).

26 The trumpets of the Last Judgment can be interpreted both as a sign of Henchard's quasi divine status and as a harbinger of his downfall.

In "keacorn" (whose meaning is "wind-pipe, gullet") we overhear "corn" (a central theme in the novel), but also "horn" (another recurrent signifier in the novel, which is full of "horns" of all kinds, including those of bulls and other "horned beasts," *MC* p. 205). A horn, like a keacorn, is some kind of "wind-pipe," or at any rate a tube for the passage of air. What also invites the association of "keacorn" with "horn" is its proximity to "trumpet." "Raw" is a homonym of "roar" in British English, and Henchard's "keacorn" becoming "raw" suggests that, when the trumpet of judgment day is sounded, Henchard's "roar" will be muted—which is exactly what happens. Thus the rhizomatic text connects Henchard's voice to his corn trade (thus binding his voice as "primeval" to his being "corn-factor," the origin of the seed of life), to the bellowing of horned beasts, and ultimately to the voice of God in the Bible.

But then the narrative stages the "murder of the father," which in real life is what conditions symbolic castration.[27] Henchard's voice becomes "softened" (*MC* p. 234), his tones "low" (*MC* p. 234), "subdued" (when he is "unmanned" by Lucetta, *MC* p. 250). His "roar," the roar of "a bull breaking fence"[28] becomes muted. Only "the tune of the roaring weir" (*MC* p. 127), the "terrific roar" of a cascade (*MC* p. 221), or the "roars of sarcastic laughter," the "uproar" of the skimmity-ride (*MC* p. 279), are heard once Henchard's downfall has begun. The "bull-roarer" is now silent. A scene is crucial in the novel: that in which Lucetta and Elizabeth are saved by Henchard mastering a bull which has broken loose—and critics have pointed out the fact that the bull in this scene is Henchard's double,[29] so that Henchard "wrenching" the animal's head is an act of self-mutilation:

> He ran forward towards the leading-staff, seized it, and wrenched the animal's head as if he would snap it off. The wrench was in reality so violent that the thick neck seemed to have lost its stiffness and to become half-paralyzed, whilst the nose dropped blood. The premeditated human

27 The symbolic murder of the Father, in the Lacanian logic, turns the father into a dead Father, and that murder achieves symbolic castration, which means that the Other is castrated: S(Ⱥ). But here, we are in the world of tragedy, and the murder of the father is not symbolic, it is not "metaphorized," it is real.

28 "He drove me back as if I were a bull breaking fence" (*MC* p. 269). Such a "bull" knows no limits, his *jouissance* (like that of the father of the primitive horde) is unbounded. But "breaking fence" suggests that a limit is being introduced.

29 Holloway points out similarities between two struggle scenes, which are struggles between a man and an animal: the struggle between Henchard and Farfrae in the barn, and the struggle between Henchard and the bull. The symmetry shows that Henchard occupies the place of the bull (as well as of the man) in the second scene (Holloway, p. 345).

> contrivance of the nose-ring was too cunning for impulsive brute force, and the creature flinched.
>
> *MC* p. 206

The scene is the exact reiteration of the Freudian scene commented on by Lacan in his pages about *schofar*: as Henchard "wrenches" the animal's head, literally *wringing its neck*, we understand that what is being performed metaphorically is a murder of the father. And, in a most striking way, the scene takes place *in complete silence*. Not a sound is uttered by the terrified women (though Lucetta is said to be "hysterical" *MC* p. 207), no bellowing of the excited bull resonates, no cry is released by the brutalized animal. Silence prevails, but sound is insistently referred to, obliquely, by the mention of words connoting it, like "horn," "brass," or "ring":[30]

> His *horns* were thick and tipped with *brass*; his two nostrils like the Thames Tunnel as seen in the perspective toys of yore. Between them, through the gristle of his nose, was a stout copper *ring*, welded on, and irremovable as Gurth's collar of *brass*. To the *ring* was attached an ash staff about a yard long, which the bull with the motions of his head flung about like a flail.
>
> *MC* p. 205, my emphasis

What this silence makes us hear is the "bellowing of the stunned bull" (*beuglement de taureau assommé*) that Lacan writes about (Lacan, 2004, p. 295). The bellowing of the stunned animal which, in normal life, is the foundation of the law and also a senseless left-over from the suppressed *jouissance*. Here we hear the silent cry of the muted "bull-roarer."[31] What is reached is the point of absolute silence, the pure silence that the object-voice aspires to but never attains—except in Munch's *Scream*.

---

30 These signifiers, particularly "horn," are used elsewhere in the novel, where they refer to wind-instruments, especially in the skimmity-ride episode: "a cow's horn" (*MC* p. 281), "rams' horns" (*MC* p. 280), "the lanterns, horns, and multitude" (*MC* p. 284), etc.

31 Interestingly, Lacan includes the "bull-roarer" in the category of instrument comparable to *schofar* and used to produce the same sound in ritual ceremonies. Cf Lacan, 2004, p. 289: "J'eusse pu aussi [...] vous rappeler la fonction du *bullroarer*, instrument [...] qui, dans les cérémonies de certaines tribus australiennes, fait surgir un certain type de ronflement que le nom de l'instrument compare à rien de moins qu'au mugissement d'un boeuf. L'étude de Reik le rapproche du son du chofar, parce qu'il est lui aussi mis en équivalence à ce que d'autres passages du texte biblique appellent le mugissement de Dieu."

Michel Poizat notes that it is not just the “sonorous materiality” of voice in itself which is desired, “but rather sonorous materiality as it frees itself from the domination of signification through a process of purification or expurgation that is never attained except as the asymptote of silence” (Poizat, 1986/1992, p. 105). If we go back to *Tess of the d’Urbervilles*, that formulation is perfectly relevant: Tess’s voice is a *suppressed* feminine voice, a strangled voice that attempts to free itself from the domination of *logos*. It is not just that male domination prevents Tess from clearly “explaining herself,” it is not just that she is ascribed a gender-role in which she fails to make use of *logos* to describe the oppression suffered at the hands of men.[32] In fact, it is quite the other way round: what Tess’s voice aspires to is not the capacity to make itself heard but “the asymptote of silence,” the “pure” voice expurgated from all signification in which the inaudible object-voice might be overheard. And what causes the resistance, the strange frictional effect, is the domination of language exerted on the “pure” woman. Tess’s voice is strangled, stuck in the throat, because of the repression she has to endure. But the appeal of that voice to the reader (and to Hardy) is very precisely an *effect* of that repression: it lies in the peculiar tone of Tess’s voice, poised between silence and audibility, both constrained and unbridled, a voice which in spite of the “violence of language” (Lecercle 1990) retains in its innermost reaches something of Tess’s original “purity,” something of an object irrevocably lost—the object-voice. The Bacchic scene at Chaseborough illustrates this point very well: the carpet of peat and hay which covers the ground and mutes all sound is both a metaphor for repression and the means used to approach the pure, unattainable silence of the vocal object. The remarkable poetic quality of the passage, already noted, makes us hear the sound of silence—like an echo of Tess’s voice.

The narrator has told us right from the start that phases of Tess’s childhood are still “lurking” in her aspect, that she is yet “untinctured by experience.” And it is in her voice that this peculiar quality is traceable:

> Tess Durbeyfield at this time of her life was a mere vessel of emotion untinctured by experience. The dialect was on her tongue to some extent, despite the village school: the characteristic intonation of that dialect for

32 In that, Bathsheba is the exact reverse of Tess: to Gabriel, who ventures that it is probably “too soon” and “absurd” for her to think of re-marrying, she replies with perfect clarity, cogency, and “unflinching determination” that she is now ready to consider the question (*FFMC* p. 302).

> this district being the voicing approximately rendered by the syllable UR, probably as rich an utterance as any to be found in human speech.
>
> *TESS* p. 21

As Jean-Jacques Lecercle has judiciously pointed out, Tess is the object of "the violence of language": violence in the novel is "primarily linguistic" he writes, it is the "pedagogic violence" of Angel's teaching, through which Tess's "natural" language is "repressed by the articulate language of dominant culture" (Lecercle, 1993, p. 149), the "standard language"[33] taught at school. Following Deleuze and Guattari, J.-J. Lecercle speaks of a process of "deterritorialisation/ reterritorialisation" (Lecercle, 1993, p. 151). Indeed the dialect still "on her tongue to some extent," whose characteristic intonation could be approximately rendered by the syllable "UR," far from being a corruption of pure English, is "the rich *Ur-sprache* in which meaning is preserved" (Lecercle, 1993, p. 151), a full, mellow, archaic, originary language, the language of ballads, folklore, story-telling, etc. —in other words what I have already referred to as *lalangue,*[34] repressed by the dominant idiom, the official *la langue.* To my mind it is not "meaning" which is preserved in Tess's rich, archaic speech, but the *sonorousness* which the signifier attempts to evacuate. It is the object-voice which resists the imperialism of the signifier, and lingers in the dialectal inflexions of Tess's voice. Michel Poizat writes:

> The accent tends to bring to the surface vocal materiality, the vocal object as such; it becomes, as we have seen, an object of *jouissance* and this intrusion of *jouissance* into language subverts the signifying action of the spoken words.
>
> POIZAT (1986/1992, p. 105)

33 "Mrs. Durbeyfield habitually spoke the dialect; her daughter, who had passed the Sixth Standard in the National School under a London-trained mistress, spoke two languages; the dialect at home, more or less; ordinary English abroad and to persons of quality" (*Tess* p. 26). "Between the mother, with her fast-perishing lumber of superstitions, folklore dialect, and orally transmitted ballads, and the daughter, with her trained National teachings and Standard knowledge under an infinitely Revised Code, there was a gap of two hundred years as ordinarily understood" (*Tess* p. 28).

34 In the Norton edition of Lacan's XXth seminar, Bruce Fink translates *lalangue* as "llanguage": "Llanguage serves purposes that are altogether different from that of communication. That is what the experience of the unconscious has shown us, insofar as it is made of llanguage, which, as you know, I write with two l's to designate what each of us deals with, our so-called mother tongue (*lalangue dite maternelle*), which isn't called that by accident" (Lacan, 1975/1998, p. 138).

Poizat starts his demonstration by showing how the *cri pur* ("pure cry") of the new-born infant turns into the *cri pour* (a cry for someone, inscribed in the order of the signifier). What is lost in the process is the material quality of the cry, the pure sound-effect devoid of meaning or intentionality. The infant is somewhat dispossessed of its cry. That lost object is of course *objet petit a*, declined in the acoustic register as the object-voice. Perhaps that is the reason why Tess is called "a pure woman" by Hardy in his subtitle to the novel: because her silent cry, "the asymptote of silence," is the "pure cry" not fully suppressed by the signifier—and it is quite remarkable that the two letters supposed to be characteristic of Tess's voicing ("Ur") should have found their way into the adjective "pure," as well as into "d'Urberville," and into words like "lurked" or "untinctured," found in close proximity to "Ur" (*Tess* p. 21). There would be logic in that hypothesis: for Tess has been allotted a place, the locus of origin—the very locus where Henchard has positioned himself in an act of *hubris* that dooms him.[35] Entrusted with the mission to "claim kin," Tess has no choice but to identify with her aristocratic origin, to rejoin the "d'Urberville vault" where she belongs.[36] And there is something indomitable and dangerous in that "pure cry" of hers, that "rich *Ur-sprache*" untamed by language, something that has to be hushed if phallic order is to be preserved. That may well be the reason why she *has to* be hanged: to eject the object "stuck in her throat." To silence the disturbing object-voice, such might be the function of the executioner's rope—another function being to make it audible in the silence of the literary text. In which case one might argue that Tess has to be hanged not because she is guilty but *because she is pure*. The end of the novel shows silence prevailing again, while the crimson stain, the substance of enjoyment which we had felt palpitating all along the novel, turns into a black cipher, the black flag announcing the heroine's execution and the restoration of phallic order. The surplus object in the visual field has been "extracted," the voice has been purged of its object (in an act that has achieved the purgation of passions), so it would seem that voice could be resonant again—but at this point the novel comes to an end, and the rest is silence.[37]

---

35 Such a position, at the locus of origin, is essentially tragic, as we have seen.

36 Her destiny is similar to that of Sygne de Coûfontaine in Paul Claudel's play *L'Otage*, to which Lacan devoted four chapters in *Le Séminaire*, "Le Transfert." Here are a few words quoted by Lacan from Claudel's text: "*Et moi je serai la Patrie entre tes bras, la Douceur jadis quittée, la terre de Ur, l'antique*" (Lacan, 1991, p. 351).

37 This silence is "linguistic" in that it cuts the continuum of the text and achieves its closure. One may wonder if the silence of the two "speechless gazers," or the silence of the flag waving "silently," is "a positive entity rather than [...] the mere negation of noise." That of course is an open question.

5.4 The Muted Voice and Hardy's Poetics

The voicing particular to Tess's lips, which tends to bring to the surface the materiality of the vocal object and thus marks the intrusion of *jouissance* into language, leads one to wonder about Hardy's own personal relation to the muted voice. If we stick to the approach defined in section 16, that is to say if we accept Barthes's view of style as "an imagery, delivery, vocabulary [which] spring from the body and the past of the writer" (Barthes, 1977, p. 10), if we pay heed not to an author's biography but to his "biology" (Barthes, 1977, p. 10), then it becomes possible to consider the muted voice in its relation to Hardy the man.

One first question could be: what did it mean to Hardy when he had to renounce his *lalangue*, the Dorset dialect that had been his mother tongue, in order to become an established writer in Standard English? For after all English was not the language in which ballads had been sung and stories told to him when, as a child, he sat by the fire-side with his family and listened, enraptured, to the rich musical voice that stirred such strange emotions in him. There is, writes Jean-Jacques Lecercle, "a striking parallel between Tess's relation to language and Hardy's" (Lecercle, 1993, p. 153). Was Hardy, like Tess, subjected to "the violence of language"? What was Hardy's relation to his *lalangue*? A poem by Hardy, "The Spring Call," provides invaluable information about regional accents, and about what must have been Hardy's own accent:

> Down Wessex way, when spring's a-shine
> The blackbird's 'pret-ty de-urr!'
> In Wessex accents marked as mine
> Is heard afar and near.
> He flutes it strong, as if in song
> No R's of feebler tone
> Than his appear in 'pretty dear'
> Have blackbirds ever known.
> Yet they pipe 'prattie deerh!' I glean
> Beneath a Scottish sky,
> And 'pehty de-aw!' amid the treen
> Of Middlesex or nigh [...]
> Well: I'll say what the listening birds
> Say, hearing 'pret-ty de-urr!' —
> However strangers sound such words,
> That's how we sound them here.
> Yes, in this clime at pairing time,

> As soon as eyes can see her
> At dawn of day, the proper way
> To call is 'pret-ty de-urr!'.
>
> THOMAS HARDY, "The Spring Call"

In this poem, the reader finds a confirmation of what all linguists know: that Dorset native speakers pronounce /r/ in all instances (like the Scots), whereas in "Middlesex or nigh" "R" is a letter of "feebler tone"; it is in fact a silent letter when it occurs at the end of a word or before a consonant. In the learned words of linguists, Standard English is a "non-rhotic" language, dialectal pronunciation in the South West is said to be "rhotic." More importantly, the poem makes us fully realize that "Ur," the strange pair of letters characteristic of Tess's "voicing" and *also* contained in her name, must have had a special resonance to Hardy's ear: for the "r" of "Ur" is mute in Standard English, but fully pronounced in dialectal speech. Therefore "Ur" carries in its silent letter some remainder of an original *jouissance* that was lost to Hardy when he gave up his *lalangue* (*lalangue dite maternelle, et pas pour rien dite ainsi*, Lacan, 1975, p. 126) to be taught Standard English "under an infinitely revised code." That primeval enjoyment derived from the vibratory substance of *lalangue*, an object irrevocably lost to whoever enters language, is bound up with the Mother as the original object of desire. It is Hardy himself who makes the connection when he has "pret-ty de-urr!" rhyme with "her" in his poem.[38] No wonder the two letters supposed to define Tess's particular voicing were a stumbling-block for translators, as shown by a letter from Madeleine Rolland to Hardy in 1921. Hardy's reply is very interesting:

> I think you could explain it by saying it was something like the UR in 'h*ur*ler' or '*ur*gence' '*r*hum', much prolonged & deeper—though this would, after all, be obscure. In English the nearest approach I can think of is '*urh*' (It is very noticeable in the word 'her', which the rustics pronounce 'hurrr').
>
> Letter to Madeleine Rolland, 14 March 1921, MILLGATE & PURDY, vol. 6, p. 76

Again Hardy makes a parallel between "Ur" and "her," and in his attempt at representing the unrepresentable (the vocal object), he suggests the French "hurler" as the "nearest approach" he can think of: a remarkable suggestion,

38 "pret-ty de-urr!" is placed so as to rhyme with "her," "here," and "near." No other form of "pretty dear" is placed in rhyming position at the end of a line. Only "pret-ty de-urr!" rhymes.

which connects Tess's voice to a cry—and thereby to silence, if we remember Lacan's assertion that "the cry is the abyss for silence to rush into" (*le cri fait gouffre où le silence se rue*). All is condensed in those two simple letters, the "Ur" of Tess of the d'Urbervilles, a "pure woman": in a nutshell we have the origin, the maternal Other, the lost *lalangue*, and Tess's silent cry.

Quite remarkably, the phonic and graphic pair "ur" is found in the titles of three major novels by Hardy: *Tess of the d'Urbervilles, The Return of the Native, Jude the Obscure*—whose title was to have been "Hearts Insurgent." *The Return of the Native* is the novel in which the play on "ur" is most insistent, in a phonematic chain that repeats words like "urn," "turn," "return," and "burn"—all of them major signifiers in the narrative. Repetition, if we follow Lacan, always occurs at the point of some traumatic encounter with the Real, for "the real is that which always returns to the same place—to the place where the subject, in so far as he thinks, where the *res cogitans*, does not meet it" (Lacan, 1973/1986b, p. 49). We should then pay special attention to the signifier "urn," which insists in the novel. The funerary "urns," dug out from barrows and used as flower-pots on the window-sills by the Egdon inhabitants, may seem to be an insignificant little detail. Yet we have seen that those incongruous objects, which arrest the gaze like the hollow bone in Holbein's painting, are an anamorphic representation of death (a *memento mori*) as well as a surplus object in the visual field—in other words a figure of the "unspecularizable" object-gaze. The "urn" as object makes us glimpse "the thing that lies beneath the semblance of the thing" (Woolf, 1931/2005, p. 138), but one may suspect that "more is heard" in the signifier "urn" than its mere signified. Mrs Yeobright's angry outburst when she discovers that her son has offered such an object to Eustacia ("the urn you had meant for me you gave away" *RN* p. 191) is rather puzzling. Why should Clym's mother be so angry with her son for giving the urn to a woman who has "a cannibal taste for such ch*ur*chyard f*ur*nit*ur*e" (*RN* p. 191, my italics)? Isn't it because she somehow feels that the urn is a womb as well as a tomb, and that she who bore Clym in her womb is the only person entitled to sharing a womb/tomb with him? That Eustacia with her "cannibal" appetite is coveting an object *in flesh and blood* which rightly belongs only to her? We begin to understand that some *jouissance* is involved here, that the bones contained in the urn are an object both awesome and desirable—exactly like the bone at the bottom of Holbein's *Ambassadors*, or like the skull on the window-ledge in an engraving by Dürer, *Saint Jerome in his Study*. The urn on the window-ledge in Hardy's novel works as an "object-cause" of desire, to which the son (like every speaking subject) aspires to return. Then of course we should distinguish between the diegetic level, in which the "urn" functions as Mrs Yeobright's own flesh and blood, and where "return" to the womb-tomb is an absolute necessity (as well as a sheer impossibility), and the textual level where we derive exquisite pleasure from the signifier "urn" because it allows us to overhear a remainder of the vocal object, a precious left-over from the (supposed) bliss of origin which the poetics of the text makes audible. Like the signifier "dress" in *The Woodlanders*, "urn" in *The Return of the Native* is a nodal point around which much seems to revolve, an obscure kernel that conveys little signification, yet is loaded with affect and sends out poetic resonances throughout the text.

A paronomasia then runs all along the novel, repeating "urn," "turn," "return," and "burn."[39] Clym's fate is of course sealed by his *return* to his native country: "if you had never returned to your native place, Clym, what a blessing it would have been for you" (*RN* p. 276). "Return," or "turn," refer to actions both necessary and impossible, and therefore they insist. As Clym walks back home after a day's work on the heath he never turns his head (*RN* p. 279), fails to see his mother following him, then falls asleep in his cottage, an unfortunate circumstance that results in his mother being "turned from his door" (*RN* p. 300).[40] Estranged from his wife, he sends her a letter begging her to return (*RN* p. 351), but no "sound or signal of her return" ever reaches him (*RN* p. 362). Only the current will "return" in the vortex where Eustacia is drowned ("the vortex formed at the c*ur*l of the ret*urn*ing c*urr*ent" *RN* p. 375, my italics). "Burn" is another major signifier in a novel where bonfires (bone-fires) are given a prominent place and where "a species of incineration" (*RN* p. 277) is the fate that awaits Mrs Yeobright on the heath when she attempts to visit her son. To burn is both something dreaded and "a consummation devoutly to be wished." All those signifiers are loaded with *jouissance*, a *jouissance* that Hardy's style breaks up into the "mere nothings" of poetry, those "silk mouthfuls" (*W* p. 269) that can be shared and enjoyed by a multiplicity of readers.

---

39 Other recurrent signifiers could be added to the list: words like "fern" ("the dying ferns" *RN* p. 336), "earn" ("he likes to earn a little" *RN* p. 301), "earnest" ("Yeobright resumed his reading in earnest" *RN* p. 241), "learn" (what Clym is desperately trying to do, wearing his eyes out through reading too much), "nocturnal" (*RN* p. 268, p. 358), "taciturnity" (RN p. 319), "burnished" (*RN* p. 291), "furniture," "furnishing," "furnace," etc. One should also consider the insistent use of the letters of "urn" in "furze" (often coupled with "fern"), "mournful," etc. It is worth noting that the French song sung by Clym as he works cutting furze on the heath contains the letters "ur" in ten rhymes out of twelve: "jour," "parure," "retour," "amour," "nature," "court" (*RN* p. 255).

40 Another example: the dice-players' luck turns ("I said it would turn, and it has turned" *RN* p. 234), in a fantastic night scene where thirteen little lamps are formed by glow-worms ranged in a circle ("Why don't you burn, you little fools?" *RN* p. 234).

In other novels by Hardy, "ur" is a graphic and phonematic pair worthy of attention. Little is noticeable in *Tess of the d'Urbervilles*, rather surprisingly, if one sets apart phrases like "a fresh and virginal daughter of Nature" (*Tess* p. 124), "phases of her childhood lurked in her aspect still...a picturesque country girl" (*Tess* p. 21), "the murmur of unspeakable despair (*Tess* p. 368), "she murmured,"[41] "the curves of her mouth" (*Tess* p. 21), the curves of those lips" (*Tess* p. 152), "a roguish curl coming upon her mouth" (*Tess* p. 184), etc. No word containing the phonematic pair is uttered by Tess in direct style (to my knowledge), as if the suppression of Tess's *lalangue* had been totally effective. *Far from the Madding Crowd* repeats "ur" in "purl," "gurgle," "gurgoyle," "guttural," "concurritur," etc. Strikingly, Hardy chose "gurgoyle" in preference to the more common "gargoyle"—"gurgoyle" being "a variant spelling[42] of gargoyle" (*FFMC*, note p. 241), a sort of portmanteau word conjoining "gargoyle" and "gurgle."

In *The Mayor of Casterbridge*, what is repeated is the consonant "r" in various combinations, as for instance in the paradigm already mentioned that runs from "reverberation" (*MC* p. 275) to "riveted," "reverie" (*MC* p. 277), "revel," "roar," "uproar" (*MC* p. 279), "rivalry" (*RN* p. 301), "revelation" (*MC* p. 302), and "revelry" (*MC* p. 325). "Weir" rhyming with "near" and "hear" is a frequent pattern in Hardy's poetic prose,[43] as for instance in this passage from *The Mayor of Casterbridge*, also remarkable for alliterations and the haunting repetition of /r/ and /i/:

> To the east of Casterbridge lay moors and meadows through which much water flowed. The wanderer in this direction, who should stand still for a

41 A few examples show the frequency of "she murmured": pp. 39, 49, 74, 75, 82, 86, 98, 109, 146, 153, 173, 176, 184, 186, 192, 196, 198, 205, etc...

42 I have doubts about "gurgoyle" being just "a variant spelling" of "gargoyle." It seems to me that the variant chosen by Hardy involves *voice*, predominantly.

43 Cf similar rhymes in *The Return of the Native*: "it was the fall of a body into the stream adjoining, apparently at a point near the weir [...] make him send down to me any men who may be living near. Somebody has fallen into the weir" (*RN* pp. 374–375). In "The Melancholy Hussar of the German Legion," the first word of the short-story is "here," which occurs three times on the first page, close to "hearing" and to "attentive ear." The last word of the short-story is "near." The purpose of the story-teller is clearly "to make you hear," the emergence of a voice is the subject of his tale (See Maisonnat, 2013, pp. 66–77). The play on "here," "near," "hear," "ear" ("ear-ring"), "tear," "rear," "peer," "appear" is most conspicuous in *A Pair of Blue Eyes*. ("peer" being both the verb "to peer" and the noun referring to the title of Lord Luxellian, a noun also related to the central theme of "the pair"). The "ear-ring" is a metaphor for the text, which is a "hear-ring": a resonant voice that makes you hear something.

> few moments on a quiet night, might hear singular symphonies from these waters, as from a lampless orchestra, all playing in their sundry tones from near and far parts of the moor. At a hole in a rotten weir they executed a recitative; where a tributary brook fell over a stone breastwork they trilled cheerily; under an arch they performed a metallic cymballing, and at Durnover Hole they hissed. The spot at which their instrumentation rose loudest was a place called Ten Hatches, whence during high springs there proceeded a very fugue of sounds.
>
> *MC* p. 296

The reader (who identifies with "the wanderer") is invited to "hear" the singular symphonies played by water "from near and far," especially at a "weir," so that the metatextual dimension of the passage cannot be doubted: the "fugue of sounds" is the self-same one which the writer of the text is playing, causing a sonorous "ring" to be heard "du*ring* high sp*ring*s." The paragraph is *about a voice*, made audible by the obsessive repetition of /r/ and /i/, a voice which is both that of the tumultuous waters and that of the text—as the use of onomatopoeia makes plain.

So "to hear" is what the text is about. Yet the "r" of "hear" is mute in Standard English, so is the "r" of "weir," that of "water," of "singular," "far," "parts," "moor," "arch," "Durnover" etc. Could it be that a core of silence lies at the heart of this beautiful poetic passage? That all the resonant noise produced by the text, its alliterations, assonances, and consonances, only serves the purpose of making audible the "asymptote of silence" to which the Hardyan voice aspires? For the mute "r" in Standard English must have carried for Hardy some remainder of the lost vocal object, just as Tess's strangled voice allows us to overhear something of the "pure" cry that it tends to (but never attains). Poetry, writes Lacan, is a "hole-effect" (as well as a "meaning-effect"[44]). A "centre of complete emptiness" (Woolf, 1927/1995, p. 193) is a prerequisite for any creation, which is always a creation *ex nihilo*: as Lacan argues in his comment on Heidegger's vase, "all art is characterized by a certain mode of organization around this emptiness" (Lacan, 1986a/2008, p. 160). "R" to Hardy is perhaps a silent spot in his poetic prose, the centre of emptiness around which everything revolves.[45] Such a

---

44 "La poésie [...] qui est effet de sens, mais aussi effet de trou." *Ornicar*, n° 17–18, May 1977, p. 22.

45 The sentence from *The Woodlanders* that I have already quoted could be studied in the same perspective: it is the cry uttered by a man, Fitzpiers, when he discovers what he believes to be the mangled form of his wife caught in a mantrap: "'O my own—my darling—O cruel heaven—it is too much this!' he cried, writhing and rocking himself over

"hole-effect" is comparable to the "blue note" that Poizat writes about,[46] the climactic point reached by the voice in opera when it turns into a pure cry.

A parallel has been drawn between young Hardy's fascination with hanging scenes and the fate of Tess (Gittings, p. 60). But rather than see "distinctly sexual overtones" (Gittings, p. 58) in Hardy's recollections of public executions, I would like to underline the *sublimation* at work in them, as well as the part played by the vocal object in the emotion he felt at the time and remembered all his life. When he was in his eighties, Hardy wrote this about the execution of Martha Brown in 1856:

> What a fine figure she showed against the sky as she hung in the misty rain, and how the tight black silk gown set off her shape as she wheeled half round and back.
>
> Quoted in GITTINGS, p. 58

In my view the woman here is "sublime" in the sense defined in section 16 of this book: an object is said to be "sublime" when it is "raised to the dignity of the Thing." Here the black silk gown clinging to the woman's body both veils and reveals the horror of the Thing, as it gives Hardy a "negative" picture of it. Beauty functions as "an ultimate barrier prohibiting access to a fundamental horror,"[47] and in my opinion Hardy's response to the hanging is an artist's, his enjoyment has probably more to do with the "feminine" Other *jouissance* than

---

the sorry accessories of her he deplored" (*W*, p. 268). His cry is a typical example of the cry as "an abyss for silence to rush into," for the paronomastic series ("cruel" / "cried" / "writhing" ...), which loudly repeats consonants (/r/ mostly, also /k/) as well as the letters "o" and "r" ("rocking", "sorry", "accessories"—almost a repetition of "sorry") stumbles against the silent "r's" in "her he deplored." See Ramel, 2013a. The blind spot lodged in the silent letter opens a void in the sentence.

Another striking example, given by my colleague Michel Cusin [...] (in an unpublished seminar held in Lyon in 2008), shows that such "hollowing out" of a text may also occur in French. The passage is from Bossuet's "Oraison funèbre d'Henriette d'Angleterre": "Ô nuit désastreuse! Ô nuit effroyable, où retentit tout à coup, comme un éclat de tonnerre, cette étonnante nouvelle: Madame se meurt! Madame est morte!" The obsessive repetition of /t/ stumbles over a mute "t," the one in "meurt," which introduces a core of silence into the sentence. Precisely at the point where death is announced. The "hole-effect" is remarkable.

46 See the chapter entitled "'The Blue Note'" in *The Angel's Cry*, pp. 31–39. For this Poizat is indebted to Chopin and Alain Didier-Weill.

47 "[...] ce que nous avons démontré, dans la tragédie, de la fonction de la beauté: barrière extrême à interdire l'accès à une horreur fondamentale" (Lacan, 1966, pp. 774–775). My translation.

with sexuality.[48] Another report on this very scene, by someone who knew Hardy, was printed in *The Sketch* (2 November 1904):

> Young Hardy with another boy, came into Dorchester and witnessed the execution from a tree that overlooked the yard in which the gallows was placed. He never forgot the rustle of the thin black gown the woman was wearing as she was led forth by the warders. A penetrating rain was falling: the white cap was no sooner over the woman's head that it clung to her features, and the noose was put round the neck of what looked like a marble statue. Hardy looked at the scene with the strange illusion of its being unreal, and was brought to his complete senses when the drop fell with a thud and his companion on a lower branch of the tree fell fainting to the ground. The tragedy haunted Hardy, and, at last, provided the emotional inspiration and some of the matter for 'Tess of the d'Urbervilles'.
>
> Quoted in GITTINGS, pp. 58–59

As in Hardy's recollection, a veil both prohibits and shows the horror: a white cap clings to the woman's features because of the drizzle. But sound has its importance too: the "thud" heard when the drop fell (redoubled by the fall of Hardy's friend from the tree), and the rustle of the thin black gown the woman was wearing, a sound which Hardy "never forgot." This, writes Gittings, shows that "the rustle of a woman's dress had enormous sexual meaning for Hardy" (Gittings, p. 59). Gittings refers to a passage in Hardy's *Life* about the strong emotion he felt when (after the success of *Far from the Madding Crowd*) he received a letter signed by Mrs Julia Augusta Martin, a *grande dame* for whom he had had great fondness as a child ("his feeling for her was almost that of a lover" *Life* p. 24):

> By signing her letter 'Julia Augusta', she revived throbs of tender feeling in him, and brought back to his memory the thrilling 'frou-frou' of her four grey silk flounces when she had used to bend over him, and when they brushed against the font as she entered church on Sundays.
>
> *Life* pp. 104–105

48 What shows that Hardy's strange enjoyment cannot be reduced to sexual arousal is the account of another hanging scene given in Hardy's *Life* (pp. 32–33; also in Gittings, p. 60). This time it is the hanging of a man (James Seale), which Hardy attended two years later, from a distance. The scopic drive is clearly involved (with the boy Hardy placing his telescope to his eye). But here too sound (and therefore voice) is important: when Hardy's emotion reaches a climax, what makes him (almost) "faint" is the "the faint note" of the town clock striking eight.

Beside the poetic dimension of the text (which proceeds through paronomasia, from "feeling" to "frou-frou," "four," "flounces," "font"...), we note that Hardy's feeling was aroused in his childhood by the "frou-frou" of the lady's dress. Not by her shape, not by her body, not by anything he had *seen*, but by this faint sound produced by her dress brushing against the font at church.[49] Of course the French "frou-frou" has sexual connotations, but I wish to emphasize the extraordinary appeal which such a dry, husky, papery sound exerted on Hardy. The impression made on Hardy by the hanging scenes was not only caused by their visual impact, it cannot be reduced to some kind of sexual arousal. The "sound of silence" probably affected Hardy the poet more than anything else, silence as a "positive entity" and not just as the negation of noise, silence as the absolute *jouissance* aimed at (and dreaded) by whoever has entered language and been bereft of the "pure cry" of origin. Those muffled sounds, subtly poised between audibility and inaudibility, which are akin to a voice but cannot be "subjectivized" as they do not proceed from a human body (but from metonymic objects contiguous to a human body), sounds that float in the intermediate domain between life and death, between the human and the inhuman (like Michel Chion's acousmatic voice), such sounds must have exerted an extraordinary fascination on Hardy because they allowed him to overhear something of the inaudible vocal object. No wonder Tess has to be hanged: to eject the disturbing object-voice (approximately rendered by the syllable "UR") which has remained stuck in her throat, and to make it audible as the "pure cry" exhaled by the strangled woman as she breathes her last. The final chapter of *Tess of the d'Urbervilles* reaches that "pure cry" in the moment of absolute silence that marks the termination of life: nobody speaks (except the large red-brick building "bespeaking captivity") and the two "speechless gazers" watch the black flag as it continues to "wave silently." That moment when the hangman's rope puts and end to life releases the "cri pur" of the new-born infant, the object-voice silenced by the imperialism of the "cri pour." One question has always puzzled me: did Hardy the new-born child, who was thrown aside into a basket while the surgeon tried to save his mother, utter a cry at birth? The answer to that question is immaterial, for the only

49 In *Tess of the d'Urbervilles*, Mrs Brooks hears the "rustle" of Tess's garments (*Tess* pp. 368, 369). In "The Withered Arm," the lady's gown "whewed and whistled so loud when it rubbed against the pews that the lady coloured up more than ever for very shame at the noise." Fitzpiers in *The Woodlanders* confesses that he remembers Grace by the rustle of her dress: "the old familiar rustle of your dress often returns upon my mind till it distracts me" (*W* p. 252). "I heard you rustling through the fern before I saw you" (*FFMC* p. 143) are Troy's words when Bathsheba reaches him in "the hollow amid the ferns."

important fact is that *nobody heard the cry* (since the child was considered dead). That "unhistorical kernel" in the history of Thomas Hardy must have had a long-lasting impact on the man, and may explain Hardy's particular relation to silence and to the voice—a relation which could very well have determined his literary career. Hardy's style may have been his own particular way of retrieving the missing "pure cry" of origin, in the silence of the texts that he wrote. For, as Jacques Rancière has noted, a literary work is "a rich resting-place of silence" (Rancière, 2011, p. 32).

Conclusion

This book has shown that a major characteristic of Hardy's prose is the fascination for muffled sounds, for a delicately-poised state of quasi audibility, in which silence is not "the mere negation of noise" but "a positive entity." To make audible the inaudible object-voice is the prime impulse at work in Hardy's writing, a creative force that gives his prose its special resonance.

Rustles, hisses, whispers, murmurs, gurgles, gushes, rumbles, grumbles, thuds, there is a whole range of subdued sounds in Hardy's fiction, sounds that are half-way between the mute voice and the cry. Inanimate things seem to have a voice, while human beings utter sounds that are mechanical, inhuman. "Hiss," for instance, is used for Boldwood's voice when he replies to Troy (*FFMC* p. 183), but also for the sound of Prince's blood spouting in a stream from his wound "and falling with a hiss into the road" (*Tess* p. 37). At Flintcomb Ash during the threshing scene, the only audible "speech" is the "hiss" of the black engine ("and there was another indistinct figure, this one black, with a sustained hiss that *spoke* of a force very much in reserve" *Tess* p. 315, my italics)—while the hum of the red thresher prevents speech[1] (*Tess* p. 317). The wind is said to have a voice, the "shrivelled voice of the heath" (*RN* p. 69). Its major characteristic is its being *restrained* by all sorts of obstacles that it has to strive through, so that it is "as if the night sang dirges with clenched teeth": for instance on Egdon Heath, a pause in the discussion between Wildeve and Eustacia is filled up "by the intonation of a pollard thorn a little way to windward, the breezes filtering through its unyielding twigs as through a strainer" (*RN* 80). In *Far from the Madding Crowd* the voice of the wind has to cross a barrier of trees: "To-night these trees sheltered the southern slope from the keenest blasts, which smote the wood and floundered through it with a sound as of grumbling, or gushed over its crowning boughs in a weakened moan" (*FFMC* p. 11).[2] Sometimes the cause of a sound cannot be determined, as when Angel

1 The hum of the thresher "increased to a raving when the supply of corn fell short of the regular quantity" (*Tess* p. 317). It is the voice of the Other, uttering its cruel injunction to work ceaselessly, the voice of the "red tyrant" which the women are here to serve.

2 Other examples from *Far from the Madding Crowd*: Gabriel's footsteps are deadened by the soft grass he is treading (*FFMC* p. 43); so are the notes of his flute: "the tune was not floating unhindered into the open air: it seemed muffled in some way, and was altogether too curtailed in power to spread high or wide" (*FFMC* pp. 12–13). The ring of the sheep-bells has more mellowness than clearness, "owing to an increasing growth of surrounding wool" (*FFMC* p. 14). Fanny trying to throw lumps of snow at Troy's window only causes "dull blows" to resonate, because the sound is heard "with difficulty in the fluffy atmosphere" (*FFMC* p. 70).

 | DOI 10.1163/9789004296626_008

and Tess reach Stonehenge and hear a strange, uncanny, monstrous sound: "'It hums', said she. 'Hearken!'" In fact "it" refers to the wind which, "playing on the edifice," produces "a booming tune, like the note of some gigantic one-stringed harp" (*Tess* p. 379). Water in Hardy's novels roars, purls, gurgles, it is often endowed with a voice that we are invited to hear: like the voice of the "weir" in *The Mayor of Casterbridge* and in *The Return of the Native*, like the sound of a mill-pond "tricking hoarsely through a hatch, and suggesting gloomy possibilities of drowning" (*FFMC* p. 165), or like the voice of the gurgoyle in *Far from the Madding Crowd*, a creature "too human to be called a dragon, too impish to be like a man," a "horrible stone-entity" which for four hundred years had "laughed at the surrounding landscape, voicelessly in dry weather, and in wet with a gurgling and snorting sound" (*FFMC* p. 241).

As a conclusion to this book I would like to focus on a passage from *The Return of the Native*, because it contains in a nutshell all the constitutive elements of Hardy's fiction, thus giving me a chance to summarize my argument. Chapter VI in *The Return of the Native* ("The Figure Against the Sky") begins with a description of the voice of the heath, its very special tone and its "linguistic peculiarity" (*RN* p. 51). Then a human voice mingles with it, as if arising from its very modulations: it is the sigh exhaled by Eustacia as she looks at the faint shine of Wildeve's window. We have here a perfect example of the "acousmatic" voice, whose origin is untraceable, a voice that is in-between, neither human nor inhuman:

> Suddenly, on the barrow, there mingled with all this wild rhetoric of night a sound which modulated so naturally into the rest that its beginning and ending were hardly to be distinguished. The bluffs, and the bushes, and the heather-bells had broken silence; at last, so did the woman; and her articulation was but as another phrase of the same discourse as theirs. Thrown out on the winds it became twined in with them, and with them it flew away.
>
> *RN* p. 52

That voice has to put in a tremendous effort to make itself heard in spite of impediments of all kinds: "a dwindled voice strove hard at a husky tune" (*RN* p. 51). It takes myriads of individual sounds from the mummied heath-bells of the past summer to produce an audible sound, which again is described as "shrivelled":

> So low was an individual sound from these that a combination of hundreds *only just emerged from silence*, and the myriads of the whole declivity reached the woman's ear but as a shrivelled and intermittent recitative.
>
> *RN* p. 51, my italics

Eustacia's voice too is restrained, it only just emerges from silence (like Tess's voice), for she has been existing "in a suppressed state." Allowing herself to utter the sigh is "a spasmodic abandonment," "as if the woman's brain had authorized what it could not regulate" (*RN* p. 52). Here we find again a woman trying to free herself from the domination of language "through a process of purification or expurgation that is never attained except at the asymptote of silence" (Poizat, 1986/1992, p. 105). What Eustacia's voice aspires to is not the capacity to express herself but the "pure" voice (like Tess's syllable "UR"), the voice which lies half-way between silence and a cry, and which contains in its inmost reaches some trace of the inaudible vocal object—the voice both *contains* it and *constrains* it.

But what makes this passage exemplary is its metatextual dimension. For we cannot fail to realize the mimetic relation between the voice of the heath and the voice of the text: in fact, the textual voice bears a great resemblance to the "shrivelled voice of the heath." Both have some difficulty in emerging from silence—for a literary text is nothing but silence[3] until the reader lends it his voice, and it returns to silence once we close the book. The note wherein lies "the linguistic peculiarity of the heath" is described in terms that suggest that the passage is a *mise en abyme* of the speech act producing the text:

> Throughout the blowing of these plaintive November winds that note bore a great resemblance to the ruins of human song which remain to the throat of fourscore and ten. It was a worn whisper, dry and *papery*, and it brushed so distinctly across the ear that, by the accustomed, the material minutiae in which it originated could be realized as by touch.
>
> *RN* p. 51, my italics

Couched on dry paper, the textual voice retains something of the lost vocal object which Lacan has called *objet a*—for it is, as Maisonnat has demonstrated, "a fictional version of the Lacanian object-voice" (Maisonnat, p. 167). Yet it has lost its fullness, its mellowness, it has been dispossessed of its original richness, the "rich Ur Sprache" of the "pure cry." Like the voice of the heath, and like the voice of Eustacia, it is but a remainder from a lost *jouissance*, a metonymic "ruin" from a youthful tune that can no longer be sung, a left-over from the heath-bells of last Summer, once "tender and purple," now "washed colourless" and "dried to dead skins" (*RN* p. 51). The literary voice has to (partially) free itself from the "suppressed state" which is the condition of whoever

3 Poetry, writes Poizat, "is the silence of prose," just as "music is the silence of words," in that it "lightens the weight of logos, eases the crushing hegemony of language" (Poizat, 1986/1992, p. 86).

inhabits language, if it is to offer the reader "a rich resting-place of silence" (Rancière, 2011, p. 32). A work of art is like an openwork fence: it keeps jouissance at bay, yet allows fragments of it to filter through its interstices "as through a strainer" (*RN* p. 80)—like Hardy's straw hat.

Thus we have reached a point where we find that the very subject of Hardy's fiction is the voice that produces it—in Higonnet's formulation, one may very well read *Tess of the d'Urbervilles* as "a metanarrative about voice" (Higonnet, p. 26). But if we wish to retrace the steps that we have followed so far, we have to go back one step, to the question of the object-gaze. For after all the "madder stain" is the subject of this book—not voice. Then the beginning of "The Figure Against the Sky" will also be of great interest to us, for it closely binds up the question of voice with the question of the gaze. The chapter opens with an image of the perishing fire (the fire lit up by the villagers on Blackbarrow hill) whose red coals "greeted her like living eyes in the corpse of day" (*RN* p. 50)—an image which continues the theme struck up in Chapter III with the "Dureresque" picture of "shadowy eye-sockets deep as those of a death's head" (*RN* p. 15), continued with the "steady unaltering eyes" of the most enduring fires (*RN* p. 26), the "quiet eye" of Eustacia's persistent fire (*RN* p. 27), and the little bonfire on Mistover Knap meeting Wildeve's eye at the end of Chapter V (*RN* p. 49), just before the passage we are focusing on. The minute and lengthy description of the voice of the wind (to which the woman is said to be listening) ends with a few lines that reintroduce the scopic drive, with "the faint shine from the window of the inn" (another "quiet eye" shining in the night), and with Eustacia's telescope, which she raises "to her eye" (*RN* p. 52). And the narrative insists on the *connection* between gaze and voice, for "the window, or what was within it, *had more to do with* the woman's sigh than had either her own actions, or the scene immediately around" (*RN* p. 52, my italics)—that connection being repeated phonematically by "the woman's sigh" which is a near homophone of "the woman's eye."

That gaze and voice should be inextricably entwined is essential to the argument of this book: for we have seen that for a sound to resonate, there must be a void somewhere. If no gap hollows out the visual field, if the object-gaze is a persistent presence, a surplus object filling up the vacuum of *objet a*, then sound cannot reverberate, the voice can only be muffled, "stuck in the throat." In Žižek's very clear formulation, "*we hear things because we cannot see everything*" (Žižek, 1996, p. 93). If, equipped with a telescope, I aim at the unspecularizable point from which the Other sees me, I am entering a process (which is structurally psychotic) that can only tend to the absolute, deadly silence of the vocal object. We have seen how Eustacia, like Tess, forms a "madder stain" on the vacuity of the perspective. It is therefore perfectly logical that the voice of the heath, *and the voice of the woman*, should be hardly audible, "stuck in the throat," as if the night "sang dirges with clenched teeth." The end of The *Return of the Native* makes this point clear: once the surrounding air at Bloom's End is "free from every taint" (*RN* p. 390), that is when the stain, the surplus object, has been removed, voice can be resonant again, Clym can find his "vocation," there is "no defect in the tones of his voice," which are "rich, musical, and stirring" (*RN* p. 411). We can hear the crystal-clear sound of the shoes of an ancient pony, which "clashed like cymbals at every tread" (*RN* p. 410). But then a pre-condition for sound to reverberate is that the preacher should wear a shade over his eyes: for only a man "who could not see [to do anything else]" (*RN* p. 412, my italics) could turn preacher on Blackbarrow hill.

So we now understand the crucial importance of the "madder stain" in the creative process that produced Hardy's style, his voiceprint: for the voice "stuck in the throat"—whether it is the worn whisper of the wind on Egdon heath, dry and papery like the ruins of human song, or the mute voice of Hardy's heroines, or the textual voice which aspires to the condition of silence—is born of that "spot" which intrudes on the white vacuity of the perspective. It is the "madder stain" which makes audible the inaudible vocal object, and thus turns Hardy's poetic fiction into "a rich resting-place of silence."

If, retracing our steps, we go back to the first chapter of this book, we find that the "missing blank" dealt with in section 3, that is to say the lack of a structural hole in the diegesis that could serve as the initial gap in the signifying chain (or as nought in the chain of numbers), is at the core of Hardy's fiction. The urge to fill up the void of origin—in defiance of the paternal metaphor which prohibits return to the origin—is the direct cause of tragedy, because it produces "this solidity, this mass seizure of the primitive signifying chain" (Lacan, 1973/1986b, p. 238). The "ring" which Henchard finds among odds and ends the morning after the fair is not a "hollow" ring (as the King's crown in *Richard II* is a "hollow crown"): it is both a tragic gash and a solidified mass, "welded on" to the flesh, like the "stout copper ring" (*MC* p. 205) welded onto the nose of the bull mastered by Henchard—we could say that the wife sale has disrupted the Symbolic and incarnated the signifier. The word has been made flesh. No structural gap hollows out Henchard's reality. As a consequence silence prevails at the Ring, a place which is "emphatic of the absence of every living thing" (*MC* p. 249), the spot chosen for "appointments of a furtive kind," where a woman was "*half* strangled" by the executioner (*MC* p. 71, my italics). Sound cannot reverberate there, only the sound of silence can be heard in the arena. Yet nothing bears a greater resemblance to that inhuman voice than the textual voice that reports on it and turns the silent Ring of Casterbridge into a resonance chamber. The "ring" then becomes audible, a "peculiar poetical like murmur" (*MC* p. 281) which is a delight to the reader's ear.

Bibliography

André, S. (1986). *Que veut une femme?* Paris: Navarin.

Barthes, R. (1977). *Writing Degree Zero* (A. Lavers & C. Smith, Trans.). New York: Hill and Wang (Original work published 1953).

———. (2000). *Camera Lucida* (R. Howard, Trans.). London: Vintage Books (Original work published 1980).

Beer, G. (2000). *Darwin's Plots*. Cambridge: Cambridge University Press (Original work published 1983).

Bernard, S. (2013). "Women of Letters and the Irony of Life: 'An Imaginative Woman' and 'On the Western Circuit'." *FATHOM, a French E-Journal of Thomas Hardy Studies*, 1 ("The Letter"). Retrieved from http://fathom.revues.org/137.

Blake, K. (1982). "Pure Tess: Hardy on Knowing a Woman." *Studies in English Literature, 1500–1900*, 22, 4, Nineteenth Century, Autumn, 689–705.

Boumelha, P. (1985). *Thomas Hardy and Women, Sexual Ideology and Narrative Form*. Madison: University of Wisconsin Press.

———. (1993). "*Tess of the d'Urbervilles:* Sexual Ideology and Narrative Form." In *Tess of the d'Urbervilles, Thomas Hardy*. P. Widdowson (Ed.), 44–62. London: New Casebooks.

Braunstein, N. (1992). *La jouissance, un concept lacanien*. Paris: Point Hors Ligne (Original work published 1990).

Bronfen, E. (1993). "Pay As You Go: On the Exchange of Bodies and Signs." In *The Sense of Sex: Feminist Perspectives on Hardy*. M. Higonnet (Ed.), 66–86. Urban and Chicago: University of Illinois Press.

Bullen, J.B. (1986). *The Expressive Eye*. Oxford: Clarendon Press.

Burgin, V. (1990). "Geometry and Abjection." In *Abjection, Melancholia and Love: The Work of Julia Kristeva*. John Flechter & Andrew Benjamin (Eds.), 104–123. London: Routledge.

Camus, A. (1957). "The Adulterous Woman." In *Exile and the Kingdom* (J. O'Brien, Trans.). [book online] New York: Vintage Books. Accessed 3 November 2014; available from dhspriory.org: http://www.dhspriory.org/kenny/PhilTexts/Camus/Exile%20and%20the%20Kingdom.pdf.

Claridge, L. (1993). "Tess: A Less Than Pure Woman Ambivalently Presented." In *Tess of the d'Urbervilles, Thomas Hardy*. P. Widdowson (Ed.), 63–79. London: New Casebooks.

Conrad, J. (1990). *Heart of Darkness and Other Tales*. Oxford: The World's Classics (Original work published 1899).

Dolar, M. (1996). "The Object Voice." In *Gaze and Voice as Love Objects*. S. Zizek & R. Salecl (Eds.), 7–31. Durham: Duke University Press.

———. (2006). *A Voice and Nothing More.* Cambridge (Mass.): MIT Press.

Dor, J. (1985). *L'inconscient structuré comme un langage* (Introduction à la lecture de Lacan, 1). Paris: Denoël.

Eliot, G. (1998). *The Mill on the Floss.* Oxford & New York: The World's Classics (Original work published 1860).

Escuret, A. (1983). "L'œuvre romanesque de Thomas Hardy (1840–1928): lectures." Thèse de Doctorat d'État, Université Paul Valéry (University of Montpellier 3).

Estanove, L. (2013). "Thought and Silence, The 'Pensive Mutes' of Hardy's Verse." *FATHOM, a French E-Journal of Thomas Hardy Studies,* 1 ("Silence"). Retrieved from http://fathom.revues.org/397.

Freud, S. (1917). *Delusion and Dream.* New York: Moffat, Yard and Company.

Gadoin, I. & Ramel, A. (2013). "Liminality – Introduction." *The Hardy Review,* XV-i, 5–10.

Garson, M. (1991). *Hardy's Fables of Integrity: Woman, Body, Text.* Oxford: Clarendon Press.

———. (2006). "Written in Stone: Hardy's Grotesque Sublime." In *Thomas Hardy Reappraised, Essays in Honour of Michael Millgate.* K. Wilson (Ed.), 96–114. Toronto: University of Toronto Press Incorporated.

Gittings, R. (1978). *Young Thomas Hardy.* London: Penguin.

Goater, T. (2008). "'The Letter Killeth': The Text as Fetish in *Jude the Obscure.*" *The Hardy Review,* Xii, 129–137.

Golan, R. (2006). *Loving Psychanalysis: Looking at Culture with Freud and Lacan.* London: Karnac Books.

Gordon, J.B. (1976). "Origins, History, and the Reconstitution of Family: Tess's Journey." *ELH,* 43, 366–388.

Gossin, P. (2007). *Thomas Hardy's Novel Universe: Astronomy, Cosmology, and Gender in the Post-Darwinian World.* Aldershot: Ashgate.

Gribble, J. (2006). "The Quiet Women of Egdon Heath." In *The Return of the Native.* P. Mallett (Ed.), 524–542. New York and London: W.W. Norton.

Hardy, Thomas (1978–1988). *The Collected Letters of Thomas Hardy,* 7 volumes. M. Millgate & R.L. Purdy (Eds.). Oxford: Clarendon Press.

———. (1985a). *A Pair of Blue Eyes.* Oxford & New York: The World's Classics (Original work published 1872).

———. (1985b). *The Woodlanders.* Oxford & New York: The World's Classics (Original work published 1887).

———. (1985c). *Jude the Obscure.* Oxford & New York: The World's Classics (Original work published 1895).

———. (1986). *Far from the Madding Crowd.* R.C. Schweik (Ed.). New-York & London: W.W. Norton (Original work published 1874).

———. (1987). *The Mayor of Casterbridge.* Oxford & New York: The World's Classics (Original work published 1886).

———. (1988a). *Tess of the d'Urbervilles.* Oxford & New York: The World's Classics (Original work published 1891).

———. (1988b). *Collected Short Stories*. D. Hawkins & F.B. Pinion (Eds.). London: Macmillan.

———. (1988c). "An Imaginative Woman." In *Collected Short Stories*. Desmond Hawkins & F.B. Pinion (Eds.). London: Macmillan.

———. (1989). *The Life and Work of Thomas Hardy*. M. Millgate (Ed.). London: Macmillan.

———. (1990). *The Return of the Native*. Oxford & New York: The World's Classics (Original work published 1878).

Higonnet, M.R. (1993). "A Woman's Story: Tess and the Problem of Voice." In *The Sense of Sex: Feminist Perspectives on Thomas Hardy*. M. Higonnet (Ed.), 14–31. Urbana: University of Illinois Press.

Hillis Miller, J. (1982). *Fiction and Repetition*. Cambridge: Harvard University Press.

Holloway, J. (1977). "Hardy's Major Fiction." In *The Mayor of Casterbridge*. J.K. Robinson (Ed.), 342–346. New York: W.W. Norton.

Homer, S. (2005). *Jacques Lacan*. Abingdon: Routledge.

Ingham, P. (1993). "Fallen Woman as Sign, and Narrative Syntax in *Tess of the d'Urbervilles*." In *Tess of the d'Urbervilles, Thomas Hardy*. P. Widdowson (Ed.), 80–89. London: New Casebooks.

Jacobus, M. (1976). "Tess's Purity." *Essays in Criticism*, 26, 318–338.

James, H. (1920). *Letters of Henry James*. P. Lubbock (Ed.). London: Macmillan.

Julien, P. (1995). *L'étrange jouissance du prochain*. Paris: Seuil.

Kaye, S. (2003). *Slavoj Žižek: A Critical Introduction*. Cambridge: Polity Press.

Lacan, J. (1966). *Écrits*. Paris: Seuil.

———. (1973). *Le Séminaire*, livre XI: "Les quatre concepts fondamentaux de la psychanalyse." Paris: Seuil.

———. (1975). *Le Séminaire*, livre XX: "Encore." Paris: Seuil.

———. (1977). *Écrits: A Selection* (A. Sheridan, Trans.). London: Tavistock Publications (Original work published 1966).

———. (1986a). *Le Séminaire*: livre VII: "L'éthique de la psychanalyse." Paris: Seuil.

———. (1986b). *The Seminar*, Book XI: "The Four Fundamental Concepts of Psychoanalysis" (A. Sheridan, Trans.). Harmondsworth: Peregrine Books (Original work published 1973).

———. (1991). *Le Séminaire*: livre VIII: "Le Transfert." Paris: Seuil.

———. (1994). *Le Séminaire*: livre IV: "La relation d'objet." Paris: Seuil.

———. (1998). *The Seminar of Jacques Lacan*, Book XX: "On Feminine Sexuality, the Limits of Love and Knowledge" (B. Fink, Trans.). New York: W.W. Norton & Company (Original work published 1975).

———. (2001a). "Lituraterre." In *Autres Écrits*. Paris: Seuil.

———. (2001b). "Hommage fait à Marguerite Duras." In *Autres Écrits*, Paris: Seuil.

———. (2004). *Le Séminaire*, livre X: "L'Angoisse." Paris: Seuil.

———. (2005). *Le Séminaire*, livre XXIII: "Le sinthome." Paris: Seuil.

———. (2006). *Le Séminaire*, livre XVI: "D'un Autre à l'autre." Paris: Seuil.

———. (2008). *The Seminar of Jacques Lacan*, Book VII: "The Ethics of Psychoanalysis" (D. Porter, Trans.). Abingdon: Routledge (Original work published 1986).

———. (2011). *The Seminar of Jacques Lacan*, Book XIX: "*...ou pire*." Paris: Seuil.

———. (2013). *Le Séminaire*, livre VI: "Le désir et son interprétation." Paris: Éditions de la Martinière.

Lanone, C. (2010). "Without Throwing a Nymphean Tissue over a Milkmaid: From Bathsheba Everdene to Tess of the d'Urbervilles." *Cycnos: Thomas Hardy, Far from the Madding Crowd*, 26, 2, 103–110.

Lecercle, J.-J. (1990). *The Violence of Language*. London and New York: Routledge.

———. (1993). "The Violence of Style in *Tess of the d'Urbervilles*." In *Tess of the d'Urbervilles*. Peter Widdowson (Ed.), 147–156. London : New Casebooks.

———. (2013). "Thomas Hardy's Silences." *FATHOM, a French E-Journal of Thomas Hardy Studies*, 1 ("Silence"). Retrieved from http://fathom.revues.org/354.

Lodge, D. (1966). "Tess, Nature, and the Voices of Hardy." In *Thomas Hardy: The Tragic Novels*. R.P. Draper (Ed.), 164–181. London: Casebook Series.

Louvel, L. (2010). *Le tiers pictural*. Rennes: Presses Universitaires de Rennes.

———. (2011). *Poetics* of *the Iconotext* (L. Petit, Trans.), K. Jacobs (Ed.). Farnham: Ashgate.

Maisonnat, C. (2012). "The Voice of Darkness." In *Conrad's "Heart of Darkness" and Contemporary Thought. Revisiting the Horror with Lacoue-Labarthe*. N. Lawtoo (Ed.), 164–180. London: Continuum.

———. (2013). "*Arkhè*, Archive and the Textual Voice in 'The Melancholy Hussar of the German Legion'." *The Hardy Review*, XV-i, Spring, 66–77.

Maleval, J.-C. (2000). *La Forcluson du Nom-du-Père*. Paris: Seuil.

Mallett, P. (2010). "Hardy and Masculinity: *A Pair of Blue Eyes* and *Jude the Obscure*." In *The Ashgate Research Companion to Thomas Hardy*. R. Morgan (Ed.), 387–402. Farnham: Ashgate.

Marret, S. (2010). "L'objet du ravissement: de Lol V. Stein à Marguerite Duras." *Quarto*, 97, April, 28–36.

Meisel, P. (1972). *Thomas Hardy: The Return of the Repressed*. Newhaven and London: Yale University Press.

Merleau-Ponty, M. (1962). *Phenomenology of Perception* (C. Smith, Trans.). London: Routledge and Kegan Paul (Original work published 1945).

Miller, J.-A. (1994). "Jacques Lacan et la voix." *Quarto*, 54, June, 47–52.

———. (2008). "L'image du corps en psychanalyse." *Notre sujet supposé savoir, La Cause freudienne*, 68, 94–104.

———. (2009). Introduction à la lecture du séminaire "L'angoisse" de Jacques Lacan. 17 March. Retrieved from http://fr.scribd.com/doc/13344816/Introduction-a-la-lecture-du-Seminaire-Langoisse-de-Jacques-Lacan-JacquesAlain-Miller (20 May 2014).

Montrelay, M. (1977). *L'ombre et le nom*. Paris: Les Éditions de Minuit.

Morgan, R. (1991). *Women and Sexuality in the Novels of Thomas Hardy*. London & New York: Routledge.

———. (2013). "Hardy and Epignetics: the case of 'San Sebastian' and 'An Imaginative Woman'." *The Hardy Review*, XV-i, 33–43.

Paccaud-Huguet, J. (2006). "Psychoanalysis after Freud." In *Literary Theory and Criticism, An Oxford Guide*. P. Waugh (Ed.), 280–297. Oxford: OUP.

Paris, J. (1969). "'A Confusion of Many Standards'. Conflicting Value Systems in *Tess of the d'Urbervilles*." *Nineteenth Century Fiction*, 24, June, 157–179.

Poizat, M. (1992). *The Angel's Cry, Beyond the Pleasure Principle in Opera* (A. Denner, Trans.). Ithaca: Cornell University Press (Original work published 1986).

———. (2001). *L'Opéra ou le cri de l'ange*. Paris: Métailié (Original work published 1986).

Quignard, P. (2007). *La nuit sexuelle*. Paris: Flammarion.

Radford, A. (2010). "Hardy and Scientific Humanism." In *The Ashgate Research Companion to Thomas Hardy*. R. Morgan (Ed.), 253–268. Farnham: Ashgate.

Ramel, A. (1991). "'Poor Wounded Name': Le Nom blessé dans *Tess of the d'Urbervilles*." *Études Angaises*, XLIVth year, 4, 385–398.

———. (1997). "Texts and Textiles in *The Mayor of Casterbridge*." In *De la littérature à la lettre*. A. Haberer & J. Paccaud-Huguet (Eds.), 75–89. Lyon: PUL.

———. (1998). "The Crevice in the Canvas: A Study of *The Mayor of Casterbridge*." *Victorian Literature and Culture*, 259–272.

———. (2008a). "Tess's Silent Cry: The Vocal Object in *Tess of the d'Urbervilles*." *English Text Construction*, 1.1, 113–124.

———. (2008b). "L'objet en trop dans *Tess d'Urberville*." In *Méthode!* (agrégation de Lettres 2009). Valérie Fasseur (Ed.), 317–324. Bandol (France): Vallongues.

———. (2009). "A peculiar poetical-like murmur: répétition et poéticité dans *The Mayor of Casterbridge*." *Cahiers Victoriens et Édouardiens*, 69, April, 267–281.

———. (2013a). "The Letter that vivifies in Hardy's texts." *FATHOM, a French E-Journal of Thomas Hardy Studies*, 1 ("Silence"). Retrieved from http://fathom.revues.org/139.

———. (2013b). "Introduction: the 'rich resting-place of silence'." *FATHOM, a French E-Journal of Thomas Hardy Studies*, 1 ("Silence"). Retrieved from http://fathom.revues.org/477.

Rancière, J. (1998). *La parole muette*. Paris: Hachette.

———. (2011). *Mute Speech* (J. Swenson, Trans.). New York: Columbia University Press (Original work published 1998).

Ray, M. (1997). *Thomas Hardy: A Textual Study of the Short-Stories*. Aldershot and Vermont: Ashgate.

Reinhard Lupton, J. (2009). "Tragedy and Psychoanalysis: Freud and Lacan." In *Blackwell Companion to Tragedy*. R. Bushnell (Ed.). London: Blackwell.

Rimmer, M. (1993). "Club Laws: Sex and the Construction of Gender in *A Pair of Blue Eyes*." In *The Sense of Sex: Feminist Perspectives on Thomas Hardy*. M.R. Higonnet (Ed.), 203–220. Urbana: University of Illinois Press.

Showalter, E. (1987). "The Unmanning of the Mayor of Casterbridge." In *Thomas Hardy's* The Mayor of Casterbridge (Modern Critical Interpretations). Harold Bloom (Ed.), 53–68. New York & Philadelphia: Chelsea House Publishers.

Silverman, K. (1993). "History, Figuration, and Female Subjectivity in *Tess of the d'Urbervilles*." In *Tess of the d'Urbervilles, Thomas Hardy*. Peter Widdowson (Ed.), 129–146. London: New Casebooks.

Strauss, M. (1987). "La vraie fonction du père, c'est d'unir un désir à la loi." In *Lacan*. Gérard Miller (Ed.), 61–76. Paris: Bordas.

Tanner, T. (1975). "Colour and Movement in *Tess of the d'Urbervilles*." In *Thomas Hardy: The Tragic Novels*. R.P. Draper (Ed.), 182–208. London: Casebook Series.

Thomas, J. (2013). *Thomas Hardy and Desire: Conceptions of the Self*. Basingstoke: Palgrave Macmillan.

Thomson, C. (1993). "Language and the Shape of Reality in *Tess of the d'Urbervilles*." In *Tess of the d'Urbervilles, Thomas Hardy*. Peter Widdowson (Ed.), 109–128. London: New Casebooks.

Wajcman, G. (1998). *L'objet du siècle*. Paris: Verdier.

———. (2010). *L'Œil absolu*. Paris: Denoël.

Widdowson, P. (1993). *Tess of the d'Urbervilles, Thomas Hardy*. London: New Casebooks.

Woolf, V. (1953). "The Novels of Thomas Hardy." In *The Common Reader*, second series. London: Hogarth Press (Original work published 1932).

———. (1978). "A Sketch of the Past." In *Moments of Being*. London: Triad Granada (Original work first published 1976).

———. (1995). *To the Lighthouse*. Hammersmith: Flamingo (Original work published 1927).

———. (1998). *Between the Acts*. Oxford: Oxford World's Classics (Original work first published 1941).

———. (2005). *The Waves*. London: Collector's Library (Original work first published 1931).

Žižek, S. (1989). *The Sublime Object of Ideology*. London: Verso.

———. (1992). *Looking Awry*. Cambridge (Mass.): MIT Press.

———. (1996). "'I Hear You with My Eyes': or, The Invisible Master." In *Gaze and Voice as Love Objects*. S. Žižek & R. Salecl (Eds.), 90–126. Durham & London: Duke University Press.

———. (1999a). "Otto Weininger, or 'Woman Does Not Exist'." In *The Žižek Reader*. Elizabeth Wright & Edmund Wright (Eds.), 127–147. Oxford: Blackwell.

———. (1999b). "Courtly Love, or Woman as Thing." In *The Žižek Reader*. Elizabeth Wright & Edmund Wright (Eds.), 148–173. Oxford: Blackwell.

———. (2001). *Enjoy your Symptom*. New York & London: Routledge.

———. (2002). *Welcome to the Desert of the Real*. New York & London: Verso.

Index of Names

Index of Subjects